句法-韵律界面
——以汉语方言连读变调为例

On the Syntax-Prosody Interface
—Evidence from Tone Sandhi Processes in Chinese Dialects

李谷慧　著

苏州大学出版社

图书在版编目(CIP)数据

句法-韵律界面：以汉语方言连读变调为例 = On the Syntax-Prosody Interface—Evidence from Tone Sandhi Processes in Chinese Dialects：英文／李谷慧著. --苏州：苏州大学出版社，2023.9
ISBN 978-7-5672-4522-8

Ⅰ.①句… Ⅱ.①李… Ⅲ.①汉语方言-韵律(语言)-方言研究-英文 Ⅳ.①H17

中国国家版本馆 CIP 数据核字(2023)第 166757 号

书　　名：	句法-韵律界面：以汉语方言连读变调为例 On the Syntax-Prosody Interface—Evidence from Tone Sandhi Processes in Chinese Dialects
著　　者：	李谷慧
责任编辑：	汤定军
策划编辑：	汤定军
装帧设计：	吴　钰
出版发行：	苏州大学出版社(Soochow University Press)
社　　址：	苏州市十梓街1号　邮编：215006
印　　装：	江苏凤凰数码印务有限公司
网　　址：	www.sudapress.com
邮　　箱：	tangdingjun@suda.edu.cn
邮购热线：	0512-67480030
销售热线：	0512-67481020
开　　本：	700 mm×1 000 mm　1/16　印张：15.75　字数：254千
版　　次：	2023年9月第1版
印　　次：	2023年9月第1次印刷
书　　号：	ISBN 978-7-5672-4522-8
定　　价：	68.00元

凡购本社图书发现印装错误，请与本社联系调换。服务热线：0512-67481020

Chapter 1　Introduction

1.1　Motivations　/ 001

1.2　Three Accounts on Syntax-Phonology Interface　/ 002

1.3　Prosodic Phonology　/ 005

1.4　Tone Sandhis Across Chinese　/ 0012

1.5　Aims & Data　/ 018

1.6　Organization　/ 021

Chapter 2　Theoretical Foundations

2.1　Match Theory of Syntactic-Prosodic Constituency Correspondence　/ 022

2.2　Optimality Theory　/ 024

2.3　Basics of Morphology and Syntax in Chinese　/ 030

2.4　Tonal Representation　/ 034

Chapter 3　Correspondence Between X and PWd

3.1　Promoting PWd　/ 038

3.2　Factors Intervening in X-ω Correspondence　/ 039

3.3　Tone Sandhi in Tianjin Dialect　/ 044

3.4　Tone Sandhi I in Shaoxing Dialect　/ 068

3.5　Tone Sandhi in Yuncheng Dialect　/ 089

3.6　Summary　/ 113

Chapter 4 Correspondence Between XP and PPh

4.1 Promoting PPh / 118

4.2 Tone Sandhi in Xiamen Dialect / 125

4.3 Phonological Domain Structure of Tone Sandhis / 134

4.4 Phonetically-Conditioned PPh Restructuring / 140

4.5 Summary / 146

Chapter 5 Correspondence Between CP and IP

5.1 Promoting IP / 152

5.2 Quick-Tempo Tone Sandhi in Zhenjiang Dialect / 154

5.3 Tone Sandhi II in Shaoxing Dialect / 160

5.4 Tone Sandhi in Wenzhou Dialect / 183

5.5 Summary / 200

Chapter 6 Typology

6.1 Summary / 205

6.2 Prosodic Properties and S-P/P-S Correspondence / 212

6.3 Syntactic Properties and Construction of PPh / 226

6.4 Conclusion / 234

6.5 Areas for Future Research / 236

Bibliography / 238

Chapter 1

Introduction

✳ 1.1　Motivations

The interaction between syntactic structure and prosodic structure has been a heated topic in contemporary linguistic studies. This book intends to re-examine syntactic-prosodic interface through addressing the domain of application of tone sandhi rules in some Chinese dialects. When talking about the Chinese tone sandhi rules, we find it difficult but important to identify the domain to which a sandhi rule applies, which is always hardly formulated directly through morphological or syntactic constituents. A typical example of such is tone sandhi in Shanghai Wu dialect. It is reported in Zhu (2006) that there are two types of tone sandhi operating at two syntactic levels, traditionally labelled as word-level tone sandhi and phrasal-level tone sandhi, but morphosyntactic structuring is not a sufficient criterion to tell one from the other. Take word-level tone sandhi for instance. The so-called word-level tone sandhi typically applies to words as the examples shown in (1.1) i, which, however, are witnessed on phrasal level as well. Both phrases in (1.1) ii are pronounced with word-level tone sandhi with the entire string forming a single domain of tone sandhi.

(1.1) Word-Level Tone Sandhi in Shanghai Dialect (Selkirk & Shen 1990; Zhu 2006)

    i. Words or Compounds   Gloss

    a. [tsùŋ-kue?]   China

    (   )$_{\text{T.S.}}$

    b. [sir-mi?-dao]   juicy honey peach

    (   )$_{\text{T.S.}}$

    c. [ti?-ku?-sir-foŋ]   square

    (   )$_{\text{T.S.}}$

    ii. Phrases

    d. [djieu [i-zoŋ]]   old clothes

    (   )$_{\text{T.S.}}$

    e. [lao [ŋae-kuoŋ]]   old view

    (   )$_{\text{T.S.}}$

    iii. Sentence

    f. [[mo   ku   [noŋ] va]]   Has someone scolded you?

    (   )$_{\text{T.S.}}$

    scold   EXP 2^{nd}sg   ?

Note: (   )$_{\text{T.S.}}$ = a tone sandi domain

A sentence may constitute a single domain of tone sandhi as well as shown in (1.1) iii. Selkirk & Shen (1990) proposes that the nonsyntactic character of constituents corresponding to the domain of tone sandhi in Shanghai dialect on word level proves the existence of an additional set of structure independent from syntactic structure. A crucial question arises: In what way do phonological rules refer to morphosyntactic information?

❋ 1.2 Three Accounts on Syntax-Phonology Interface

As formulated in Truckenbrodt (1999), phonology relates to syntax in two ways essentially: direct reference to syntax and indirect reference to syntax. Direct Reference Theory holds that the domain structure of a phonological rule is purely composed of syntactic constituents (Cinque 1993; Odden 1990), while Indirect Reference Theory holds that the domain structure of a phonological rule is purely composed of phonological constituents, prosodic constituents to be specific (Selkirk 1984, 1996, 2011; Nespor & Vogel 1986, 2007; Truckenbrodt 1995, 1999).

1.2.1 Direct Reference

Direct Reference Theory suggests that the domain of application of a phonological rule should be the output of syntax, which means the construction of the domain of application of a phonological rule can and only can refer to syntactic constituency (Cinque 1993; Odden 1990). See Figure 1.1 for an illustration of Direct Reference:

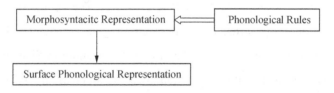

Figure 1.1 Direct Reference (cit. Seidl 2002)

If there is a phonological rule which applies to an utterance, Direct Reference predicts that the construction of the domain of this rule refers to morphsyntactic information of this utterance. It is an obvious defect that Direct Reference fails in reasoning the nonsyntactic characteristics of domain structure of phonological rules.

1.2.2 Indirect Reference

Indirect Reference Theory suggests that the phonological domain of a phonological rule is a certain prosodic constituent which is a component of a set of strictly layered universal prosodic hierarchy. There is a set of rules (or constraints) which creates a set of prosodic constituents from syntactic constituents (Selkirk 1984, 1996, 2011; Nespor & Vogel 1986, 2007; Truckenbrodt 1995, 1999).

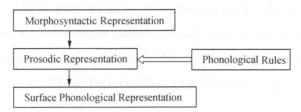

Figure 1.2 Indirect Reference (cit. Seidl 2002)

Indirect Reference Theory proposes that syntactic structure is incapable of directly defining the domain structure of a phonological rule which actually refers to prosodic constituents that are derived but independent from syntactic structure.

Indirect Reference Theory also holds that the set of prosodic constituents make up a prosodic hierarchy which is the prime of prosodic phonology (Selkirk 1984, 1996, 2011; Nespor & Vogel 1986, 2007). The basic assumption made by prosodic phonology is that phonology has its own structure which serves to explain certain mismatch data (like the case of tone sandhi in Shanghai dialect), because phonology and syntax have their own hierarchical structures and it is a natural consequence that there should be times when these two structures do not match up.

1.2.3 Kaisse's (1985) Connected Speech

Kaisse's (1985: 5 – 15) interface-theory Connected Speech (CS) distinguishes two levels of phonological rules: P1 rules and P2 rules. According to CS, only P1 rules may be sensitive to syntactic conditions such as adjacency or c-command. P2 rules on the other hand have no access to syntax but are sensitive only to prosodic information such as pause, location or elements in the prosodic hierarchy.

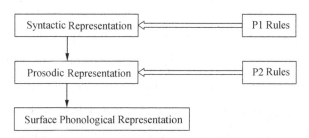

Figure 1.3　The Connected Speech architecture for
the postsyntactic component (cit. Seidl 2002)

CS assumes that P1 rules are sensitive to syntax, but all syntactic information will disappear after the application of P1 rules, hence, P2 rules have no access to syntactic information and only refer to prosodic information. Thus the domains of P2 rules are purely defined through prosodic constituents.

The three major syntax-phonology interface theories introduced above actually have their own research targets respectively. Kassie's (1985) CS intends to categorize phonological rules into two sets: purely syntactically-conditioned ones and purely prosodically-conditioned ones. The construction of the domain of the formers only refers to morphosyntactic information sharing the same research targets with Direct Reference in essence, while the construction of the domain of the latters only refers to prosodic information. Whereas, the case of tone sandhi in Shanghai dialect proves that it is just ideal to abruptly set syntax and prosody apart. Indirect Reference Theory, or prosodic phonology to be specific, holds that the domain structure of phonological rules is defined through prosodic constituents which are constructed from syntactic constituents. To put it another way, phonological rules reveal the interaction between syntax and prosody, two independent but closely-related structures of language. Phonological activities like tone sandhis in Shanghai dialect that fall into the regime of prosodic phonology are the research objects of this book.

❋ 1.3　Prosodic Phonology

Prosodic phonology, initiated and formulated by Selkirk (1980, 1984) and

Nespor & Vogel (1986), advocates that grammatical utterances are endowed with a hierarchical prosodic structure and that prosodic constituents are constructed on the basis of the morphosyntactic structure of sentences. Prosodic phonology concerns the phonological rules whose domain structures cannot be predicted from morphosyntactic structure but rather have to be defined through prosodic constituents. Prosodic constituents are constructed from syntactic constituents through a set of corresponding constraints. Language-specific prosodic structure well-formedness constraints also serve in shaping the structure of prosodic constituents. Prosodic structure well-formedness constraints may conflict with the corresponding constraints between prosodic constituents and syntactic constituents, thus leading to nonisomorphism between them. Prosodic phonology also maintains that the various kinds of prosodic constituents constitute a prosodic hierarchy which is universal and whose components are universal even though "... languages seem to differ in how an utterance is rhythmically and prosodically organized" (Jun 2005).

1.3.1 Prosodic Hierarchy

Prosodic Structure Theory holds that a sentence is endowed with a hierarchically organized prosodic structure that is distinct from the morphosyntactic structure of the sentence. Selkirk (1984), Nespor & Vogel (1986, 2007) and others developed a full-scale phonological constituent structure:

(1.2) Prosodic Hierarchy (Nespor & Vogel 1986, 2007)
      Syllable < Foot < Phonological Word / Prosodic Word (PWd, ω) < Clitic Group (CG) < Phonological Phrase (PPh, φ) < Intonational Phrase (IP, ι) < Utterance (Utt, υ)

The PWd is the lowest constituent that interacts with morphosyntax. The prosodic category Foot and the categories smaller than it are pure metrically-constrained constituents. To handle language-specific phenomena, researchers extended the range of prosodic domain, for example, Major Phrase and Tone Group (Ladd 1986), Minor Phrase and Major Phrase (Selkirk, 2000), Accentual Phrase and Intermediate Intonational Phrase (Pierrehumert & Beckman, 1988) and so on. Opposing the view that there should be more distinct prosodic categories to account for typological diversity, there are also attempts to eliminate particular phonological domains from the hierarchy. For instance, among the prosodic categories above foot level, the CG is the most controversial. The CG was originally proposed by Hayes (1989) which placed it between the Phonological Word / Prosodic Word and the Phonological Phrase. According to Nespor & Vogel (1986), "... the domain of CG consists of a PWd plus a directional clitic or a plain clitic such that there is no possible host with which it shares more category memberships". Vogel (2009: 18 – 19) admits that frequent overlap with PWd, and over-assignment of PWd status to morphemes such as affixes and clitics, severely threaten the justification of CG. See the examples about overlap and over-assignment below:

(1.3) a. Overlap of CG and PWd Structures   b. Over-Assignment of PWd Status

```
    CG   CG  CG   CG   CG                    CG
    |    |   |    |    |                  ╱ ╱ ╲ ╲
    PWd  PWd PWd PWd  PWd               PWd PWd PWd PWd
    Foreign green ideas sleep fast.      te  lo  ri  seleziona
                                         (He) re-selects it for you.
```

In (1.3) a, it is ambiguous whether a constituent is supposed to be parsed as PWd or CG. In the Italian sentence in (1.3) b, it is awkward to promote the two clitics (*te*, *lo*) and the prefix (*ri-*) to PWd status so as to satisfy Strict Layer Hypothesis (SLH) (to be introduced in 1.3.3).

A well-accepted solution was the introduction of recursion into prosodic constituents (Ito & Mestor 2003; Selkirk 1996; Booji 1996; Peperkamp 1997; Hall 1999; Anderson 2005). With the notion of recursion introduced in, the sentence in (1.3)b would have structures as (1.4)a or (1.4)b:

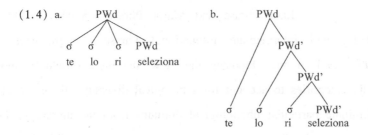

With the recursively-built PWd introduced in, there are also empirically-based claims that clitics can adjoin to prosodic constituents higher than PWd and IP (Inkelas 1990; Selkirk 1995). Since recursion was introduced in to eliminate the prosodic category CG, a large amount of empirical research has proved the existence of recursion at least in PWd, PPh and IP (Ito & Mestor 2013). The reduction of the distinction between CG and PWd, PPh and IP to subcategorization drives scholars to reevaluate the justification of the numerous prosodic constituents proposed in the traditional framework of prosodic hierarchy.

Selkirk (2011) developed a vastly simplified model to the syntax-prosody mapping which distinguishes only three levels (word, phrase and clause) where syntactic constituents are systematically made to correspond to phonological domains. Explicitly, she proposes a syntactically grounded prosodic hierarchy:

(1.5) Syntactically Grounded Prosodic Hierarchy (Selkirk 2011)
    PWd < PPh < IP

According to (1.5), PWd, PPh and IP are the suprafoot prosodic category types that are involved in syntactic-prosodic constituency correspondence. Only these three syntactically grounded prosodic constituents are universal, and all other types of prosodic category above the Foot are subtypes of the primitive, syntactically grounded category PWd, PPh and IP (Ito & Mestor 2007).

1.3.2 Construction of Prosodic Constituents

Selkirk (2011) proposes the Match Theory of syntactic-prosodic constituency correspondence which explicitly calls for a match between syntactic and prosodic constituents:

(1.6) The Match Theory of Syntactic-Prosodic Constituency Correspondence (Selkirk 2011: 439)

i. Match Clause

A **clause** in syntactic constituent structure must be matched by a corresponding prosodic constituent, call it ι, in phonological representation.

ii. Match Phrase

A **phrase** in syntactic constituent structure must be matched by a corresponding prosodic constituent, call it φ, in phonological representation.

iii. Match Word

A **word** in syntactic constituent structure must be matched by a corresponding constituent, call it ω, in phonological representation.

This set of universal constraints connects syntactic structure and prosodic structure and predicts that (Selkirk 2011: 439) phonological domains mirror syntactic constituents. On this stand, recursion in prosodic constituents is in consequence a reflection of syntactic structure, which is also firmly held in Kabak & Revithiadou (2009). So Match constraints ideally allow the fundamental syntactic distinctions between clauses, phrases and words to be detectable from IP, PPh and PWd.

Highly-ranked prosodic structure well-formedness constraints may lead to the violation of Match constraints and to nonisomorphism between syntactic constituents and prosodic constituents.

The independence of phonological domain structure of sentence-level phonological phenomena provides the essential arguments for the prosodic structure theory of this domain structure.

The Match Theory, on the one hand, identifies that prosodic structure should display formal properties that are inherited from syntactic structure, but on the other hand, predicts that prosodic structure may diverge from syntactic structure. In the Match Theory, prosodic categories are reduced to three basic syntactically grounded ones: PWd, PPh and IP, and further types of prosodic categories above the Foot level are essentially the subtypes of the three primitive ones (Ito & Mestor 2007). Further, the three primitive prosodic categories are universal because they are solidly syntactically-grounded. But the Match Theory predicts that highly/lowly-ranked prosodic structure well-formedness constraints may prevent the realization of one or more of them in specific languages.

1.3.3 Properties of Prosodic Structure

Prosodic hierarchy is at the core of the theory of prosodic phonology. Selkirk (1996) expresses the basic principles of the organization of prosodic structure in the form of constraints:

(1.7) Prosodic Hierarchy Well-formedness (Selkirk 1996: 190)
    a. LAYEREDNESS: No C_i dominates a C_j, $j > i$
        Lower levels cannot dominate higher levels.
    b. HEADEDNESS: Any C_i must dominate a C_{i-1}
        All parts of the prosodic hierarchy except the syllable must dominate something.
    c. EXHAUSTIVITY: No C_i immediately dominates a constituent C_j, $j < i-1$
        There is no skipping of levels within the hierarchy.
    d. NONRECURSIVITY: No C_i dominates C_j, $j = i$
        Phrases are not recursive.

EXHAUSTIVITY does not allow level-skipping, for instance, PWd immediately dominates a syllable or a PWd immediately dominates another PWd. The latter case also incurs the violation of NONRECURSIVITY. LAYEREDNESS prohibits a lower layered prosodic constituent from dominating a higher layered one, for example, a syllable cannot dominate a foot. HEADEDNESS requires that a prosodic constituent (except for syllable) must dominate a prosodic constituent irrespective of their prosodic categories. LAYEREDNESS and HEADEDNESS together produce strictly layered prosodic constituents (Selkirk 1981, 1995; Nespor & Vogel 1986; Pierrehumbert & Beckman 1988; Hayes 1989; Inkelas 1990).

(1.8) The SLH (Selkirk 2011: 437)

    A constituent of category-level n in the prosodic hierarchy immediately dominates only a (sequence of) constituents at category-level n-1 in the hierarchy.

The SLH constitutes a purely phonological theory of the formal relations holding between different prosodic categories in a prosodic structure demonstrated in (1.9)a. So a recursive prosodic constituent which is produced by observing Match constraints (1.6) incurs the violation of SLH demonstrated in (1.9)b.

(1.9) a. Strict Layering   b. Recursion: Violation of SLH

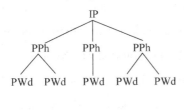 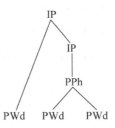

(Selkirk 2011)

If the contexts in which a phonological rule applies cannot be directly predicted through morphosyntactic constituency, and regular prosodic properties are detectable at the same time, then a prosodic account of the domain construction of this phonological rule is advocated, just like the case of tone sandhi in Shanghai dialect.

1.4　Tone Sandhis Across Chinese

1.4.1　Dialects in China

Ever since Yuan (1960, 2001) which is still accepted as a standard reference of Chinese dialectology, linguistists have carried out intensive research in the genetic classification and geographical distribution of Chinese dialects, and *Language Atlas of China* (1987) is one of the representative achievements. According to the *Atlas* (1987), there are ten families of dialects in Chinese: Mandarin, Jin, Wu, Hui, Gan, Xiang, Min, Yue, Pinghua and Hakka. Mandarin-based nouthern dialects have the vastest distribution—the entire region north of the Yangzi River and the four southwestern provinces. Jin (represented by Pingyao dialect and so on) surrounded by Mandarin-based dialects is mainly spoken in Shanxi, north Shaanxi and west Hebei. The Wu group (represented by Suzhou dialet, Wenzhou dialect and so on) covers south Jiangsu, Zhejiang and southeastern Anhui. Hui (represented by Tunxi dialect and so on) is scattered around southeastern Anhui and western Zhejiang. Gan (represented by Nanchang dialect and others) is spoken in Jiangxi and the east part of Hunan, while Xiang (represented by Changsha dialect and others) is restricted to Hunan. The Min family (represented by Fuzhou dialect, Xiamen dialect and so on) is distributed among Fujian, Taiwan, Hainan and east Guangdong. Yue (represented by Cantonese and others) is spoken in Guangdong and eastern Guangxi. Pinghua (represented by Nanning dialect and so on) is only spoken in southern Guangxi. Hakka (represented by Meixian dialect, Changting dialect and others) is scattered around southern Guangxi, western Fujian, eastern Guangdong and part of Taiwan. Enormous phonological diversities exist not only among the ten dialect families, but also within a dialect family, for instance, Wujiang North Wu and Wenzhou South Wu which are not mutually intelligible (Zhang 2015).

Mandarin-based dialects typically have smaller tonal inventory than the other dialect families; tone sandhis are more common in the Mandarin-based family, Wu family, Jin family, Min family, and Hakka family than in the rest (Chen 2000).

1.4.2 Tonal System

Tone is the use of pitch in language to distinguish lexical or grammatical meanings. Tones in Chinese are typically associated with individual syllables and distinguish lexical meanings. (Yip 2002: 1 – 3) Tones in Chinese are distinguished by their distinctive contour shapes, in the sense that each tone has its unique internal pattern of rising and falling pitch. (Yip 2002: 178 – 184) Traditional Chinese phonology represented by *Qieyun* (AD 601) categorizes tones into four tonal categories, namely *ping* tone, *shang* tone, *qu* tone and *ru* tone:

Table 1.1 Middle ancient Chinese tonal categories (Chen 2000: 2)

	Tonal Category	Gloss
I	*ping*	level
II	*shang*	rising
III	*qu*	departing
IV	*ru*	entering

Ru tone distinguishes with the other three tonal categories in that it exclusively connects to "checked" syllables with stops /-p, -t, -k/ or glottal stop /-ʔ/ in coda position. Exact pitch values of the four types of tones in middle ancient Chinese are elusive from *Qieyun* which nevertheless suggests tonal shapes in the most general sense that *ping* tone is level tone, *shang* tone is rising tone and *qu* tone is falling tone.

Ting (1982) argues that it is traceable that the four middle ancient Chinese tones have experienced processes of splitting and then merging. There a stage during which each of the middle ancient Chinese tonal categories was split into two registers—a *high* register labelled as *yin* tone and a *low* register labelled as *yang* tone conditioned by the voicing contrast in syllable onset in the sense that syllables with voiceless onset carry *yin* tone while syllables with voicing onset carry *yang* tone. At this stage, a rather symmetrical eight-tone system was born which is still maintained in many south dialects, for example Shaoxing North Wu:

Table 1.2 Eight tones in Shaoxing dialect (Zhang 2006: 196)

	Ping (I)	Shang (II)	Qu (III)	Ru (IV)
Yin (a)	52	35	33	5
Yang (b)	31	13	22	3

The pitch values of tones in Table 1.2 are marked with Chao's (1928) five-digit-scale method. The tonal space is divided into five scales, with 5 representing the highest pitch and 1 representing the lowest pitch. So in Shaoxing dialect, there are four tonal categories—*Ping* (I) tone has falling pitch contour, *Shang* (II) tone has rising pitch contour, and *Qu* (III) tone and *ru* (IV) tone are level tones. All the four tonal categories are evenly divided into two registers—*Yin* (a) tones have higher pitch value while *Yang* (b) tones have lower pitch value.

According to Ting (1982), with the full-ranged eight-member system, the evolution of the tonal system switched to merging, typically exemplified by Mandarin-based dialects. Take the most familiar Mandarin for illustration:

Table 1.3 Four tones in Mandarin (based on Chen 2000: 8)

yinping Ia	yangping Ib	shang II	qu III
55	35	213	51

From Table 1.3 it can be seen that only the *ping* tonal category is distinct in register height which is no longer detectable in the *shang* and *qu* tonal categories. Stop coda has entirely disappeared, hence all checked syllables have evolved into unchecked syllables as a dramatic consequence. The merging of tones is not restricted to Mandarin-based dialects. In Shaoxing dialect, checked syllables are still preserved, but the distinctions among stops i. e. /-p, -t, -k/ have disappeared, all of which are debuccalized into the glottal stop /-ʔ/ (Zhang 2006: 150). Evolution of the tonal system towards merging is believed to be in progress, but with individualized rates and individualized fashions in individual dialects.

1.4.3 Typology of Tone Sandhis in Chinese

With such a rich and diversified tonal system, it is of extremely great linguistic importance that tones in sequence may undergo changes which are referred to as tone sandhi. Tone sandhi is a phonological change occurring in tonal languages. Tone alternation takes place caused by adjacent tones or the prosodic/morphorsyntactic environment in which a tone appears, which is commonly referred to as tone sandhi. (Yip 2002; Zhang 2014: 443) A series of questions lie behind such phonological changes and they have aroused great interest among linguists.

From the angle of the trigger of tone sandhi, Li (2004) claims that basically tone sandhis in Chinese can be divided into two major groups: i) grammatical-related tone sandhi; and ii) phonological-context conditioned tone sandhi. For the first kind, tone sandhi has become regarded as a phonological marker of grammatical changes, e. g. tone sandhi in reduplication, tone sandhi in diminutive forms, tone sandhi marking parts of speech, as a symbol of grammaticalization and so on. Phonologists are interested in the second kind, hence it is what my research relies on. So in the following analysis, I will use the term "tone sandhi" to refer to the phonological-context conditioned tone sandhi.

Supported by cross-dialectal data, Bao (2011: 2583) proposes the follwing tone sandhi typology in Chinese:

(1.10) a. Contextual sandhi, e. g. Tianjin
      b. Positional sandhi, e. g. Xiamen

c. Templatic sandhi, e. g. Wenzhou

d. Tone spread, e. g. Shanghai

For (1.10) a, conditioned by neighboring tones, tone sandhi rules will cause changes to register, contour, or both features of a tone. This kind of sandhi is most commonly found in Mandarin-based dialects. For (1.10) b, the position of a tone in a certain string is of vital importance, while tonal context plays no role. Min (note: South Min, to be specific) is the representative of this kind of tone sandhi. For (1.10) c, tone sandhi is not derivable without referring to a prespecified tonal template. Wenzhou dialect, a South Wu dialect is a typical example. For (1.10) d, a lexical specified tone spreads from a periphery syllable to neighboring syllable(s). This kind of tone sandhi can be found in North Wu. Bao (2011) essentially asserts a typology of phonological rules of tone sandhis in Chinese.

Yue-Hashimoto (1986) tries to testify the prosodic structure from tone sandhi. If the citation form of the leftmost syllable is preserved, then this dialect is left-prominent. If the citation form of the rightmost syllable is preserved, then this dialect is right-prominent. However, this deduction is controversial. First, tone sandhi in Shanghai dialect belongs to (1.10)c and d, and it is the tone of the leftmost syllable retained. According to Yue-Hashimoto (1986), Shanghai dialect is supposed to be left-prominent. Nevertheless, the native scholar Zhu (2006) falsifies this assumption on the ground that sandhi patterns are not uniformly perceived as left-prominent. Second, Yip (2002) argues that every full-toned syllable is a stressed syllable, so a syllable with sandhi tone is not unstressed as long as it is still a full-toned syllable. Take Mandarin for instance. In Mandarin, it is the right syllable that keeps the citation tone. But Yue-Hashimoto's (1986) criterion is far away from asserting that Mandarin is right-prominent. However, Yue-Hashimoto (1986) account is still referential, for it closely connects with the directionality of tone sandhi.

Directionality is another language-specific property of tone sandhi. Word-level tone sandhi in Shanghai dialect proceeds rightward (Qian 1992), while tone sandhi in Xiamen sweeps leftward (Li 1962). Tianjin dialect is a more complicated case as tone sandhi processes from both directions (Li & Liu 1985).

As long as a domain of tone sandhi is established, tone sandhi will apply either cyclically or iteratively. Mandarin is a typical example in which tone sandhi applies cyclically by respecting the morphosyntactic structure of its domain of application (Chen 2000). Tone sandhi in Tianjin dialect is insensitive to the morphosyntactic structure and instantiates iterative application (Ma 2005a, 2005b).

Regularities of phonological rules of tone sandhi have attracted tremendous attention from scholars, while studies on the domain structure of tone sandhi are comparatively impoverished.

1.4.4 Domain of Tone Sandhi

As pointed out by Bao (2011), most descriptive field reports and theoretical works on tone sandhi in Chinese linguistics focus on word level, which seems to be unanimously taken as the default domain of tone sandhi. Chen (2000) pays attention to the domain structure of tone sandhi. It is very insightful and inspiring of Chen that he extended the environments of tone sandhi from word level to sentence level which enables us to examine tone sandhi comprehensively.

Ever since Chen (1987), Chen has noticed that the domain of tone sandhi in Xiamen dialect is sensitive to the syntactic structure, without being entirely conditioned by syntax. From Wenzhou dialect, Chen (2000) finds that the domain of tone sandhi may be structured due to either prosodical or nonlinguistic factors. Tone sandhi in Wu dialects is well-known for its complexity. Recall the case of Shanghai that encountered at the very beginning of this chapter. Wu dialects distinguish themselves with two separate levels of tone sandhi, roughly speaking, word level and phrasal level (Qian 1992). In traditional Chinese dialectology, it is seldom made explicit what conditions the construction of domains of both levels of tone sandhi in essence. The reason might lie in Bao's account which is stated at the beginning of this subsection: The polysyllabic compound is conventionally preconceived as the default domain of tone sandhi.

The phonological domain structure of tone sandhi is the focus of our discussion in the following chapters, which ultimately serve to explore the corresponding relationship between syntax and phonology.

✣ 1.5 Aims & Data

1.5.1 Aims

Through decades of development, it has been established that phonology is not a homogeneous system, but is composed of a set of interacting self-governed subsystems, such as metrical phonology, lexical phonology, autosegmental phonology and prosodic phonology (Nespor & Vogel 2007; Wang 2008). This book will dig deeper into syntax-phonology interface problems based on the theory of prosodic phonology. In this chapter I have already introduced that prosodic components are hierarchically layered blocks, so by nature, prosodic phonology is a theory of domains. Prosodic phonology proposes that on the one hand, each prosodic constituent serves as the domain of application of specific phonological rules and phonetic processes, and on the other hand, each prosodic constituent is constituted with raw materials from morphosyntactic constituents through a set of mapping rules or constraints (Nespor & Vogel 2007; Selkirk 2011). The Match Theory of prosodic phonology states the regularity of mapping from syntax to prosody. Nonisomorphism between syntactic constituents and prosodic constituents is frequently the case on all the three levels of prosodic categories, as a consequence of language-specific rankings of syntactic-prosodic constituency faithful mapping constraints with respect to universal prosodic structure markedness constraints, language-particular syntactic structuring, and phonology proper. The phonological domain structure of phonological rules assigned to a sentence diagnoses language-particular rankings between these faithfulness constraints and markedness constraints and specific requirements from phonological rules. This book is dedicated to an exploration of the correspondence between syntactic constituency and prosodic constituency on all the three levels of prosodic categories diagnosed by phonological phenomena—tone sandhis in Chinese—ranging from word level to sentence level. As this book is built on the analysis of tone sandhis in some Chinese dialects, I will seek answers to the following questions:

a) How do we diagnose a domain of tone sandhi? What systematic properties does the phonological domain structure of tone sandhi possess?

b) Do these properties originate solely from morphosyntactic structures? If not, what are the other intervening factors, prosody, tone sandhi rules, or what else?

c) Do the morphosyntactic-dependent properties interact with those morphosyntactic-free properties? If so, how?

d) Is the interaction between these factors unanimous across Chinese dialects? To be specific, how shall we explain the typological differences in the phonological domain structure of tone sandhis?

I will try to deliver a theoretical analysis of these questions based on a large amount of empirical data. With the help of my partners, I have collected data pertaining to Tianjin dialect, Shaoxing dialect and Chenghai dialect. In adition, Li & Liu (1985), Wang (2003), Shi & Wang (2004), Wang (2015), Zhang (2006), Lin (1995, 1996) and others are also taken as important references. Data pertaining to Yuncheng dialect, Zhenjiang dialect and Wenzhou dialect are chiefly based on Lü (1989), Zhang (1985), Chen (2000) and Zheng-zhang (1964, 1980, 2007, 2008).

1.5.2 Data Collection and Processing

Besides the data collected from literature, I have collected data pertaining to Tianjin dialect, Shaoxing dialect and Chenghai dialect in the past two years, with the help of my partners.

Investigations into these three dialects covered tone sandhis from the word level to the sentence level. The samples on the word level were selected and grouped according to their syllable count. Simplex words, compounds and coordinate-structured strings were all included in. The samples on the phrasal level covered the structures of subject-predicate, verb-object, coordinate, subordinate, verb-adverbial, etc. Samples on sentence level ranged from the most basic SVO-structured ones to more complicated ones, like topiclization, focus, double-object, passive and so on.

The informants previewed and read the lists of sample words, phrases and sentences. All their readings were recorded then. The informants from Tianjin and Shaoxing exceeded 30 respectively, and those from Chenghai exceeded 10, all of whom are native speakers. As the focus of the investigation was the phonetic manifestation of tone sandhi, it was necessary to eliminate other potential influences on fundamental frequency (F0) and duration. So the informants were required to read at normal speech rate without expressing any personal sentiments.

Perceptual annotation and phonetic analysis of tone sandhi were conducted afterwards. Perceptual judgments of tone sandhis were conducted first. Three people annotated the surface tones of all the sample strings independently. For different annotations, the three people gave re-judgments together with the help of Praat. All the recordings were sent to phonetic annotations for the next step. F0 contours and string durations (calculated syllable by syllable) were extracted, and pauses between syllables within string were also annotated. All the perceptual and phonetic data collected were then sent to statistical analysis with the help of SPSS and Excel.

Both the perceptual and phonetic data obtained were then taken to diagnose the domain of application of tone sandhi.

1.6 Organization

This book will address one fundamental issue of the syntax-phonology interface: the relation between syntactic constituency and the prosodic constituent defined the domains of sentential-level phonological phenomena. Tone sandhis in Chinese are chosen as the carriers of my research here.

Chapter 1 introduces the motivations for writing this book. A brief review of prosodic phonology and the revelevant studies of tone sandhis in Chinese are delivered afterwards.

Chapter 2 introduces the theories that this book rests on. The entire book is guided by the Match Theory of syntactic-prosodic constituency correspondence, the latest development in prosodic phonology. The Optimality Theory offers a typology of domain structure of tone sandhis.

Chapters 3 – 5 are the core of this book. I will examine the correspondence between the syntactic constituency and the prosodic constituent domains for sentence-level tone sandhi phenomena. Chapter 3 will discuss the correspondence between syntax and prosody on prosodic word level exemplified by tone sandhis in Mandarin-based Tianjin dialect, Shaoxing North Wu dialect and Yuncheng South Jin dialect. It will be argued that prosodic markedness constraints, known as size effects, constitute a major source of X-PWd mismatch. Chapter 4 will focus on tone sandhis on phrasal level exemplified by the dialects of South Min. Correspondence between Syntactic Phrase and PPh is typically syntactically-conditioned. Correspondence between clause and IP is even more flexible greatly influenced by linguistic and nonlinguistic factors. Tone sandhis in Zhenjiang dialect, a heavily Wu-colored Mandarin-based dialect, Shaoxing dialect and Wenzhou South Wu dialect will provide us with empirical evidence. This will be examined in Chapter 5.

Chapter 6 summarizes the arguments established in the previous three chapters. A typology of domain construction of tone sandhis on different prosodic levels will be arrived at within the framework of the Optimality Theory.

Chapter 2

Theoretical Foundations

In this chapter I will introduce the theoretical foundations that this book rests on.

2.1 Match Theory of Syntactic-Prosodic Constituency Correspondence

My research is essentially carried out in the framework of prosodic phonology, especially based on the Match Theory of syntactic-prosodic constituency correspondence. Hence, it is fundamentally confirmed in this book that:

i. the domains of phonological phenomena are defined through phonological constituents, rather than directly from syntactic representations;

ii. the phonological representations are organized into prosodic constituents which are mapped from syntactic constituents;

iii. syntactic properties may be reflected in prosodic constituents;

iv. prosodic constituents, which are organized in the form of a prosodic hierarchy, are independent from syntactic constituents;

v. prosodic structures may converge with or diverge from syntactic structures.

Phonological phenomena on sentence level will be taken as diagnosis of the construction of prosodic constituent structure, which is largely grounded in the syntactic constituency of the sentence. The Match Theory of syntax-prosody constituency correspondence predicts that: (1) above the Foot level, there are basically three levels of distinct prosodic constituents—PWd, PPh and IP; and (2) there may be systematic recursivity and level-skipping in the construction of prosodic constituents in violation of strict layering, since a prosodic constituent is mapped from a syntactic constituent.

Selkirk (2011: 453) is explicit that the functional-lexical distinction is important for syntactic-prosodic correspondence at both PWd level and PPh level: lexical words and their projections can be parsed as PWd and PPh respectively, while functional words (especially mono-syllabic ones) and phrases headed by them cannot on the ground that it is frequently the case cross-linguistically that a FncP is not delimited by PPh boundaries. Truckenbrodt (1999) expresses the idea that prosodic structures, ignoring functional syntactic constituents, are based on only lexical syntactic constituents, as the Lexical Category Condition (LCC):

(2.1) The Lexical Category Condition (Truckenbrodt 1999: 226)
  Constraints relating syntactic and prosodic categories apply to lexical syntactic elements and their projections, but not to functional elements and their projections, or to empty syntactic elements and their projections.

Functional elements and their projections are excluded from the interaction between syntactic constituents and prosodic constituents by LCC. A potential but uninevitable related problem is how functional elements and their projections are prosodically parsed as long as all syllables must participate in prosodic construction. Both empirical and theoretical evidence drives Werle (2009) to propose that functional-element-headed projections are endowed by their lexical complements with lexicalness so that constraints relating syntactic and prosodic categories can refer to functional elements and their projections as well. Sentence level phonological phenomena, tone sandhi in Xiamen dialect—South Min dialect to be specific, which are going to be examined in Chapter 4, support Werle's (2009) theoretical refinement to LCC.

2.2 Optimality Theory

The Optimality Theory (OT) (Prince & Smolensky 1993; McCarthy & Prince 1993) is a theory of human language capacity, which basically assumes that each linguistic output form is optimal, in the sense that it incurs the least serious violations of a set of conflicting constraints. For a given input, the grammar generates and then evaluates an infinite set of hierarchically ranked constraints, each of which will eliminate some candidate outputs, until a point is reached at which only one output candidate survives.

OT organizes two types of constraints, faithfulness constraints and markedness constraints, which are universal and violable. Each individual constraint evaluates one specific aspect of output markedness or faithfulness. Markedness constraints require that output forms meet some criterion of structural well-formedness. Faithfulness constraints require that outputs preserve the properties of their basic lexical forms, requiring some kind of similarity between the output and its input. Markedness constraints and faithfulness constraints are inherently in conflict: markedness constraints trigger changes, while faithfulness constraints reject changes. The grammar of OT is a system of ranked constraints. Differences between languages are reducible to language-particular differences in the ranking of the constraints. (Kager 2000)

2.2.1 Correspondence Theory

The Correspondence Theory (McCarthy & Prince 1995) includes constraints requiring identity between elements in pairs of representations:

(2.2) Correspondence (McCarthy & Prince 1995)

>Given two strings S_1 and S_2, related to one another as input-output, base-reduplicant, etc., correspondence is a relation R from the elements of S_1 to those of S_2. Elements $\alpha \in S_1$ and $\beta \in S_2$ are referred to as correspondents of one another when $\alpha R \beta$.

Given this general definition of correspondence, the correspondence constraints (MAX, DEP, IDENT, etc.) must be relativized for different values of S_1 and S_2. McCarthy & Prince (1995) crucially points out that correspondence is not a relationship that is "established" by constraints, but rather a relationship that is evaluated by constraints. Constraints which evaluate the correspondence relationships produced by the generator are violable, giving rise to optimal candidates displaying imperfect correspondence relations.

Selkirk's (2011) Match Theory of syntactic-prosodic constituency correspondence in essence states the correspondence relation between syntactic constituents and prosodic constituents analogous to input-output faithfulness or base-reduplicant identity. In the case of correspondence between syntactic constituency and prosodic constituency, a constituent in syntax must have a corresponding constituent in prosody, while on the other hand, every prosodic constituent must correspond to a constituent in syntax. Hence, Selkirk (2011: 451) makes it explicit that there are two sets of constraints that evaluate the correspondence between syntactic constituency and prosodic constituency, one set examines whether the edges of a syntactic constituent correspond to the edges of a prosodic constituent; while the other set examines whether the edges of a syntactic constituent correspond to the edges of a prosodic constituent:

(2.3) Constraints on Syntax-Prosody Correspondence (Selkirk 2011: 451)
>a. Match (α, π)
>>The left and right edges of a constituent of type α in the input syntactic representation must correspond to the left and right edges of a constituent of type π in the output phonological representation.

b. Match (π, α)

    The left and right edges of a constituent of type π in the output phonological representation must correspond to the left and right edges of a constituent of type α in the input syntactic representation.

Corresponding relation between syntactic constituents and prosodic constituents is formalized through the correspondence constraints. The Match Theory of syntactic-prosodic constituency correspondence primitively proposes three levels of prosodic constituents, namely PWd / ω, PPh / φ and IP / ι, see (1.6) reference. Hence, we can further subcategorize the correspondence constraints Match (α, π) and Match (π, α) into the following three groups:

(2.4) a-i) MATCH-X-ω: A X must correspond to a ω.
    a-ii) MATCH-ω-X: A ω must correspond to a X.
    b-i) MATCH-XP-φ: A XP must correspond to a φ.
    b-ii) MATCH-φ-XP: A φ must correspond to a XP.
    c-i) MATCH-CP-ι: A CP must correspond to a ι.
    c-ii) MATCH-ι-CP: A ι must correspond to a CP.

In consistence with the IO-faithfulness constraints (Prince & Smolensky 1993; McCarthy & Prince 1993), another set of faithfulness constraints penalizing syllable epenthesis is also promoted:

(2.5) a) DEP-X-ω: Correspondent X and ω have identical syllable number.
    b) DEP-XP-φ: Correspondent XP and φ have identical syllable number.
    c) DEP-CP-ι: Correspondent CP and ι have identical syllable number.

Syntactic-prosodic constituency correspondence constraints are vital in identifying prosodic constituency. Markedness constraints on prosodic representation interact with these correspondence constraints. Language-particular rankings give rise to cross-language typology of corresponding relationship between syntactic constituents and prosodic constituents.

2.2.2 Markedness Theory

The term "markedness" has been used to refer to many different linguistic concepts. One of the most common uses relates to observations about the outputs, undergoers, and triggers of some processes (Trubetzkoy 1939). De Lacy (2006) developed the concept into a new "markedness theory" with the following four leading ideas:

(2.6) Markedness Theory (de Lacy 2006: 1 – 2)
    a. Competence Markedness
        Markedness is part of grammatical Competence (i-language). Markedness in Competence is distinct from sometimes apparently similar Performance-related phenomena.
    b. Preservation of the Marked
        There is grammatical pressure to preserve marked elements. If x is more marked than y, x can be unaffected by a process while y is forced to undergo it.
    c. Markedness Conflation
        Markedness distinctions can be conflated (i.e. ignored), but never reversed. If a language treats x as more marked than y, another language can treat x and y as being equally marked; however, no language will treat y as less marked than x.
    d. Hierarchy Conflict
        Markedness hierarchies can conflict: one hierarchy may favor x over y while another favors y over x.

De Lacy's (2006) Markedness Theory is based on the proposal that markedness hierarchies are universal. For example, the hierarchy for the major place of articulation / PoA is given in (2.7):

(2.7) The Major Place of Articulation Markedness Hierarchy / PoA Hierarchy (Lombardi 1995, 1998)

| dorsal > labial > coronal > glottal |

In Ulu Muar Malay, in codas, /p/ may become [ʔ], but /ʔ/ never becomes [p]; therefore, [p] is more marked than [ʔ]. Similarly in Cantonese, /p/ may become [t], but /t/ never becomes [p]; also /t/ may become [ʔ]. Empirical evidence reveals a markedness hierarchy: "| labial > coronal > glottal |". Furthermore, from inspecting dorsals, we find a full-range PoA hierarchy: "| dorsal > labial > coronal > glottal |". This PoA hierarchy is related to a set of output constraints:

(2.8) Output Constraints for the Major Place of Articulation (de Lacy 2006: 2)
    a. *{dors}: Assign a violation for each [dorsal] feature.
    b. *{dors, lab}: Assign a violation for each [dorsal] and each [labial] feature.
    c. *{dors, lab, cor}: Assign a violation for each [dorsal], each [labial], and each [coronal] feature.
    d. *{dors, lab, cor, gl}: Assign a violation for each [dorsal], each [labial], each [coronal], and each [glottal] feature.

The PoA hierarchy is conveyed through these output constraints in (2.8). For example, dorsals are more marked than labials, coronals and glottals in the PoA hierarchy. Dorsals like [k] incur the violation of *{dorsal}, but segments like [p], [t], and [ʔ] do not. So every constraint is violated by labials, coronals and glottals is also violated by dorsals (i.e. *{dors, lab}, *{dor, lab, cor}, *{dors, lab, cor, gl}). In this way relative markedness relations are translated into violations of the PoA output constraints. Parallel with the output constraints, there is a set of faithfulness constraints for the major place of articulation:

(2.9) Output Constraints for the Major Place of Articulation (de Lacy 2006: 2)

a. IDENT{dors}: If x is dorsal, then x' has the same PoA as x.
b. IDENT {dors,lab}: If x is dorsal or labial, then x' has the same PoA as x.
c. IDENT {dors,lab,cor}: If x is dorsal, labial or coronal, then x' has the same PoA as x.
d. IDENT {dors,lab,cor,gl}: If x is dorsal, labial, coronal, or glottal, then x' has the same PoA as x.

Faithfulness constraints aim to preserve the marked features. For example, constraint IDENT{dors} serves to prevent dosals from undergoing a PoA-altering process like neutralization or assimilation. Because dorsals are the most marked in PoA hierarchy, if dorsals are preserved, less marked labials, coronals and glottals have also to be preserved. This hierarchical relationship is expressed through the series of constraints: IDENT {dors,lab,cor,gl}, IDENT {dors,lab, cor} and IDENT {dors,lab}.

De Lacy's Markedness Theory (2006) primarily focuses on establishing the fundamental mechanisms behind markedness reduction, preservation, and conflation. Marked elements can be the specific targets of preservation. The desire to preserve marked elements can conflict with the pressure to eliminate marked elements ("markedness reduction"). To sum up, there are two major influences in markedness:

(2..10) Markedness Pressures (de Lacy 2006: 23)
    a. Markedness Reduction
        There is pressure for output segments to have unmarked features.
    b. Preservation of the Marked
        There is pressure for marked inputs to be preserved faithfully.

(2.10) a is formally expressed through the constraints, for example, (2.8) disfavouring marked segments. (2.10) b is expressed through constraints, for example, (2.9) favouring faithful presence of marked features.

Markedness Hierarchies are universal across languages, but individual languages and even individual processes can collapse markedness distinctions. For the marked elements that are preserved or eliminated, their distinction in terms of markedness may be conflated. In the general sense, markedness conflation will be shown to occur when two markedness categories incur the same violations of active constraints. For example, if *{dorsal, labial} is the only active constraint, the distinction between dorsals and labials is eliminated as they both incur the same violations of this constraint. The distinction between dorsals and labials may also be conflated by the high-ranking of IDENT {dors, lab} which preserves both elements.

Markedness Hierarchies may conflict. Exactly which segment is favored in which environment in a particular language depends on which Markedness Hierarchy dominates in that language. For example, Mabalay Atayal has epenthetic [ʔ], but Axininca Campa has [t] (Payne 1981). It seems that languages can choose between "coronal" and "glottal" as the least marked. De Lacy (2006) introduced in the Sonority Hierarchy "| glottal > stops |", for glottals [ʔ, h] consistently act as highly sonorous in many phonological phenomena. Hierarchical relation between glottals and other stops essentially conflict in PoA (| coronal > dorsal |) and in Sonority Hirarchy (| glottal > stops|). [ʔ] is chosen as epenthetic segment in Mabalay Atayal because glottals are the least marked in PoA hierarchy, while in Axininca Campa [t] is chosen as epenthetic segment because it is the least sonorous coronal in Sonority Hirarchy. To summarize, Markedness Hierarchies are universally consistent. There are no language-specific hierarchies; apparent markedness disagreements arise through different choices about which hierarchies take precedence in a particular language.

What concerned in my research is markedness reduction and preservation during the construction of PWd.

❋ 2.3 Basics of Morphology and Syntax in Chinese

As long as our research examines the corresponding relation between morphosynactic constituency and prosodic constituency, it is necessary to state briefly the basic principles of the morphosyntactic correlates.

2.3.1 Compounding

Since syntactic word and syntactic phrase map into distinct prosodic constituents which serve to define the domain of application of phonological rules, it is of vital importance to distinguish words from phrases decisively. However, defining "word" in Chinese is difficult all the time, so it is by no means an easy job to make a clear cut between phrase and word in Chinese (Chao 1968; Lü 1963).

Linguistics often distinguishes two basic types of morphological patterns: concatenative and non-concatenative. Affixation and compounding fall into the regime of concatenation. (Haspelmath & Sims 2010) Though affixation has been evolving prosperously in Modern Chinese, compounding is the major mechanic of word-formation (Chao 1968). With high level of productivity, the distinction between word and phrase actually refers to the distinction between compound and phrase.

In Chinese literature, quite a lot of criteria have been proposed for testing wordhood in Chinese. Nevertheless, no unified conclusion has been reached. Duanmu (2007: 99 – 115) has reviewed the most notable ten tests for wordhood in Chinese, focusing on [M N] norminals. The result is stated here for reference (Table 2.1):

Table 2.1 Ten tests for Wordhood in Chinese (Duanmu 2007: 115)

	Tests	[M N]	[M de N]
1.	Conjunction Reduction (Huang 1984: 60)	word	phrase
2.	Freedom of Parts (Chao 1968: 361)	both	phrase
3.	Semantic Composition (Chao 1968: 363)	both	phrase
4.	Syllable Count (Lü 1979: 21 – 22)	both	phrase
5.	Insertion (Lu 1964: 21)	both	phrase
6.	Exocentric Structure (Chao 1968: 362)	??	phrase

	Tests	[M N]	[M de N]
7.	Adverbial Modification (Fan 1958: 214)	word	phrase
8.	XP Substitution (Fan 1958: 214)	word	phrase
9.	Productivity	word	phrase
10.	Intuition (Lü 1979: 21-22)	??	phrase

By these tests, [M de N] is always a phrase. Results for [M N] differ. Duanmu (2007) then argues against Syllable Count, Insertion, and Intuition serving as tests for wordhood in Chinese. In consequence, all [M N] should be accepted as nominals, as well as their iterative derivatives, such as [M [M N]] and [[M N] N], are compounds. Basically, I am on the same ground with Duanmu (2007) in holding that taking the appearance of [de] as an overt marker of phrases.

2.3.2 X'-Theory

Ever since Chomsky (1970), X'-theory came into shape, which consolidated all individual phrase structures of particular categories into a general schema. I will give a very brief introduction to this theory chiefly based on Radford (2004) and Huang, Li & Li (2009) on which the Match Theory rests. See the schematic illustration of a VP as given in (2.11):

(2.11)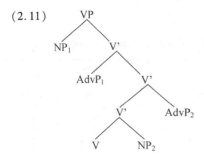

Complement (Comp for short) NP_2 combining with V forms V', the intermediate "sub-phrase". Comp is where the object of VP locates. NP_1, the sister to the highest V', also the daughter of VP, is the specifier (Spec for short). Spec is where the subject of VP locates. There is no restriction to the category of phrase head, for all kinds of phrases—NPs, VPs, APs, PPs, CPs, DPs, TPs, etc.—have their syntactic structure built in the same way as illustrated by (2.11). The schema for phrases is called X'-structure.

Various significant consequences follow the X'-structure. Still take VP for illustration. Firstly, V' effectively distinguishes the subject from the object; secondly, Modifiers, $AdvP_1$ and $AdvP_2$ adjoin to this verb phrase without changing the structural nature of it.

Modifiers, regardless of their categories and the categories of the words they modify, are referred to as adjuncts. Adjuncts adjoin to X'. Hence, a phrase XP may have any number of X's in it depending on how many modifiers adjoin in.

It is firmly held that syntactic phrases are intrinsically recursive. Firstly, because XP can consist of another XP, there is no intrinsic limitation on the number of XPs inside the phrase. Secondly, there is no limitation on the number of X's inside XP. However, XP eventually must terminate with X, the head of the phrase.

2.3.3 Argument Structure

In a VP, the object and subject hold intrinsic semantic relations with the verb. Borrowing the concept from logic, every verb has to take arguments. Arguments are usually classified into Agent for the doer party of an event, Patient for the do-ee party, and a few others such as Theme, Benefactive, Goal and Source to accommodate various roles that an argument may represent in linguistic environments relevant to syntax. (Radford 2004: 128)

Agent, Patient, etc. are called thematic roles (θ-roles); a lexical word (typically a verb) is said to have a certain number of θ-roles to assign; θ-roles are typically assigned to arguments—the phrases that function as subject and objects. (Chomsky 1981: 36) The set of θ-roles that a lexical word has to assign is its argument structure which is treated as an intrinsic lexical property of a lexical word.

The system of θ-roles is ranked so that Agent is the highest in the thematic hierarchy (Radford 2004: 193), Patient is next, followed by a few others. The system of syntactic arguments is also ranked, with the subject placed higher than the object in the tree diagram. As the highest θ-role in an argument structure, Agent must go to the subject, the highest argument in a clause; Patient is the next in the thematic ranking and must be assigned to the object, etc.

2.4 Tonal Representation

In traditional Chinese dialectology, Chao's (1928) five-digit-scale framework is the most commonly and widely adopted in the description of pitch values of tones. Phonologists (Hyman 1986; Snider 1990; Yip 1989; Bao 1999) endeavor to mark tones with autosegmental features. Based on data from Chinese dialects, Yip proposed that a tone should be not an indivisible entity, but it could be decomposed into two parts, namely Register and Tone. Register indicates the imaginary pitch band in which a tone is realized, and tone specifies the way the tone behaves over the duration of the tone-bearing unit (Bao 1999: 22). Refining Yip (1989), Bao (1999) proposes a geometry of tone in which a tonal root node T dominates both a register r and a contour c node. Under the root node, the register node can dominate either H or L, the contour node can dominate either h or l. If the contour node branches, it may dominate a sequence of lh or hl.

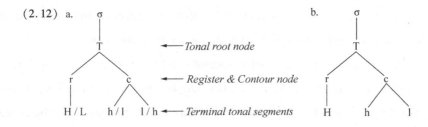

So, with this tonal framework illustrated in (2.12) a, for instance, *yinping* / Ia tone in Shaoxing dialect can be represented as shown by (2.12) b. In this book, tonal representation will be formalized under Bao's (1999) framework.

Chapter 3

Correspondence Between X and PWd

PWd / ω is the most basic prosodic constituent that interacts with the syntactic constituents. The Match Theory of syntactic-prosodic constituency correspondence (Selkirk 2011: 439) proposes: A word in syntactic constituent structure must be matched by a corresponding constituent, call it ω, in phonological representation.

The Match Theory predicts that the prosodic structures mirror syntactic structures since they are mapped from the syntactic counterparts. The syntactic terminal element, i. e. syntactic word then corresponds to ω. If a prosodic constituent is supposed to mirror the structure of a syntactic constituent it corresponds with, then recursion in prosodic constituent is the result of morphosyntactic recursion (Kabak & Revithiadou 2009; Selkirk 2011). A subgroup of the phonological domain structure of tone sandhi in Tianjin dialect provides empirical evidence supporting this proposal. Meanwhile, unique phonological properties of this subgroup of tone sandhi in Tianjin dialect being crucially conditioned by the readjustment in metrical structure testifies to Kabak & Revithiadou's (2009: 5) deduction that "... an extended domain such as PWd involves an additional layer of structure on the metrical grid to which rhythmic rules are naturally sensitive."

It is also theoretically predicted that the intrinsic properties in prosodic structure may lead to divergence between prosodic structure and syntactic structure. (Nespor & Vogel 2007; Selkirk 2011). Take PWd for illustration. Since it is the smallest prosodic constituent that maps the morphsyntactic structure, X-ω correspondence requires it to correspond to the syntactic terminal element, the syntactic word. Nevertheless, being composed of pure metrical units, namely Feet, a well-formed ω has limitations on its size which could be reducible to pure rhythmic motivations. Languages may vary on whether X-ω faithful mapping takes priority or ω structure well-formedness is dominant. Shaoxing dialect has two layers of tone sandhi rules, one of which has its phonological domain structure defined through ω and presents the dominance of ω structure well-formedness over X-ω correspondence.

The phonological domain structure of tone sandhi in Tianjin dialect exemplifies that language-specific syntactic structure (to be specific, recursion here) may impact the formation of prosodic structure; while that of Shaoxing dialect distinguishes itself in the sense that prosodic structure well-formedness constraints (to be specific, size effects on ω) gives prominence. Tone sandhis of Tianjin dialect and Shaoxing dialect are both domain-sensitive phonological rules, which do not refer to any syntactic or prosodic information. Tone sandhi in Yuncheng dialect, in contrast, not only has its phonological domain structure configured through the interaction between X-ω correspondence and ω structure well-formedness constraint, but also is sensitive to the integrity of immediate morphosyntactic constituency. So, from tone sandhi in Yuncheng dialect, we see that, besides syntactic-prosodic constituency correspondence and prosodic structure well-formedness constraints, phonological rules themselves may express requirements on the construction of their domain structure.

As early as in the edge-based theory, Selkirk (1986, 1995: 188) has insightfully pointed out, through observing the prosodic behavior of functional words in English, that the mapping from syntactic structure to prosodic structure is sensitive to the distinction between lexical categories (i. e. nouns, verbs, adjectives) and functional categories (i. e. determiners, prepositions, auxiliaries, modals, conjunctions, complementizers, etc.). This basic principle has been repeatedly testified through cross-language data (Truckenbrodt 1999) and maintained in the Match Theory. Our research on the formation of phonological domains of tone sandhis in Tianjin, Yuncheng and Shaoxing dialect also support this important theoretical assertion.

Distinction between lexical category and functional category will be further illustrated in Chapters 4 and 5 through tone sandhis of South Min dialects and Wenzhou dialect, a well-described dialect of South Wu.

3.1 Promoting PWd

In the prosodic hierarchy, ω is the smallest constituent that interacts with syntactic constituents. According to the Match Theory (Selkirk 2011), PWd is mapped from the syntactic terminal element X, with the refinement that X belongs to lexical categories (i.e. X = N, V, A). Nespor & Vogel (2007: 110 – 114) reports that in Demotic Greek, the PWd has the same extension as the syntactic terminal lexical element, which is revealed through two phonological rules Nasal Assimilation (NA) and Stop Voicing (SV). Greek NA and SV are ω span rules and only obligatory within the ω regardless whatever the morphological structure of X that maps into the ω is. See (3.1) for illustration:

(3.1) a. [tembélis]   lazy
    b. [tsambunízo]   (I) shout
    c. [simbonó] < [sin + ponó]   (I) have compassion
    d. [simbíno] < [sin + píno]   (I) drink in company
    e. [embiría] < [en + piría]   experience
    f. [siŋgataléγo] < [sin + kata + léγo]   (I) include among
    g. [siŋgatavéno] < [sin + kata + véno]   (I) condescend

Examples in (3.1) show that NA and SV apply in underived words (a, b), in derived words, between the prefix and the stem (c, d, e), and between prefixes of a word (f, g). Segmental changes prove the isomorphism between the syntactic terminal elements X and PWd in Demotic Greek. In fact, it is ideal, however frequently not the case, that ω is isomorphic with X from which it is mapped.

3.2 Factors Intervening in X-ω Correspondence

3.2.1 Strict Layering

The Match Theory, as an interface theory, states the correspondence between syntactic constituency and prosodic constituency. It inherits the core spirits of McCarthy & Prince's (1995) Theory of Correspondence which holds that correspondence has dual-effects.

(3.2) Syntax-Prosody Correspondence (Selkirk 2011: 451)
 a. S-P Faithfulness
  The left and right edges of a constituent of type α in the input syntactic representation must correspond to the left and right edges of a constituent of type π in the output phonological representation.
 b. P-S Faithfulness
  The left and right edges of a constituent of type π in the output phonological representation must correspond to the left and right edges of a constituents of type α in the input syntactic representation.

Syntactic constituency is required to be faithfully reflected in prosodic constituency and prosodic constituency must faithfully reflect syntactic constituency (Selkirk 2011: 437). [1] A major consequence of faithful syntactic-

---

[1] The notion of syntax-prosody correspondence will be explicitly developed in Chapter 6 in which an OT-based typological account on the domain structure of tone sandhi will be delivered.

prosodic mapping is the emergence of prosodic constituents with recursive structure in violation of the Strict Layer Hypothesis:

(3.3) Strict Layer Hypothesis (Selkirk 1995; Nespor & Vogel 2007; Pierrehumbert & Beckman 1988; Hayes 1989; Inkelas 1990)

A constituent of category level n in the prosodic hierarchy immediately dominates only a (sequence of) constituents at category level n-1 in the hierarchy.

Strict Layer Hypothesis conveys purely phonological relations holding between different levels of prosodic constituents. So a recursively-built PWd out of the requirement of S-P faithful mapping as illustrated in (3.4) violates Strict Layer Hypothesis because: firstly, a prosodic constituent at category level n (i.e. ω here) immediately dominates another prosodic constituent at the same category level (i.e. ω here); secondly, a prosodic constituent at category level n (i.e. ω here) immediately dominates a prosodic constituent at category level lower than level n-1 (i.e. σ here) thus resulting into level-skipping (Selkirk 2011).

(3.4)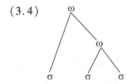

A subgroup of tri-syllabic tone sandhi in Tianjin dialect exactly diagnoses the recursive property of ω which is inherited from syntax. The domination of S-P faithful mapping over strict layering of prosodic structure is assumed to take the responsibility.

3.2.2 Size Constraints

In Prosodic Hierarchy, the pure rhythmic unit, namely, the Foot is universally minimally bimoraic or bi-syllabic, as a consequence, a ω, consisting of minimally one foot, must itself be minimally bisyllabic (Hayes 1995). Hayes's idea is carried further in Selkirk (2011: 468) where she proposes that "prosodic minimality effects will be common across languages both at the φ-level and at the ι-level", and two sets of prosodic markedness constraints are formulated then: for instance, BinMin (φ, ω) requires that a φ minimally consist of two ωs, and BinMin (φ, ω) requires that a φ maximally consist of two ωs. Hence, size effect is transmissive in the sense that the limitation on the size of a certain prosodic constituent may still be visible in the prosodic constituent of the immediate upper level into which it composes.

Let us turn to rhythmic grouping in Chinese. Take the most well studied Mandarin Chinese, as the starting point.

Lü (1963) points out that while bi-syllabicity has become the general tendency in Modern Chinese, the mono-syllabic fragment is no longer favorable, so it either becomes a di-syllabic unit with resorts to morphological compounding or adjoins to the adjacent di-syllabic unit thus forming a tri-syllabic fragment which is also quite common in Modern Chinese. Feng's (1996: 162 – 163, 167) successive research clarifies the prosodic status of Lü's (1963) di- and tri-syllabic fragments. Chen (2000: 367) labels the di-syllabic prosodic unit as Minimal Rhythmic Unit (MRU). The tri-syllabic rhythmic unit comes into existence because a mono-syllabic fragment is too weak to stand alone prosodically so that it incorporates into an MRU in juxtaposition. Feng (1996) also argues that there are cases in which mono-syllabic fragments do stand alone on their own; however, with their rhyme lengthened, or with an empty beat inserted to their right, which are apparently resolutions ad hoc.

Based on Feng's (1996) insightful work, Wang (2000) argues that ω in Mandarin Chinese consists of either one foot (bi-syllabic or tri-syllabic) or two feet (bi-syllabic only). So, in Mandarin Chinese, a legitimate ω could be minimally bi-syllabic, tri-syllabic, and maximally quarto-syllabic as shown in (3.5) a, b, d.

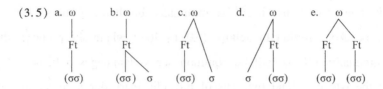

(3.5)

Wang's (2000) deduction on the configuration of ω in Mandarin converges with Hayes's (1995) and Selkirk's (2000, 2011) theoretical prediction. A ω is minimally di-syllabic, i.e. (3.5) a required by BINMIN—"a ω consists of at least one foot which must itself be binary" (Selkirk 2011), but maximally quarto-syllabic, i.e. (3.5) d, as a consequence of BINMAX (ω, Ft) requiring there be no more than two Ft in a ω. Ito & Mestor (2003) has, based on Japanese loanwords, argued that it is not necessarily the case that the requirement of binarity on ω must be rigidly realized through Feet, but a Ft and a single syllable could compose a ω as well, i.e. (3.5) c, (at the expense of Strict Layering, obviously). Tri-syllabic ω is also legitimate in Chinese. But, whether it is composed of a tri-syllabic Ft, i.e. (3.5) b, or an independent Ft plus a syllable, i.e. (3.5) c, d, it needs further empirical proof and theoretical computation, and situations vary from dialect to dialect. A subgroup of tone sandhi in Tianjin dialect proves the computation of (3.5) d, while tone sandhi in Shaoxing dialect not only supports the ω structure of (3.5) e, but also allows ω being composed of a di-syllabic Ft and a tri-syllabic Ft, which constitutes typological difference to ω formation in Mandarin. The regulation on the organization of a ω expresses itself explicitly as Size Constraint—a legitimate ω has lower and upper limits on syllable count. The outranking of size constraints over P-S faithfulness mapping results in nonisomorphism between ω and X which will be the focus of this chapter.

3.2.3 Domain-Sensitive Phonological Constraint

Besides syntactic structure and prosodic structure well-formedness constraints,

Selkirk (2011: 448 – 449) proposes that another source of S-P nonisomorphism comes from phonology itself.

In Xitsonga, a Bantu language, H-tone spreading is a sentence-level phonology (Kisseberth 1994; Cassimjee & Kissberth 1998). Though its phonological domain structure is defined through its prosodic constituent, PPh/φ, H-tone spreading itself is also sensitive to prosodic structures (Selkirk 2011: 9): "A lexical hightone spreads rightward from its underlying position, but it is (i) blocked from spreading onto the final, rightmost, syllable of a φ-domain as illustrated by (3.6) a and (ii) blocked from spreading across the left edge of a φ-domain as illustrated by (3.6) b."

(3.6) Prosodic Domain of H-Tone Spreading (Selkirk 2011: 443)

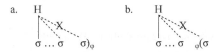

H-tone spreading in Xitsonga exemplifies that phonological domain may refer to prosodic information. Tone sandhi in Yuncheng dialect, on the other hand, helps with developing Selkirk's proposal in the sense that phonological rules interact with both prosody and syntax.

In Section 3.3 we will explore the recursivity in PWd inherited from syntax through tone sandhi in Tianjin dialect; in Section 3.4 we will discuss how prosodic structure markedness constraints (appearing as size effects) undermine the correspondence between the syntactic word and PWd through the investigation of the phonological domain structure of tone sandhi in Shaoxing dialect; in Section 3.5 tone sandhi in Yuncheng dialect will show us how phonology interacts with prosody and syntax.

3.3 Tone Sandhi in Tianjin Dialect

3.3.1 Basics

The city of Tianjin is located 120 kilometers away from Beijing. Tianjin dialect is greatly Mandarin-based and its tone and tone sandhi is distinct from nearby dialects. There are four citation tones in Tianjin dialect: *yinping*, *yangping*, *shangsheng* and *qusheng*. From Li (1956) to Shi & Wang (2004), consecutive studies reveal that the pitch values of the four citation tones have been undergoing slight changes over the past 50 – 60 years. Disregarding the trivial phonetic details, phonologically-oriented, they can be formalized as follows (Table 3.1):

Table 3.1 Citation tones in Tianjin dialect (Wang 2002)

Tonal Category	Ia	Ib	II	III
Phonological Representation	LL	HH	LH	HL

In Tianjin dialect, tones in juxtaposition will undergo tone sandhi changes. Tone sandhi in Tianjin dialect is chiefly characterized by (Li & Liu 1985; Shi 1990):

i. The di-syllabic string is the minimal domain of tone sandhi, and polysyllabic strings undergo tone sandhi based on the di-syllabic ones; the quarto-syllabic string is the largest domain of application of tone sandhi.

ii. In a di-syllabic string, the first syllable puts on a new tone while the second syllable keeps its base tone.

iii. In literature, tone sandhi can proceed from both direction in polysyllabic (specifically tri-syllabic) strings.

iv. Di- and tri-syllabic tone sandhis are insensitive to strings' morphosyntactic structure, while quarto-syllabic tone sandhi shows influence from syntax.

Many phonologists (Chen 1986, 2000; Millken et al 1997; Wang 2003; Ma 2005) have conducted research on the triggers of rules of tone sandhi in Tianjin dialect; however, as far as di-directionality and phonological opacity arising from poly-syllabic tone sandhi are concerned, the disputes are far away from being resolved. Meanwhile, social investigations (Lu 1997; Shi & Wang 2004) find that tone sandhi in Tianjin dialect is undergoing significant change which requires reappraisal of the analysis of tone sandhi purely from phonology itself. Moreover, the phonological domain structure of tone sandhi has always been neglected in the previous studies, which, according to our observation, is vital in resolving the "paradox of tone sandhi in Tianjin dialect" (Chen 1986).

Our argument will be based on first-hand data collected from intensive social investigation on tone sandhi in Tianjin dialect that we conducted on our own, together with data selected from literature. In Section 3.3.2, differences in di- and tri- syllabic tone sandhis between Old Tianjin dialect and New Tianjin dialect will be first introduced, disputes over directionality and phonoligcal opacity will be resolved, evidenced by the changes in tone sandhi along with a prosodic account on the phonological domain structure of di- and tri-syllabic tone sandhi being delivered. The ω status of the domain of tone sandhi is reinforced by optional application of tone sandhi on quarto-syllabic strings. A subgroup of tri-syllabic tone sandhi testifies to recursion of prosodic constituents inherited from morphosyntactic structure and triggered by the changes in stress pattern.

3.3.2 Phonological Structure of Tone Sandhi Domain

3.3.2.1 Di-Syllabic Tone Sandhi

For di-syllabic strings, among the 4 × 4 = 16 tonal combinations, 4 of them undergo tone sandhi changes. Regulations of tone sandhi were first described in Li & Liu (1985). However, according to Lu (1997), and Shi & Wang's (2004) recent studies, di-syllabic tone sandhis have tremendously changed within the past twenty years. Data from Shi & Wang (2004) are repeated in Table 3.2:

Table 3.2 Disyllabic tone sandhis of Old Tianjin dialect and
New Tianjin dialect (Shi & Wang 2004)

	Old Tianjin Dialect		New Tianjin Dialect	Examples
a.	LL.LL→LH.LL	a'	LL.LL→HH.LL	[fei-tɕi] airplane [tṣʰəu [ian]] smoke cigarette
b.	LH.LH→HH.LH	b'	LH.LH→HH.LH	[ṣuei-kuə] fruit [ɕi [lian]] wash face
c.	HL.HL→LL.HL	c'	—	[tɕiau-ṣəu] professor [tṣʰaŋ[ɕi]] sing opera
d.	HL.LL→HH.LL	d'	HL.LL→HH.LL	[mian-pau] bread [xua-tṣuaŋ] make-up

Differences which are phonologically distinctive can be witnessed between Old Tianjin dialect and New Tianjin dialect (Lu 1997; Shi & Wang 2004):

i. Influenced by Mandarin, LL.LL→LH.LL only exists in Old Tianjin dialect, New Tianjin dialect takes HH.LH as the sandhi form.

ii. HL.HL→LL.HL has been disappearing dramatically, and can be hardly heard in Tianjin dialect.

iii. Conversely, HL.LL→HH.LL is reinforced and becomes the most prominent tone sandhi change. Indeed, our interview[①] of the non-Tianjin dialect speakers living in Tianjin has proved this tendency. Newcomers claim that the H-L melody is the mostly noticeable perceptually, and 86% of them tell that HL.LL→HH.LL is the first sandhi rule that they acquire.

Lu (1997) and Shi & Wang (2004) attribute the changes to the influence from Mandarin. Let us first look at the sandhi change of LL.LL→LH.LL. On the one hand, *shangsheng* / LH in LL.LL→LH.LL is realized in its allophonic form with the same tone shape but with higher register (i.e. 35). One the other hand, *yangping* / HH, the toneme at issue, with the phonetic value 45, lies between the allophone of *shangsheng* in Tianjin and *yinping* in Mandarin. It is

---

① The interview was conducted in Tianjin in 2014. 32 students of Tianjin Normal University from across China except for Tianjin participated in our interview.

believed that younger generations of Tianjin dialect use *yangping* / HH to replace the allophone of *shangsheng* / LH under the influence of *yinping* / HH in Mandarin. It is thus also a natural consequence that HL. LL→HH. LL is reinforced.

3.3.2.2 Chained-Up Tri-Syllabic Tone Sandhi

Multi-syllabic tone sandhi process on the base of di-syllabic tone sandhis, which means the changes of di-syllabic tone sandhis from Old Tianjin dialect to New Tianjin dialect will definitely lead to changes in multi-syllabic tone sandhis. In this section, we will chiefly introduce the divergence from Old Tianjin dialect to New Tianjin dialect exemplified by tri-syllabic tone sandhis. The domain structure of tri-syllabic tone sandhis will also be discussed in detail.

Among the $4 \times 4 \times 4 = 64$ types of tri-syllabic tonal combinations, 20 types may undergo sandhi changes in the initial or middle syllable (labelled as "σ_1 T. S." and "σ_2 T. S." respectively), while 7 types may undergo sandhi changes in both the initial and middle syllables (which is named as chained-up tone sandhi here). We will focus on the chained-up tone sandhi in this section.

Theoretically, for LL. LL. LL, LH. LL. LL, HL. LL. LL, HL. HL. HL, LL. HL. HL, HL. HL. LL, LH. LH. LH, both the initial and middle syllables can undergo sandhi changes, and tone sandhis can process from both directions (i.e. left-to-right and right-to-left). In fact, as far as directionality of tone sandhi is concerned, according to Li & Liu (1985), tone sandhis of HL. HL. LL and LH. LH. LH process from left to right (f, g in Table 3.3), while those of the other five types process from right to left (a – e in Table 3.3). Directionality directly leads to bleeding or feeding effects during the process of chained-up tone sandhi.

In the section above we have just introduced that significant changes have happened to di-syllabic tone sandhis, and it is deducible that the poly-syllabic ones will definitely not remain still. Our investigation① has proved this prediction. See the contrasts between Old Tianjin dialect and New Tianjin dialect:

Table 3.3 Tri-syllabic chained-up tone sandhi in Old Tianjin dialect and New Tianjin dialect②

	Old Tianjin Dialect		New Tianjin Dialect	Examples
a	HL. LL. LL→HL. LH. LL	a'	i. HL. LL. LL→HL. LH. LL ii. HL. LL. LL→HL. HH. LL	[uəi-ṣəŋtɕian] washroom [ta ku-ma] elder ante
b	LL. LL. LL→LL. LH. LL	b'	i. LL. LL. LL→LL. LH. LL ii. LL. LL. LL→LL. HH. LL	[tṣən-tṣu ṣuaŋ] pearl cream [kʰɛ fei-tɕi] fly a plane
c	HL. HL. HL→ HL. LL. HL→HH. LL. HL	c'	i. no sandhi changes ii. HL. HL. HL→HL. LL. HL	[i-ta-li] Italy [kʰan tian-ṣi] watch TV
d	LL. HL. HL→ LL. LL. HL→LH. LL. HL	d'	i. no sandhi changes ii. LL. HL. HL→LL. LL. HL	[uən-tu tɕi] thermometer [tʰoŋ tian-xua] make a phone call

---

① Our investigation was conducted in the summer of 2014 in Tianjin. We have selected 120 di-syllabic sample strings (that satisfy the phonological requirements of di-syllabic tone sandhi), and 339 tri-syllabic sample strings (that satisfy the phonological requirements of tri-syllabic tone sandhi) among which 127 satisfy the phonological requirements of chained-up tone sandhis. For each type of tonal combination, sample strings range from 10 to 20. The sample strings selected include both compounds and phrases with structures of subject-predicate, verb-object, coordinate, subordinate, verb-adverbial, etc. The syllable count of the syntactic terminal elements is also taken into consideration. Take tri-syllabic strings for instance. There are sample strings of both the syllabic combination of 1+2 and that of 2+1. All the sample strings are randomly listed. Subjects preview and read the samples at normal speech rate. 33 native speakers of Tianjin participated in our investigation, 12 of whom aged from 20–49, the rest 21 subjects aged from 50–79, 18 of whom are males, and 15 of whom are females. Their education backgrounds range from junior high school students to postgraduates. We recorded all the subjects' readings. 31 subjects' recordings were valid for further analysis. Perceptual judgments of tone sandhis were conducted first. Three people annotated the surface tones of all the sample strings independently. For different annotations, the three people gave re-judgments together with the help of Praat. All the recordings were sent to phonetic annotations for the next step. F0 contours and string durations (calculated syllable by syllable) were extracted, pauses between syllables within string were also annotated. All the perceptual and phonetic data collected were then sent to statistical analysis with the help of SPSS and Excel.

② Data of the tone sandhis of Old Tianjin dialect are cited from Ma (2005).

(continued)

	Old Tianjin Dialect		New Tianjin Dialect	Examples
e	LH. LL. LL→ LH. LH. LL→HH. LH. LL	e'	i. LH. LL. LL→LH. LH. LL ii. LH. LL. LL→LH. HH. LL	[fa-çi-si] fascism [zəu kaŋ-si] wire walking
f	HL. HL. LL→ LL. HL. LL→LL. HH. LL	f'	HL. HL. LL→HL. HH. LL	[ly-təu kau] mung bean cake [kuei-ʂuən-tʂai] Proper Name
g	LH. LH. LH→ HH. LH. LH→HH. HH. LH	g'	i. LH. LH. LH → HH. LH. LH→ HH. HH. LH ii. LH. LH. LH→LH. HH. LH	[pʰau-ma tʂʰaŋ] racecourse [tʂʰaŋ taŋ-uei] party committee

In thirty years' time, great changes have happened to chained-up tone sandhis, many of which are due to the changes of di-syllabic tone sandhis:

i. The change from LL. LL → LH. LL to LL. LL → HH. LL has significantly affected the tone sandhis of HL. LL. LL, LL. LL. LL and LH. LL. LL: sandhi forms of HL. HH. LL, LL. HH. LL, LH. HH. LL have emerged (see a' ii, b' ii, e' ii in Table 3.3). More specifically, 78% of the LH. LL. LL sample strings put on the sandhi form of LH. HH. LL which hence bleeds the sandhi change of LH in the string's initial position. In short, for these three tonal combinations, directionality remains as leftward, sandhi processes stop at the middle syllable.

ii. The disappearance of HL. HL→LL. HL has significantly affected the chained-up tone sandhi of HL. HL. H and LL. HL. HL. Statistical analysis show that up to 50% of subjects keep the citation forms (c' i, d' i); citation forms and sandhi forms HL. LL. HL, LL. LL. HL co-exist for the other half of the subjects. Sandhi forms HH. LL. HL and LH. LL. HL are the rare cases: (1) only one male subject (MJSL) aged over 60 can finish the sandhi process HL. **HL. HL**→HL. **LL**. HL →**HH**. LL. HL, with 2/3 of the sample strings changed to **HH**. LL. HL and the left 1/3 stop at HL. **LL**. HL. (2) Only two subjects

(MJSL and FZXL) both aged over 60 can finish the sandhi process LL. HL. HL→LL. LL. HL→LH. LL. HL, with just 11 sample strings put on the sandhi form LH. LL. HL, but the vast majority stop at LL. LL. HL. (3) It is the general tendency that young people keep the citation forms, but the sandhi forms HL. LL. HL and LL. LL. HL are still acceptable, nevertheless, it is worthy of noting that young people not only do not produce the sandhi forms LH. LL. HL and LL. LL. HL, but also find them to be weird! For these two groups, Leftward is still the default tone sandhi direction; however, the fading of HL. HL → LL. HL gives rise to citation forms being kept. Another tendency seen from these two groups is that tone sandhis halt at the middle syllable.

iii. Statistical analysis show that HL. HL. LL has undergone subversive changes: the reinforcement of HL. LL→HL. LL and the disappearance of HL. HL. → LL. HL lead to the reverse of the directionality of HL. HL. LL's sandhi processes from rightward to leftward, as 95% of sample strings put on the sandhi form of HL. HH. LL (f' in Table 3.3). Young people still accept the old-fashioned rightward tone sandhi processing, but they themselves do not produce it any more.

iv. Two groups of related statistical data reveal LH. LH. LH's sandhi process has been switching from rightward to leftward as well: (1) while most of the sample strings take the sandhi form HH. HH. LH, it is noticeable that 1/3 of the sample strings have undergone the leftward tone sandhi process as their sandhi forms are LH. HH. LH; (2) especially, for the coordinate phrases, 22% of them take LH. HH. LH as their sandhi forms. Even though rightward is still the default direction, leftward processing has been diffusing to LH. LH. LH.

In Short, for the tri-syllabic chained-up tone sandhis, the major differences between Old Tianjin dialect and New Tianjin dialect are:

i. Di-directionality has been switching to unified leftwardness.
ii. Chained-up tone sandhis have been "losing the chain" as the sandhi processes halt as soon as sandhi changes of the middle syllables have done, which at the same time reveals that the internal morphosyntactic structure is irrelevant to the application of tone sandhi.

Simplification is the general tendency in chained-up tone sandhis. Despite the significant changes from Old Tianjin dialect to New Tianjin dialect, coordinate expressions (e. g. [muə-ɕi-kə] Maxico), phrases (e. g. [kʰɛ fei-tɕi] fly an airplane) and compounds (e. g. [tʂ ən-tʂu ʂuaŋ] pearl cream) are all involved in chained-up tone sandhis, and the internal structures do not form a block to sandhi processing. Once the tonic contexts are met, tone sandhis will take place. To make it clearer, the chained-up tone sandhi takes the entire tri-syllabic string as its domain of application.

3.3.3 Prosodic Constituency of the Tone Sandhi Domain

Li (1956) claimed that tone sandhi in Tianjin dialect typically operates on di- and tri-syllabic strings. Our investigation has not only testified Li's claim but also revealed that in New Tianjin dialect tone sandhi starts to work from the right boundaries of strings and proceeds leftward irrespective of both the syntactic constituency and the strings' internal morphosyntactic structure. Tone sandhi rules of Tianjin dialect are indifferent to syntactic constituency, and there are rigid size effects to the domain of tone sandhi. Both properties point to a prosodic interpretation of the domain structure of tone sandhi in Tianjin dialect.

3.3.3.1 PWd and S-P Correspondence

Despite the phonetic changes discussed above, the morphosyntactic environments of tone sandhi remain unchanged. Di-syllabic tone sandhis range from compounds (e. g. [fei-tɕi] airplane) to phrases (e. g. [tʂʰəu [ian]] smoke cigarette). And it hence seems that the prosodic domain of di-syllabic tone sandhi is a paradox. According to the Match Theory, the compound noun of [fei-tɕi] projects into PWd, while the verb phrase of [tʂʰəu [ian]] projects into PPh. The phonological processes are the same, but prosodic-definings of their domains are different.

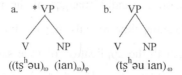

Figure 3.1 Prosodic parsing of [tʂʰəu [ian]] smoke cigarette

In Tianjin dialect, for a di-syllabic string, once the tonal context is met, tone sandhi will take place, whatever the morphosyntactic structure is. Our phonetic analysis shows that the F0 contour is continuous without any pitch reset between the two syllables, and neither pause nor prolonging can be perceived. Both phonological and phonetic clues demonstrate that BINMIN and BINMAX—prosodic structure well-formedness constraints—defeat prosodic-syntactic isomorphism, hence the two mono-syllabic syntactic terminal constituents combine and produce a di-syllabic ω as a consequence. In Tianjin dialect, for a di-syllabic string, its syntactic structure is not a blocker to tone sandhi due to the high pressure of Binarity. ω defines the di-syllabic tone sandhi domain with the possibility that the ω's domain is larger than the syntactic terminal element, as the case of [tʂʰəu [ian]] shown.

The tri-syllabic string, as well as the di-syllabic counterpart, is the obligatory domain of application of tone sandhi in Tianjin dialect, irrespective of the syntactic constituency and the string's internal morphosyntactic structure. Our investigation on sentential-level tone sandhi shows that, at a normal speech rate, a clause will map into a sequence of di- or tri-syllabic domains of tone sandhi[①]. In Section 3.2.2 we have promoted and reasoned for tri-syllabic strings' legal status as an independent ω in Mandarin. The size of the domain of tone sandhi identifies the validity of a tri-syllabic ω in Tianjin dialect. Whether a compound, a phrase or a clause, as long as tone sandhi takes it as an

---

① Sporadic quarto-syllabic domains of tone sandhi on sentence level were also found in our investigation. We will discuss quarto-syllabic tone sandhi in Section 3.3.3.2.

independent working domain, then this tri-syllabic string is granted within dependent prosodic status as ω. Hence, application of chained-up tone sandhi to VP ([kʰɛ fei-tɕi] fly a plane) in Figure 3.2 a, coordinate structured string ([fa-ɕi-si] fascism) in Figure 3.2 b and compound ([uən-tu tɕi] thermometer) in Figure 3.2 c demonstrate that the tri-syllabic strings map into independent ωs at the expense of syntactic-prosodic constituency correspondence.

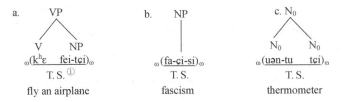

Figure 3.2 Prosodic parsing of tri-syllabic string

The fact that obligatory tone sandhi in Tianjin dialect is typically restricted to di- and tri-syllabic string irrespective of the syntactic constituency indicates that the size effects initiated by ω well-formedness requirements defeats syntactic-prosodic constituency correspondence, in another word, rhythmic grouping may destroy the integrity of syntactic constituents at the sentence level, which is diagnosed by prosodically constrained sentential phonological phenomena, i.e. tone sandhi.

3.3.3.2 Obligatory Tone Sandhi vs. Optional Tone Sandhi

We have just demonstrated that, in Tianjin dialect, irrespective of the internal morphosyntactic structure, once the tonal contexts are satisfied, tone sandhi will obligatorily take place in a di- or tri-syllabic string. However, Shi (1990) reports that tone sandhi is also witnessed in quarto-syllabic strings with reference to morphosyntactic structure. In fact, quarto-syllabic tone sandhi significantly reveals that tone sandhi may appear on two levels of prosodic constituents, i.e. PWd / ω and PPh / φ. Tone sandhi obligatorily applies leftward within ω, while optionally applies between adjacent di-syllabic ωs which are linearly ordered rightward on the sentence level. This means tone sandhi optionally applies rightward on φ-level after tone sandhi within ω is done. The

---

① T.S. =Tone Sandhi

facts stated above strongly imply that the phonological domain of the application of tone sandhi in Tianjin dialect is ω.

3.3.3.2.1　A+B+C+D and [A+B]+[C+D]

Our investigation of New Tianjin dialect reveals that, in a quarto-syllabic string with coordinate structure, if "A + B" or "C + D" meets the tonic requirements of tone sandhi, tone sandhi will apply to "A + B" and "C + D" respectively; if "B + C" (either "C" is in citation form or sandhi form) meets the tonic requirements, tone sandhi will happen only when they are of the combination of LH. LH. In Figure 3.3 we can see that tone sandhi applies to "[ny lau] woman, adged person" with the tonal context LH. LH as shown in Figure 3.3 a, but fails to take place between "[tuŋ tsʰuən] winter, spring" with the tonal context LL. LL in Figure 3.3 b.

Tone sandhi of LH. LH widely exists in Mandarin-based dialects. According to Mei (1977), its history can be traced back as early as the 16th century. It behaves noticeably different from the other three groups of tone sandhi (namely, LL. LL, HL. HL and HL. LL) in Tianjin dialect (Figure 3.3):

i. In multi-syllabic strings, HL. HL tone sandhi processes from left to right, e. g. in tri-syllabic chained-up tone sandhi "[pʰau-ma tsʰaŋ] racecourse".

ii. HL. HL tone sandhi is so powerful that it cannot be hindered by Binarity and syntactic constituency, e. g. in quarto-syllabic strings we are discussing at hand.

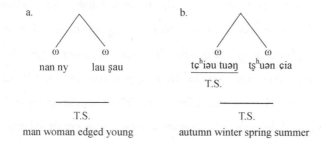

Figure 3.3　A+B+C+D structured quarto-syllabic tone sandhi

Strings with the structure of [A+B] + [C+D] behave the same as those [A+B+C+D] structured ones; the two di-syllabic syntactic terminal elements project into two independent ωs. Tone sandhis take these two ωs as domains of application respectively, but no more tone sandhi takes place across the boundary of the ω except for "B + C" being of the combination of LH. LH. For instance, in Figure 3.4 a, [li] and sandhi-formed [ʂuəi] meet the LH. LH tonal context, and undergo tone sandhi changes consequently; contrastively, in b, [tʂuəŋ] and sandhi-formed [fan] meet the LL. LL tonal context, but tone sandhi does not happen after all.

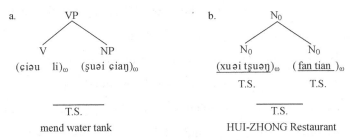

Figure 3.4 [A + B] + [C + D] structured quarto-syllabic tone sandhi

Tone sandhi of quarto-syllabic strings structured as "A + B + C + D" or "A + B + C + D" is obviously constrained by the prosodic structure wellformedness constraints—Binarity. Whether the string is a phrase or a compound, it splits into two independent di-syllabic domains of tone sandhi which are the most unmarked ω in essence. These two ωs may form a larger domain of tone sandhi if and only if the non-periphery syllables meet the tonal context of LH. LH.

3.3.3.2.2 [A + [B + C + D]]

Our investigation shows that X-ω correspondence appears to be dominant in the combination of [A + [B + C + D]], because, whether the string is left-or right-headed, "B + C + D" undergoes tri-syllabic tone sandhis as per what we have discussed in the previous section. Nevertheless, "A" does not undergo sandhi change even if "A + B" satisfies the tonic requirements of tone sandhi. As is shown in Spectrogram 3.1, [tɕiəu] keeps its citation form although [tɕiəuʂəu] meets the tonal context of HL. LL. This illusion drives us to propose that X-ω correspondence introduces in two independent ωs, i.e. (A)$_ω$

and (BCD)$_\omega$. But, obviously, the appearance of mono-syllabic PWd (A)$_\omega$ violates BINMIN. We have then conducted statistical analysis on syllable duration of [A + [B + C + D]] structured sample strings, and [[A + B + C] + D] structured strings are taken for reference (see Figure 3.5):

i. In [[A + B + C] + D] structured strings, the duration of "A" is shorter than the whole string's average syllabic duration.

ii. Conversely, in [A + [B + C + D]] structured strings, the duration of "A" which lasts almost as long as "D", is apparently longer than the whole string's average syllabic duration.

iii. The duration of "D" is the longest in the whole string in both [A + [B + C + D]] and [[A + B + C] + D] structured ones.

Syllables at prosodic boundaries may be prolonged (Liberman & Pierrehumbert 1984). Since "A" and "D" of [A + [B + C + D]] structured strings behave similarly in terms of duration, it is very possible that the locus of "A" is a certain prosodic boundary as well as that of "D". It is indeed the case that a very short un-silent pause can be perceived immediately after "A". So, "A" in [A + [B + C + D]] structured string is promoted to a "degenerate foot … through rime-prolonging or pause in postposition …" (Feng 1996: 163), and then gains independent prosodic status, as is shown in Figure 3.6 a, b.

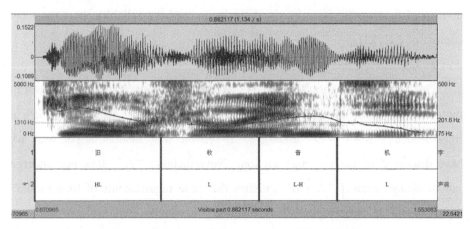

Spectrogram 3.1 [tɕiəu [ʂəu in tɕi]] **old radio**

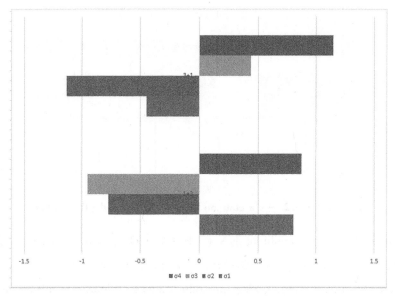

Figure 3.5 Z-score of syllable duration in $[A + [B + C + D]]$ & $[[A + B + C] + D]$

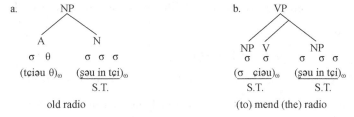

Figure 3.6 Quarto-syllabic tone sandhi of $[A + [B + C + D]]$ structured string

Although "A" can stand alone prosodically through prolonging or pause, degenerate feet are severely contextual-restricted (Feng 1996: 163). A more unmarked choice is to adjoin to a prosodic constituent in juxtaposition. For example, as Spectrogram 3.2 shows, in the penta-syllabic short clause "[tʰa çiəu ṣəu iən tçi] he mended (the) radio", there are two tone sandhi domains [tʰa çiəu] and [ṣəu iən tçi]. Even though [çiəu] and [ṣəu] satisfy the tonic requirement of tone sandhi, tone sandhi does not take place at all. Besides, a pause can be prominently perceived between [tʰa çiəu] and [ṣəu iən tçi]. Motivated by Binarity, the two mono-syllabic syntactic terminal constituents, i.e. subject [tʰa] and verb [çiəu], project into a di-syllabic PWd at the expense of X-ω correspondence as shown in Figure 3.6 b.

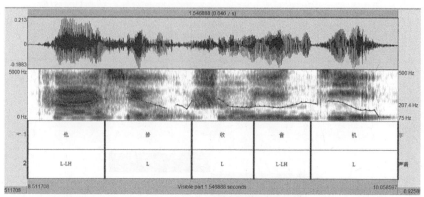

Spectrogram 3.2 [tʰa ɕiəuʂəu iɔn tɕi] he mended (the) radio①

Analysis of tone sandhi of [A + [B + C + D]] structured strings above reveals the top-ranking of BINMIN. A mono-syllabic syntactic terminal constituent can obtain independent prosodic status temporarily by observing X-ω correspondence, but in larger syntactic constituents, mono-syllabic constituents will incorporate into an adjacent constituent so as to optimize the prosodic spelling of the entire string.

3.3.3.2.3 [[A +B +C] +D]

Tone sandhi of the [[A + B + C] + D] structured string is the most complicated case in that of quarto-syllabic strings. According to our investigation, in about 1/4 of the sample strings, tone sandhi processes observing syntactic-prosodic constituency isomorphism, namely: "A + B + C" undergo tri-syllabic tone sandhi, but "D", in most cases, is deprived of the right of participating in tone sandhi, hence "C" will not undergo sandhi changes even if "C + D" meets the tonal contexts. Confusingly enough, there are indeed 4 cases that tone sandhi in "C + D" is witnessed. Moreover, in these 4 cases, all the four syllables are closely connected, without significant pause being perceived inside the string.

In Section 3.3.3.2.1, [A + B + C + D] or [[A + B] + [C + D]] structured examples in Figure 3.4 demonstrate that tone sandhi processes in a

---

① The length of the VOT of the aspirated voiceless stops is uniformally set as 50 ms in this book.

two-step way: "A + B" and "C + D" undergo tone sandhi separately, for exannple, "[xuəi ʂuəŋ] HUI-ZHONG" and "[fan tian] Restaurant" in Figure 3.4 b; then if "B + C" ("C" is either in citation form or sandhi form) meets tonic contexts of tone sandhi, the LH. LH conditioned ones will take place (compare "[li ʂuəi] (LH. LH)" and "[tʂuəŋ fan] (LL. LL)"). This two-step process is also what we see in the four [[A + B + C] + D] structured cases. ①

Let us take "[mɤ-çi-kə tsʰuən] Mexico Village" for illustration. Theoretically speaking, X-ω correspondence predicts that the entire compound [mɤ-çi-kə tsʰuən] maps into a single domain of tone sandhi which proceeds leftward syllable by syllable as is demonstrated in Figure 3.7 b. However, pitch contour in Spectrogram 3.3 denies this assumption. In Spectrogram 3.3, we see that [çi] surfaces in sandhi tone H, and [kə] surfaces in sandhi tone LH. This pattern of tone sandhi is produced through two steps: [mɤ-çi-kə tsʰuən] splits into two separate domains of application of tone sandhi, and chained-up tri-syllabic tone sandhi takes place in [mɤ-çi-kə] resulting in the tonal change of [çi]; as [çɪ kə] meets the LH. LH tonal context, [mɤ-çi-kə tsʰuən] forms a larger domain resulting in the tonal change of [kə] (see Figure 3.7 a).

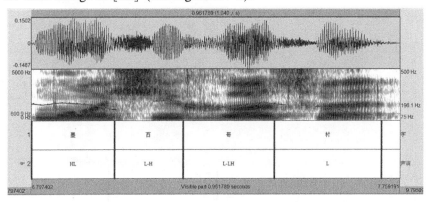

Spectrogram 3.3　　[mɤ-çi-kə tsʰuən] Mexico village

---

① A vital difference between the [A +B +C +D] / [[A +B] +[C +D]] structured ones and the [[A +B +C] +D] structured ones lies in that application of tone sandhi between "B +C" in the former is restricted to the LH. LH combination, while there is no restriction to tonic contexts on "C +D" in the latter.

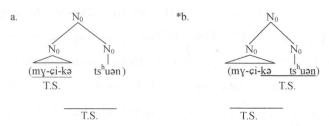

Figure 3.7 [A+[B+C+D]] structured string: [mɤ-ɕi-kə tsʰuən] Mexico

"[mɤ-ɕi-kə tsʰuən] Mexico Village" is one of the only 4 sample strings that undergo this two-step tone sandhi. In fact, the general situation is that the most unmarked di-syllabic ω completely shapes the string's tonic grouping. Take a quarto-syllabic preposition phrase "[[tɕin-ʂa]-tɕiaŋ] pian] along the Jinsha River" for example. If the domain of tone sandhi of [[tɕin-ʂa]-tɕiaŋ] pian] is built with X-ω correspondence being observed, then the compound noun [tɕin-ʂa-tɕiaŋ] and the preposition head [pian] should compose two separate domains of tone sandhi, as is shown in Figure 3.8 b. But pitch contour in Spectrogram 3.4 proves the outranking of Binarity over X-ω correspondence. In Spectrogram 3.4, [tɕin] and [tɕiaŋ] surface as LH which means [tɕin-ʂa] and [tɕiaŋ pian] form domains of tone sandhi independent from each other as shown by Figure 3.8 a.

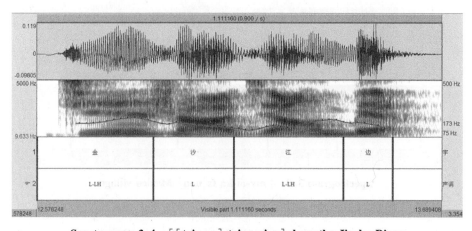

Spectrogram 3.4 [[tɕin-ʂa]-tɕiaŋ pian] along the Jinsha River

Chapter 3   Correspondence Between X and PWd

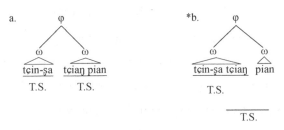

**Figure 3.8   Tone sandhi of [A + [B + C + D]] structured string:
[[tɕin-ʂa]-tɕiaŋ] pian] along the Jinsha River**

It might be argued that, in examples like [[tɕin-ʂa]-tɕiaŋ] pian], semantic or pragmatic factors, rather than prosodic structure well-formedness constraint Binarity, should take the blame that the grouping of domains of tone sandhi fails in observing the integrity of morphosyntactic structure, since "[tɕiaŋ pian] river bank" is semantically legitimate. Our investigation, however, immediately refutes this assumption. Among the vast [[A + B + C] + D] structured sample strings, 3/4 have the same parsing of the domain of application of tone sandhi as [[tɕin-ʂa]-tɕiaŋ] pian] does, regardless of whether the tone sandhi groups have legitimate semantic readings or not, for example, "[[xuəŋ [ʂi-tsi]] xuəi]→(xuəŋ ʂi)$_\omega$(tsi xuəi)$_\omega$ Association of the Red Cross", "[[ku [uən-xua]] tɕiɛ]→(ku uən)$_\omega$(xua tɕiɛ)$_\omega$ old culture street", "[[[xua tʂuaŋ] pʰin] tʂʰaŋ]→(xua tʂuaŋ)$_\omega$(pʰin ʂaŋ)$_\omega$ factory of cosmetics", etc. It suffices to say that prosodic structure well-formedness constraint Binarity is the fundamental strength that leads to nonisomorphism between syntactic constituents and prosodic constituents in [[A + B + C] + D] structured strings.

3.3.3.3   Recursion in PWd

In Section 3.3.2.2 we have introduced that, besides the 7 types of tri-syllabic tonic combinations that undergo chained-up tone sandhi, there are 20 types of tri-syllabic tonal combinations that undergo either σ_1 T. S. or σ_2 T. S. Wang (2003) is the pioneer work that studies σ_1 T. S. or σ_2 T. S., and is the first to point out the asymmetrical behaviors of tone sandhis between HL. LL. X and X. HL. LL. Our investigation has further found that LL. LL. X and X. LL. LL behave differently as well. Except for the cases just introduced, all other σ_1 T. S. and σ_2 T. S. process regularly: they range from coordinate structures (e. g. "[tɕiəu-u-i] nine five one"), compounds (e. g. "[ɕi-pei tɕiau] (the) northwest corner") to phrases (e. g. "[sau ma-lu] sweep the road", "[rən-ʂəu ʂau] short of hands"), and the strings' internal morphosyntactic structures are of no relevance, which are just the same as chained-up tone sandhis. Another way in which the strings resemble chained-up tone sandhis is that they map into an independent domain of application of tone sandhi. Our phonetic analysis shows that, as far as these tri-syllabic sandhi groups are concerned, the F0 contour is continuous without any pitch reset within the string, and neither pause nor prolonging inside the string can be perceived. Phonetic and perceptual evidence testifies to Feng's (1996) theoretical hypothesis: a mono-syllabic element (being either head or non-head syntactically speaking) is too weak to stand on its own prosodically speaking, in consequence, it incorporates into the adjacent di-syllabic constituent to gain its prosodic status, thus leading to a tri-syllabic ω, and tone sandhi processes within this ω are blind to its morphosyntactic structure (see Figure 3.9).

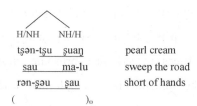

Figure 3.9 **Chained-up tone sandhi, σ_1 T. S. and σ_2 T. S.**

Turning aside from the cases just discussed above, let us turn to the focus of this subsection: the asymmetrical behaviors of tone sandhis between L. LH. X and X. L. LH, L. L. X and X. L. L.

As is shown in Table 3.4, the application of L. LH and L. L relates to their position in the tri-syllabic string. Take Type I as an example. If the left boundary of a tone sandhi group aligns with the left boundary of the string, tone sandhi will not process (a-I, c-I in Table 3.4); in contrast, if the right boundary of tone sandhi group aligns with the right boundary of the string, tone sandhi will process (b-I, d-I in Table 3.4). Up to now, the only difference between (a-I., c-I.) and (b-I., d-I.) lies in the position of the tone sandhi group in the tri-syllabic string, for instance, [la] keeps the citation tone (HL) in "[[la-tɕiau] ʂuəi] spicy water" but surfaces as a sandhi tone (H) in "[xuəŋ [la-tɕiau]] red pepper" (see pitch contour in Spectrogram 3.5 below). Meanwhile, morphosyntactic structure does not account for the asymmetrical behavior between (a-I., c-I.) and (b-I., d-I.) because [A + [B + C]] and [[A + B] + C] structured examples exist both in (a-I., c-I.) and (b-I., d-I.).

Table 3.4 Asymmetrical behaviors between HL. LL. X and X. HL. LL, LL. LL. X and X. LL. LL

	Tonal Contexts	Example I	Example II
a.	HL. LL. X→? HH. LL. X	[[la-tɕiau] ʂuəi] spicy water [mai [piŋ-kuən]] sell ice cream	[tɕʰy [lau-pʰo]] marry a woman [suəi [po-li]] fragmentized glass
b.	X. HL. LL→X. HH. LL	[pu-liɛ-tian] Britain [xuəŋ [la-tɕiau]] red pepper	
c.	LL. LL. X→? HH(/ LH). LL. X	[[tɕin-kaŋ] tɕʰiau] JIN GANG bridge [tʰin[tɕin tɕy]] enjoy Piking Opera	[tɕʰin[i fu]] new clothes [tʰan [tɕian-piŋ]] cook pan cake
d.	X. LL. LL → X. HH (/ LH). LL	[[xuəŋ pau] tuə] many red-pockets [tʂa [kuən tsi]] check salary	

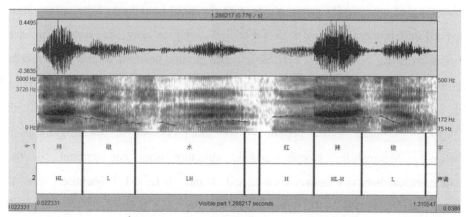

Spectrogram 3.5 "[[la-tɕiau] ʂuəi] spicy water" and "[xuəŋ [la-tɕiau]] red pepper"①

But it is not always the case that tonal combinations of Type a, c in Table 3.4 do not undergo tone sandhis. Examples of Type a-II, c-II in Table 3.4 undergo tone sandhi even though the left boundary of tone sandhi group aligns with the left boundary of the string; besides, we have also noticed that the final syllable changes into neutral tone. Take "[suəi [po-li]] fragmentized glass" (Table 3.4 a-II) for illustration. In Spectrogram 3.6 we may find that [po] surfaces with neutral tone, and [suəi] turns up with sandhi form HH. Obviously, the asymmetrical sandhi behavior between a-I, c-I and a-II, c-II is directly caused by the syllable with neutral tone in the string's final position. The neutral tone changes the stress pattern of the entire string, which then triggers tone sandhi. ②

---

① This subject has a creaky voice.
② Stress pattern is a problem in Mandarin and Mandarin-based dialects. Neither a unified conclusion nor a convincing conclusion has been reached by now. I will not go deeper on this issue here and leave it for future research.

Chapter 3 Correspondence Between X and PWd   065

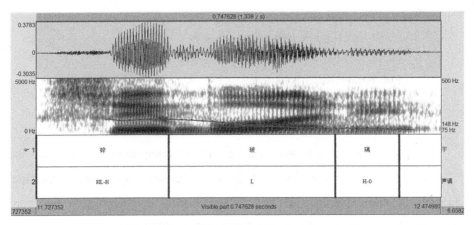

Spectrogram 3.6 [suəi [po-li]] fragmentized glass

If we take a closer look at the examples of Type II, we may find that all of them are of the morphosyntactic structure [A + [B + C]], which means that the application of tone sandhis has to refer to the string's syntactic structure—progressive neutral tone on [B + C] feeds regressive tone sandhi on [A + [B + C]]. Still take "[suəi [po-li]] fragmentized glass" for instance. Progressive neutral tone takes place to [po-li] leading to the change of stress pattern, which in turn facilitates regressive tone sandhi of [suəi [po-li]] (process as shown in Figure 3.10).

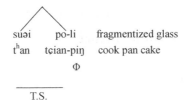

T.S.

Figure 3.10 Changes in Stress Pattern facilitate tone sandhi

In the previous analysis, we have reached the conclusion that the domain of tone sandhi in Tianjin dialect is defined through ω, but how is the domain structure of tone sandhi of the cases under discussion constructed? Penultimate vowel lengthening in Xitsonga is a very inspiring analog. In Xitsonga, all and only vowels that are penultimate in the clause are long (Selkirk 2011: 441). This process is however not purely phonologically driven, as defended by Selkirk (2011), CP, which corresponds to the intonational phrase, is the domain for penultimate lengthening:

(3.7) [[ndzi-xav-el-a [xi-phukuphuku] [fo:le]]]_CP
1st. sg. Subj-buy-appl-FV class 7-fool tobacco
I am buying tobacco for a fool.
ɩ(ndzi-xavela xi-phukuphuku fo:le)ɩ

Things become complicated with postposed components. Sentences like (3.8) containing a postposed subject show penultimate lengthening on the final word of the entire sentence as well as penultimate lengthening on the word preceding the postposed subject. As Kisseberth (1994) argues, what precedes the subject is a clause itself.

(3.8) _CP[_CP[[vá-xáv-á[tí-ho:m! ú]]_CP[vá:-nhu]]_CP
buying, Pe3pl cattle   people
They are buying cattle, the people are.

The nested syntactic structure projects into a recursively-built intonational phrase (ɩ) which is the working domain of penultimate vowel lengthening as is shown in Figure 3.11. In Xitsonga, syntactic-prosodic constituency isomorphism results in recursively-built prosodic structure.

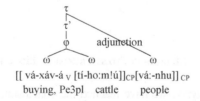

[[vá-xáv-á _V [tí-ho:m!ú]]_CP[vá:-nhu]] _CP
buying, Pe3pl cattle   people

Figure 3.11 Xitsonga: Postposed subject

I propose that in Tianjin dialect, for strings that undergo tone sandhis of the type (a, c-II) in Table 3.4, the phonological domain structure is also recursively built mirroring the string's morphosyntactic structure: [po] in [po-li] first turns into the neutral tone, [suəi] then incorporates in and undergoes tone sandhi as long as [po-li] meets the tonal context of (HL. L) (processes shown in Figure 3.12).

Nevertheless, analysis delivered up to now has adequately proven that tone sandhi in Tianjin dialect takes di- or tri-syllabic ω as its domain of application irrespective of the morphosyntactic structure. Then, why does the domain of tone sandhi of [suəi [po-li]] and the like make reference to the string's morphosyntactic structure since it is built recursively? It has to be clarified that the recursivity in the phonological domain of [suəi [po-li]] and the like is triggered by the appearance of the neutral tone.

The neutral tone in Tianjin dialect is sensitive to immediate morphosyntactic constituency, and in a di-syllabic string it is the final syllable that takes the neutral tone which is 1/4 of a full-toned syllable in terms of time duration; hence a neutral-toned syllable is an unstressed syllable (Wang 2002). If a syllable with neutral tone cannot bear stress, then [suəi [po-li]] and [tʰan [tɕian-piŋ]] in (a, c-II, Table 3.4) are fundamentally distinct from "[[tɕin-kaŋ] tɕʰiau] Jin gang Bridge" and "[mai [piŋ-kuən]] sell ice cream" (a, c-I, Table 3.4) in terms of stress pattern, because the final syllables of the formers bear neutral tone, while those of the latters bear full tone. In the second place, [suəi [po-li]] and the like differs from [mai [piŋ-kuən]] and the like in whether the initial syllables undergo tone sandhi. It is then easily detectable that if the final syllable takes on neutral tone, then the initial syllable undergoes tone sandhi. The logic of this phonological process is: In the [A + [B + C]] structured string, if "B + C" is an immediate morphosyntactic constituent, if "C" turns up with neutral tone, and if "A + B" meets either HL. L or L. L contexts of tone sanshi, then "A" will surface with sandhi form.

Take [suəi [po-li]] once again as a concrete illustration. The monosyllabic syntactic constituent [suəi] adjoins to the prosodic word (ω) [po-li], producing a recursively-built ω (as is shown in Figure 3.12). A legitimate tri-syllabic ω is born at the expense of SLH in the sense that, skipping Ft, the single syllable directly adjoins to ω.

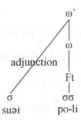

Figure 3.12 Prosodic parsing of [suəi [po-li]]

Tone sandhi of [suəi [po-li]] and the like in Tianjin dialect adds evidence to Ito & Mestor's (2003) proposal that it is not necessarily the case that a ω must be rigidly realized through Feet, but a Ft and a single syllable could compose a ω as well (at the expense of Strict Layering, obviously).

Tone sandhi of [suəi [po-li]] and the kind in Tianjin dialect adds evidence to one of the consequences of the Match Theory that recursion is not an inherent property of phonology but arises by the mirroring of recursive structures at the morphosyntactic level.

In the sections above, we have introduced the results of our investigation on tone sandhi in Tianjin dialect, finding that significant divergence has been arising between Old Tianjin dialect and New Tianjin dialect. Phonological analysis show that the tone sandhi domain of Tianjin dialect is defined through ω. Metrical well-formedness constraint—Binarity—is dominant in Tianjin dialect, hence mono-syllabic prosodic constituents are severely restricted. The prosodic structure well-formedness constraint drives mono-syllabic constituents into incorporating into adjacent prosodic ones at the expense violating of syntactic-prosodic constituency correspondence.

✳ 3.4 Tone Sandhi I in Shaoxing Dialect

3.4.1 Basics

Shaoxing dialect belongs to the Wu family. Although grouped into the subgroup of North Wu, it neither resembles Shanghai dialect and Suzhou dialect which are considered as representatives of North Wu, nor is intelligible to South Wu, Wenzhou dialect for instance. There are eight citation tones in Shaoxing dialect (Wang 2015; Wu 2007; Yang & Yang 2000). In spite of trivial phonetic differences in terms of pitch height between different versions, the distribution of tonal contour and register among the eight citation tones are rather regular.

Table 3.5 Phonological representation of citation tones (Zhang 2006: 207)

	Ping I	Shang II	Qu III	Ru IV
High register (/ Yin) a	H. hl	H. lh	H. l	H. h
Low register (/ Yang) b	L. hl	L. lh	L. l	L. h

The phonological representation of citation tones in Shaoxing dialect with tonal register features H / L and tonal contour features h / l is given by Zhang (2006). Zhang's configuration is built on Bao's (1999) tonal model. If we just look at the contour shapes of these tones, things are simpler. In Shaoxing dialect, the pitch contour of the tonal category *I* is falling, that of *II* is rising, and those of *III* and *IV* are rising except that the pitch height of the former is lower than the latter's. On the dimension of pitch height, the eight tones distribute evenly among the high register and the low register in the sense that four are featured with H and the other four are featured with L.

Bearing the phonological representation of tones in mind, we now turn to the focus—tone sandhi. Native scholars of Shaoxing dialect (Wu 2007; Wang 2015) uniformly affirm that Shaoxing dialect distinguishes two levels of tone sandhi; which are literally labeled as word-level tone sandhi and phrasal-level tone sandhi, nevertheless, it is by no means possible to draw a distinct line between them simply through syntactic constituency (Wang 2015), rather, both are prosodically-constrained sentence-level phonological phenomena in the sense that their working domains are defined through the prosodic constituents revealed by our investigation. Description of word-level tone sandhi (tone sandhi I / T. S. I) will be presented first, then non-syntactic influence on the domain of T. S. I will be discussed in detail, which actually drive me to argue for a prosodic-oriented analysis.

Phrasal-level tone sandhi (tone sandhi II / T. S. II) once again provides evidence for the interaction between prosodic structure well-formedness constraints and syntactic-prosodic constituency correspondence which will be the focus of Chapter 5.

Data relating to T. S. I with five syllables or less, as well as di-syllabic and tri-syllabic T. S. II are collected from Wang (2015); data relating to T. S. I with more than five syllables, T. S. II with more than three syllables are collected through our own investigation. ①

3.4.2 Tone Sandhi I in Shaoxing Dialect

3.4.2.1 Di-syllabic T. S. I

On word level, every syllable of a string may undergo sandhi changes, which anyhow lead no changes to the inventory of toneme. The di-syllabic string is the minimal working unit of T. S. I in Shaoxing dialect. Table 3.6 offers the tone sandhis of word-level di-syllabic tone sandhi patterns and sample words.

Table 3.6 Word-level di-syllabic tone sandhi

σ_1		σ_2			
		I	II	III	IV
		hl	lh	l	h
Ia	H. hl	H. l – H. hl	H. l – H. h	H. l – H. h	H. l – H. h
Ib	L. hl	L. l – H. hl	L. l – H. h	L. l – H. h	L. l – H. h
IIa	H. lh	H. lh – H. hl	H. lh – H. hl	H. lh – H. hl	H. lh – H. hl
IIb	L. lh	L. lh – H. hl	L. lh – H. hl	L. lh – H. hl	H. lh – H. hl
IIIa	H. l	H. l – H. l	H. l – H. l	H. l – H. l	H. l – H. l
IIIb	L. l	L. l – L. l	L. l – L. l	L. l – L. l	L. l – L. l
IVa	H. h	H. l – H. hl	H. l – H. h	H. l – H. h	H. l – H. h
IVb	L. h	L. l – H. hl	L. l – H. h	L. l – H. h	L. l – H. h

---

① Investigation on tone sandhi in Shaoxing dialect was conducted in 2016. The subjects were asked to preview and read a list of sample stings at normal speech rate. The list was arranged according to syllable count. The subjects aged 25 – 60 are all native speakers of Shaoxing dialect, who were born and now live in downtown Shaoxing. Field work, phonetic analysis, perceptive denotation and statistical analysis were conducted by the author and her classmate Gu Shengyun, a native speaker of Shaoxing dialect; the research results were then double checked and verified by Professor Zhang Jisheng, also a native speaker of Shaoxing dialect.

At a very quick glance of the di-syllabic tone sandhi listed in Table 3.6, it can be easily observed:
i. σ_1 is either level tone l / h or rising tone lh, but never falling tone hl.
ii. σ_2 is either level tone l / h or falling tone hl, but never rising tone lh.
iii. Register feature of σ_1 H / L is well preserved.
iv. σ_2 surfaces with high register H except that it is of the tonal category *qu*, whose register feature H / L remains unchanged.

Hence, di-syllabic T. S. I can be further abstracted as follows (Table 3.7):

Table 3.7 Phonological representation of di-syllabic T. S. I

σ_1	σ_2	
	hl	lh / l / h
hl / h	l – H. hl	l – H. h
lh		lh – H. hl
l		l – l

Tone sandhi changes the tonal contour of σ_1, but it does not affect its register feature. If σ_1 is in the falling tone hl or the level tone h, then it will surface into a level tone l and σ_2 will become either a high falling tone H. hl or a high level tone H. h. If σ_1 is in the rising tone lh, then it will keep its citation form and σ_2 will uniformly change into a high falling tone H. hl. If σ_1 is in the low level tone l, then both σ_1 and σ_2 will surface as level tone l with the register feature H / L of σ_1 kept and spread to σ_2. Table 3.7 reveals that patterns of di-syllabic T. S. I are predictable from the citation forms of σ_1 and that is also the case in multi-syllabic T. S. I.

3.4.2.2 Multi-syllabic T. S. I

Multi-syllabic T. S. I is chiefly a "stretched version" of di-syllabic T. S. I in the sense that the sandhi forms of the initial and final syllables in a multi-syllabic string resemble that of a di-syllabic one, and the non-periphery syllables surface with level tone. The following is the phonological representation of sandhi patterns of tri-syllabic T. S. I based on the data of Wang (2015):

Table 3.8 Patterns of tri-syllabic T. S. I

Tonal Category of σ_1	C. T. of σ_1	Sandhi Pattern	Examples
Ping	H. hl	H. 1 – H. h – H. hl	[sɤ-iŋ-tɕi] radio [səŋ-tshæ̃-lie?] productivity
	L. hl	L. 1 – H. h – H. hl	[bu-kuoŋ-iŋ] dandelion [ɕo-lo-z?] cobblestone
Shang	H. lh	H. lh – H. h – H. hl	[sE-tɕiŋ-kuoŋ] crystal palace [ɕiaŋ-dʑiai-le?] imagination
	L. lh	L. lh – H. h – H. hl	[mɤ-tæ̃-huo] peony [li-tɕia-le?] comprehension
Qu	H. l	H. 1 – H. 1 – H. 1	[tɕiŋ-kʰo-ɕy] textbook [tsæ̃-tɤ-le?] fighting capacity
	L. l	L. 1 – L. 1 – L. 1	[væ̃-huo-doŋ] kaleidoscope [da-li-zə?] marble
Ru	H. h	H. 1 – H. h – H. hl	[po?-piŋ-ɦiaŋ] the Arctic Ocean [ɕie?-tʰie?-zə?] lodestone
	L. h	L. 1 – H. h – H. hl	[ba?-mɒ-n̪y] the white-haired girl [ba?-ɦiõ?-zə?] dolomite

Note: C. T. = Citation Tone

Table 3.8 reveals that tri-syllabic T. S. I is definitely predictable once the citation tone of σ_1 is confirmed:

i. Sandhi forms of σ_1s in tri-syllabic words are exactly the same as those in di-syllabic words. To be specific, tonal categories of *ping* / I, *qu* / III and *ru* / IV neutralize into level tones H. 1 / L. 1, while tonal categories of *shang* / III keep their rising pitch contour H. lh / L. lh. The register feature of σ_1 is preserved.

ii. When σ_1 is of tonal category I / II / IV, σ_3 will turn into a falling tone H. hl; when σ_1 is of tonal category III, i.e. a middle or low level tone, σ_3 will become a level tone h / l with the register feature spread from σ_1. Hence, it is rather regular that σ_3 may surface as either a high falling tone H. hl or a level tone H. l / L. l purely conditioned by the tonal category of σ_1.

iii. A default level tone is inserted into σ_2, whose pitch height is determined by the onset of σ_3's pitch value.

By and large, sandhi patterns of both di-syllabic and tri-syllabic T. S. I are predictable from the tonal category of σ_1; tri-syllabic tone sandhi is a "stretched" version of di-syllabic tone sandhi in the sense that a default level tone is inserted between the initial and final syllables. Actually, multi-syllabic T. S. I exhibits the same characteristics as its tri-syllabic counterpart does. We have collected 123 multi-syllabic (3 < syllable count ⩽ 5) compounds / words from Wang (2015) and classified them into 8 groups according to which tonal category σ_1 belongs to. See Table 3.9 for sandhi patterns of multi-syllabic T. S. I and examples:

Table 3.9 Phonological representation of multi-syllabic T. S. I (3 < syllable count ⩽ 5)

Tonal Category of σ_1	C. T. of σ_1	Sandhi Patterns	Examples
Ping	H. hl	H. l – H. h – ... – H. h – H. hl	[ɕiŋ-vu da-n̠iaŋ] bride
		H. l – H. l – ... – H. h – H. hl	[sɤ-tsu lɒ-ɕiaŋ-kuoŋ] landlord
	L. hl	L. l – H. h – ... – H. h – H. hl	[dzE-zẽ bu-sæʔ] God of Wealth
		L. l – L. l – ... – H. h – H. hl	[dʑi-tsɿ mE-dɤ-fiu] chess-shaped preserved bean curd
Shang	H. lh	H. lh – H. h – ... – H. h – H. hl	[tʰu-di bu-sæʔ] God of Land [ɕiɒ [sɤ [tsɿ-dɤ]]] pinkie
	L. lh	L. lh – H. h – ... – H. h – H. hl	[lɒ[do ku-n̠iaŋ]] spinster [lɒ[ɕiɒ kuɤ̃-zē]]] bachelor

(continued)

Tonal Category of σ_1	C. T. of σ_1	Sandhi Patterns	Examples
Qu	H. l	H. 1 – H. 1 – ... – H. 1 – H. hl	[ku ᴇ-huo ɲiẽ -kɒ] rice cake fermented with osmanthus flowers
		H. 1 – H. 1 – ... – H. h – H. hl	[ta-kʰo? ɦiẽ -ɦiɣ-lo] snail
	L. l	L. 1 – L. 1 – ... – L. 1 – H. hl	[zɿ-1ᴇ hu-kuaŋ] match stick
		L. 1 – L. 1 – ... – H. h – H. hl	[di-dzɒŋ-ɦiʊŋ bu-sæ?] God of Hell
Ru	H. h	H. 1 – H. h – ... – H. h – H. hl	[huo?-sē ɲiaŋ-ɲiaŋ] Goddess of Lights
		H. 1 – H. 1 – ... – H. h – H. hl	[i-saŋ i-sɿ] entire life
	L. h	L. 1 – H. h – ... – H. h – H. hl	[ɦia?-sɿ di-zɒ] sanitary soap
		L. 1 – L. 1 – ...– H. h – H. hl	[ze?-çiŋ mõ-dɣ] steamed bun

It can be observed from Table 3.9 that the sandhi patterns of multi-syllabic compounds are reminiscent of tri-syllabic tone sandhi:

i. Sandhi patterns can be predicted from the tonal categories of σ_1.

ii. The tone sandhis of string-initial and final syllables behave almost the same as those of tri-syllabic compounds do.

The initial syllable, exactly as σ_1 of a tri-syllabic word (and hence σ_1 of di-syllabic word) does, will neutralize into level tone H. 1 / L. 1 if it is of tonal category I / III / IV; otherwise, it will keep its citation form if it is of tonal category II.

The final syllable, overwhelmingly, will change into high falling tone H. hl.① This differs from tri-syllabic tone sandhi. Recall that in a tri-syllabic string, σ_3 may surface with either a high falling tone H. hl or a level tone H. l / L. l conditioned by the tonal category of σ_1.

iii. We have already seen that in a tri-syllabic string, a default level tone is inserted in the position of σ_2, whose pitch height is phonetically shaped by the onset of the pitch of σ_3, i. e. regressive phonetic assimilation. Whereas, in a string longer than tri-syllabic, the effects of phonetic assimilation are bi-directional: progressive assimilation is initiated by σ_1 and regressive assimilation associated is with the final syllable.

From Table 3.9 we can see that strings begin with *ping*, *qu* and *ru*, have two alternative readings: for instance, the sandhi form of "[ta-kʰoʔ ɦiẽ-ɦiɤ-lo] snail" is H. l – H. l – H. l – H. h – H. hl, the sandhi form of "[di-dzɒŋ-ɦuɒŋ bu-sæʔ] god of Hell" is L. l – L. l – H. h – H. h – H. hl. Level tones are inserted into all non-periphery syllables, with pitch height shaped by the initial (i. e. progressive phonetic assimilation) and the final (i. e. regressive phonetic assimilation) syllable. But the working domain of progressive assimilation and regressive assimilation are not predictable either morpho-syntactically or metrically.

Finally, for a string beginning with tonal category *II*, phonetically speaking, as the pitch contour of the first syllable ends up in the high register②, and the pitch contour of the final syllable starts from high register, the non-periphery syllables will undoubtedly be featured with H. h either through progressive or regressive phonetic assimilation, e. g. "[tʰu-di bu-sæʔ] god of land" and "[ɕiɒ [sɤ [tsʅ-dɤ]]] pinkie".

---

① Phonetic analysis of the data from our investigation shows that many sample words actually end with the high level tone H. h. Native speaker Gu Shengyun (investigator) says that they do tolerate a high level ending, though they would rather perceive it as a high falling tone H. hl. This seemingly paradoxical point reveals the change of her perspective from that of a speaker to an audience. Wang (2015) delivers obviously the description from an audience's position.

② Wang (2015) reports that the sandhi form of the tonal category *II a* can rise to as high as 5 (H. h).

3.4.2.3 Phonetic Diagnosis of T. S. I

Sections 3.4.2.1 and 3.4.2.2 demonstrate that sandhi patterns of T. S. I are predictable from the citation form of σ_1. Sandhi patterns of longer strings are built on the base of di-syllabic tone sandhi. Tone sandhis of the initial syllables in multi-syllabic strings behave consistently with that seen in di-syllabic strings (Table 3.6, 3.8, 3.9), both of which surface as either the level tone h / l or the rising tone lh. Default level tones are inserted into all non-periphery syllables in multi-syllabic string with pitch values determined by the periphery syllables (Table 8). As the string grows longer, the final syllable uniformly ends up with the high falling tone H. hl. Hence, the pitch contour produced by T. S. I is rather regular: within a working domain of T. S. I, the pitch contour starts with middle level tone or rising tone, then stretches rightward without any fluctuation, and ends with a falling tail. The configuration of the T. S. I rule can be formalized as follows (Figure 3.13):

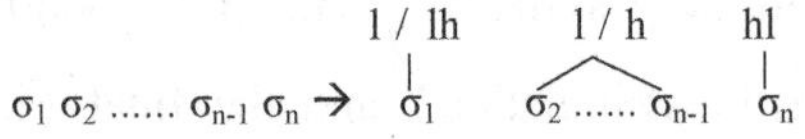

$$\sigma_1\ \sigma_2\ \ldots\ \sigma_{n-1}\ \sigma_n \rightarrow \underset{\sigma_1}{1/\text{lh}}\ \underset{\sigma_2\ \ldots\ \sigma_{n-1}}{1/\text{h}}\ \underset{\sigma_n}{\text{hl}}$$

Figure 3.13 Phonological representation of the sandhi pattern of T. S. I

This pitch contour marks a working domain of T. S. I. [①]

3.4.3 Phonological Domain of T. S. I and X-ω Correspondence

Although T. S. I, formulated as in Figure 3.13, regulates how a sequence of tones surface, it is not domain-sensitive itself at all in the sense that it delivers no information about the domain of its application. It depends on syntactic constituency or prosodic constituency to define its domain structure.

Wang (2015) strongly asserts that T. S. I typically applies to syntactic terminal elements, i.e. syntactic words. But he also points out that it cannot be neglected that T. S. I applies to certain groups of phrases as well. Although the

---

[①] Existing research (Zhang 2006) has proven that T. S. I is constrained by metrical stress, which is realized through the choice of tonal register and tonal contour. See detailed introduction in Chapter 5.

phonological domain structure of T. S. I shows a clear effect of syntactic constituency, the divergences from syntactic structure which are due to prosodic structure well-formedness constraints require the phonological domain structure of T. S. I to be prosodically-parsed.

3.4.3.1　X-ω Correspondence

The results of our investigation support Wang's (2015) assertion that, basically, a syntactic word constituents a phonological domain of T. S. I, regardless of whether it is a simple word or a (complex) compound (Spectrogram 3.7):

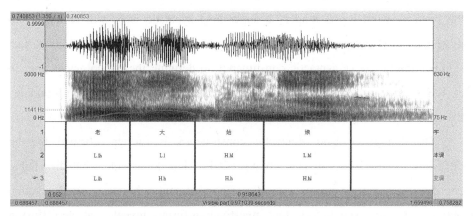

Spectrogram 3.7　[lɒ[do ku-ȵiaŋ]] spinster

Spectrogram 3.7 shows that the shape of the pitch contour of "[lɒ[do ku ȵiaŋ]] spinster" is "rising-high level-falling" (i. e. L. lh – H. h – H. h – H. hl) which is in accordance with the sandhi pattern predicted by Figure 3.13. The entire compound equates to a phonological domain of T. S. I, irrespective of the morphological structure of the compound.

Following the Match Theory, if a syntactic category X maps into the prosodic category PWd, then the working domain of T. S. I is defined through PWd. Immediately, a question arises: would it be superfluous to have prosody involved? At least up to now, it seems that there is no difference between whether the phonological domain structure of T. S. I is defined through the syntactic category X or the prosodic category PWd, taking "[lɒ [do ku-ȵeiaŋ]] spinster" for instance, since the prosodic constituent PWd and the syntactic constituent X align on both edges.

3.4.3.2 Size of Phonological Domain of T. S. I

According to Wang (2015), a single syntactic word constitutes a single domain of application of T. S. I. But the compounds documented in Wang (2015) do not exceed five syllables (see samples in Table 3.9). Following Wang's line of research, we carried out an investigation into strings with six syllables or more which had compounds and coordinate structured strings included. The results from our investigation shows very clearly that the isomorphism between the phonological domain of T. S. I and the syntactic word X is no longer solid when the syntactic word grows longer: a super long syntactic word will collapse into more than one independent domain of application of T. S. I, which in fact signifies the failure of syntactic constituency in defining the phonological domain of T. S. I. As a syntactic word could expand infinitely through cyclic-compounding, the span of phonological domain of T. S. I has its upper limits.

The divergence from syntactic constituency is further affirmed by the diffusion of T. S. I into phrases. Wang (2015) has documented that di-syllabic coordinate-structured strings, predicate-complement phrases, modifier-noun phrases, etc. undergo T. S. I. Our investigation further reveals that the diffusion of T. S. I into phrases is not restricted to di-syllabic ones, constructions mentioned above with tri-, quarto-syllables apply T. S. I as well (on the condition that the terminal elements of a phrase are closely connected).

Thus, the phonological domain of T. S. I is characterized by:

i) The span of its domain has lower and upper limits.

ii) X-ω correspondence may not be observed all the time, as the phonological domain of T. S. I could be smaller or larger than a syntactic word. This is actually the consequence of i).

The size effects give rise to a prosodic interpretation on the organization of phonological domain structure of T. S. I (which is insensitive to domain structure itself).

3.4.3.2.1 Phonological Domain of T. S. I Smaller than X

The result of our investigation into tone sandhi of di-, tri- and quarto-syllabic compounds is in accordance with Wang's (2015) description, namely, one syntactic word constitutes one domain of application of T. S. I; however, tone sandhis of penta-syllabic strings do not behave as uniformly as those documented in Wang (2015). With normal speech rate, more than one half of the penta-syllabic sample compounds from our survey project into two separate phonological domains of T. S. I, for instance, "[tsʰẽ-tɕi [ɦiø̃-doŋ-kuE]] Spring sports meeting" and "[[[pʰu-kɒŋ] tsẽ] tsəŋ-fu]] government of Pujiang District" are produced as (tsʰẽ-tɕi) (ɦiø̃-doŋ-kuE), (pʰu-kɒŋ tsẽ)(tsəŋ-fu). But our subjects do not reject the "one-word-one-T. S. -domain" reading if the speech rate is a little bit faster, i. e. (tsʰẽ-tɕi ɦiø̃-doŋ-kuE) (pʰu-kɒŋ tsẽ tsəŋ-fu). Penta-syllabicity seems to reach the upper limit of the syllable count of domain of T. S. I, since the "one-word-one-T. S. -domain" reading is not favored any more by our subjects when the syllable count of a compound exceeds five, for instance, "[[[ɦieʔ-la]kuø̃ saŋ-tsʰæ̃ ɕiẽ]] product line of pop-top can" and "[pu-n̠i-noʔ-sɿ-E-li-sɿ] Buenos Aires". See the pitch contour of [tsʰẽ-tɕieʔ liẽ-huø̃ væ̃-kuE] in Spectrogram 3.8:

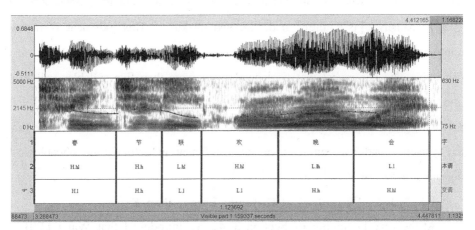

Spectrogram 3.8 [tsʰẽ-tɕieʔ liẽ-huø̃ væ̃-kuE] Spring Festival Gala Evening

In Spectrogram 3.8, the pitch contour of compound [tsʰẽ-tɕieʔ liẽ-huø̃ væ̃-kuE] starts with middle level tone H.l and rises to high level tone H.h on [tɕieʔ]; after its falling to middle level tone H.l on syllable [liẽ] again, it continues to climb up and reaches as high as H.l on syllable [væ̃] and ends in the high falling tone H. hl on string-final syllable [kuE]. The sudden dip in pitch register of syllable [liẽ] significantly indicates that [tsʰẽ-tɕie? liẽ-huø̃ væ̃-kuE] does not mirror into an independent domain of T. S. I since its phonetic behavior sharply conflicts with what Table 3.9 exemplifies and what Figure 3.13 predicts: σ_n's pitch height can not be lower than that of σ_{n-1} (which is metrically constrained in essence and will be analyzed in detail in Chapter 5). It can also be detected in Spectrogram 3.8 that there is downstep① from [liẽ] to [væ̃] due to the intervening middle-registered [liẽ]. The reset of pitch register from [tsʰẽ-tɕie?] to [liẽ-huø̃ væ̃-kuE] inspires us to inspect the application of T. S. I to [tsʰẽ-tɕie?] and [liẽ-huø̃ væ̃-kuE] separately. It is surprising, yet reasonable, that the pitch contours of [tsʰẽ-tɕie?] and [liẽ-huø̃ væ̃-kuE] (i.e. H.l – H.h and L.l – L.l – H.h – H.hl respectively) accord with the regularities of di- and quarto-syllabic T. S. I (see Tables 3.6, 3.9).② The phonetic clue stated above provides us with necessary proof that morphosyntactic structure fails in restricting the phonological domain structure of T. S. I, as is instantiated in the case of [tsʰẽ-tɕie? liẽ-huẽ væ̃-kuE] which is divided into two independent domains of application of T. S. I, namely, [tsʰẽ-tɕie?] and [liẽ-huø̃ væ̃-kuE]. This judgment is further reinforced through our perceptual experiments. Both phonetic evidence and perceptive evidence reveal that compounds with more than five syllables will map into n phonological domains of T. S. I, and each phonological domain of T. S. I will not be longer than penta-syllabic. From the analysis of this subsection we see that the syntactic condition, on its own, is insufficient in defining the phonological domain structure of T. S. I.

3.4.3.2.2 Phonological Domains Larger than X

At the very beginning of Section 3.4, we introduced that Wang (2015:

---

① Downstep refers to that an H-tone is realized at a lower pitch than a preceding H-tone if L intervenes (Gussenhoven 2004: 100).

② As soon as T. S. I have proceeded in [tsʰẽ-tɕie?] and [liẽ-huø̃ væ̃-ku E] separately, T. S. II applies vacuously between [tsʰẽ-tɕie?] and [liẽ-huø̃ væ̃-ku E] as no more changes have been aroused then.

17) has affirmatively announced that though typically taking place in syntactic words, T.S.I applies to Modifier-Noun structured, Predicate-Complement structured, and Coordinate structured di-syllabic phrases as well; moreover, phrases of this kind are typically characterized by the close juncture between the syntactic terminal elements. This characteristic is rather common among the North Wu dialects (Qian 1992), take Shanghai dialect for instance, "... there is a closer juncture between syllable undergoing ... broad sandhi than undergoing narrow sandhi ... That juncture difference leads to differences in sandhi types and pitch values." (Zhu 2006: 37)

Actually, in Shaoxing dialect, the diffusion of T.S.I into phrases is by no means restricted to di-syllabic phrases with the three kinds of structures mentioned in Wang (2015). We have collected a list of quarto-syllabic phrases, among which, 30 are constructed with M-N structure and 13 are constructed with coordinate structure. These examples are subgrouped according to the syntactic terminal element's syllable-count (see samples listed in Table 3.10 for illustration).

Table 3.10 Quarto-syllabic phrases with T.S.I applied

Phrasal Type	Construction Type	Examples	Citation Form of σ_1	Sandhi Form
M-N	2 + 2	[[dɤ-vu]ɕiŋ-dzaŋ] kind-hearted	L.l	L.l – L.l – H.h – H.hl
	1 + (2 + 1)	dʑiɤ [[ɦiaŋ-mɒ] sæ̃]] old woolen sweater	L.l	L.l – L.l – H.h – H.hl
	1 + (1 + 2)	[ɕiẽ [ɦiɤ[dɤ-vu]]] fresh fried bean curd	H.hl	H.l – H.h – H.h – H.hl
	(2 + 1) + 1	[[ɕiɒ-sø̃ kɒŋ] li] in the Xiaoshun River	H.lh	H.lh – H.h – H.h – H.hl
	(1 + 2) + 1	[[ɦiɤ[dɤ-vu] tʰɒŋ] fried bean curd soup	L.hl	L.l – L.l – H.h – H.hl

(continued)

Phrasal Type	Construction Type	Examples	Citation Form of σ_1	Sandhi Form
Coordinate	1 + 1 + 1 + 1	[tsʰẽ ɦo tɕʰuɛ tuɒŋ] spring summer autumn winter	H. hl	H. l – H. h – H. h – H. hl
	2 + 2	[tsoʔ-saŋ tsoʔ-sɿ] uninhibited	H. h	H. l – H. l – H. h – H. hl

Both perceptual and phonetic analyses reveal that pitch contours of the phrasal expressions under our research accord with the sandhi patterns of multi-syllabic words predicted in Figure 3.13. It can be seen from Spectrogram 3.9 that the coordinate sample string "[tsʰẽ ɦo tɕʰuɛ tuɒŋ] spring summer autumn winter" surfaces as H. l – H. h – H. h – H. hl which is consistent with the tone sandhi of a quarto-syllabic compound. The entire coordinate string composes an independent domain of T. S. I.

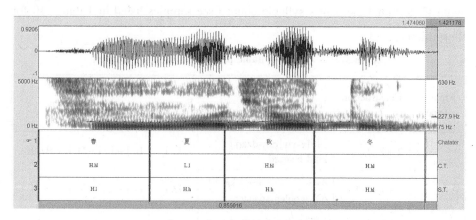

Spectrogram 3.9 [tsʰẽ ɦo tɕʰuɛ tuɒŋ] **spring summer autumn winter**

Spectrogram 3.10 presents with the pitch contour of a M-N phrase "[dʑiɤ ɦiaŋ mɒ sæ̃] old woollen sweater": [dʑiɤ], [ɦiaŋ] and [mɒ] all change into level tone l ∕ h, and [sæ̃] closes the phrase with high falling tone H. hl. Its sandhi form (i. e. L. l-L. l-H. h-H. hl) also indicates the application of T. S. I as the coordinate-structured quarto-syllabic string "[tsʰ ẽ ɦo tɕʰu ɛ tuɒŋ] spring summer autumn winte" does. In this quarto-syllabic M-N phrase, T. S. I has crossed the right boundary of the adjective [dʑiɤ] and the left boundary of the noun [ɦiaŋ mʊ sæ̃], and taken this entire phrase as its domain of application. The close juncture between the modifier and its noun head promots this entire M-N phrase mapping into an independent phonological domain of T. S. I. ①

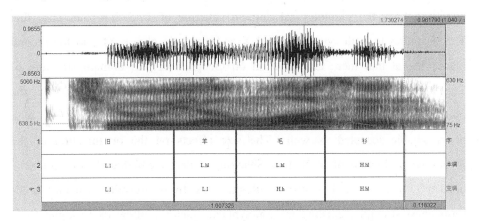

Spectrogram 3.10 [dʑiɤ[[ɦiaŋ-mʊ] sæ̃]] **old woollen sweater**

The tone sandhis of super long compounds and phrases whose terminal elements are closely connected demonstrate that syntactic constituency is insufficient in directly defining the phonological domain structure of T. S. I. When a compound is super long (more than five syllables in the most common place), such as [tsʰẽ-tɕie? liẽ-huõ væ̃-kuẽ], it corresponds to two or more phonological domains of T. S. I on the condition that each phonological domain usually does not exceed five syllables. Constituent integrity of super long syntactic word X is no longer guaranteed during the application of T. S. I because the phonological domain structure of T. S. I has upper limits in terms of syllable-count. When a phrase does not exceed penta-syllabic and its terminal

---

① Co-researcher Gu Shengyun, a native speaker of Shaoxing dialect, affirms that a phrase is intuitively accepted as a word if it is produced with T. S. I. Take "[dʑiɤ[ɕy-pʊ-tsɿ]] old books and newspapers" and "[ɕiŋ[ɕy-pʊ-tsɿ]] new books and newspapers" for illustration: [dʑiɤ[ɕy-pʊ-tsɿ]], which is frequently used in daily life and is considered to be on the way of evolving into compound, undergoes T. S. I; contrastively, [ɕiŋ[ɕy-pʊ-tsɿ]], which is definitely still perceived as a noun phrase, expectedly, undergoes tone sandhi processes (i. e. T. S. I and T. S. II apply in sequence which will be the focus of Chapter 5) different from that of [dʑiɤ[ɕy-pʊ-tsɿ]].

elements are of closer juncture, such as [dʑiɤ ɦiaŋ mɒ sæ̃], the entire phrase corresponds to a single phonological domain of T. S. I with the basic criterion—T. S. I typically applies to syntactic word X—being violated.

Cases discussed above, in the first place, deny that syntactic constituency directly defines the phonological domain structure of T. S. I in the sense that T. S. I applies to both syntactic word X and syntactic phrase XP; in the second place, reveal that there is restriction on the phonological domain structure of T. S. I in the sense that its size has lower and upper limits. To be specific, the phonological domain of T. S. I is usually di-, tri- and quarto-syllabic, with penta-syllabic accepted as well. The size effects on the organization of the phonological domain of T. S. I in Shaoxing dialect are reducible to "prosodic binarity" (Selkirk 2011: 468). Restrictions from prosodic structure well-formedness strength, existing as non-syntactic factors, allow us to argue for a prosodic-structure defined phonological domain structure of T. S. I.

3.4.4　Interaction Between Size Effects and X-ω Correspondence

Analysis up to now reveals that T. S. I in Shaoxing dialect typically takes syntactic word X (X = N, A, V) as its phonological domain of application. Nevertheless, the existence of systematic nonisomorphism between the syntactic constituent and the phonological domain constituent, empirically being evidenced by the limits to the size of a phonological domain of T. S. I and T. S. I's diffusion into phrases (that do not exceed four syllables) which are on the way of evolving into compounds, falsifies the hypothesis that the organization of phonological domain structure of T. S. I directly refers to syntactic structure. In Section 3. 2. 2 we have introduced that a limitation on size which is purely rhythmically based is one of the properties of prosodic structures (Selkirk 2011). The phonological domain structure of T. S. I possessing formal properties of prosodic structures distinct from that of syntactic structures drives a prosodic representation of itself. However, phonological domain structures defined through prosodic constituents not only present effects resulting from prosodic structure well-formedness constraints, but also mirror syntactic structures which are inherited through the mapping from syntactic constituents to prosodic constituents (Kabak & Revithiadou 2009).

According to the Match Theory of syntactic-prosodic constituency correspondence (Selkirk 2011), if a syntactic word X (X = N, A, V) maps into a Pwd / ω, then the phonological domain of T. S. I in Shaoxing dialect is defined through PWd. To put it the other way round, the phonological domain structure of T. S. I provides empirical evidence as to the interaction between X-ω correspondence and prosodic structure well-formedness constraints.

Primarily, X-ω correspondence requires that a ω aligns with an X from which it maps on both edges, regardless of the length of this X. On the other hand, prosodic structure has a restriction on the size of ω, which is purely rhythmically grounded.

It is rather obvious that X-ω correspondence differs from prosodic structure well-formedness constraints on the restriction of the syllable count of ω. And in Shaoxing dialect, the size effect on ω is more important than the faithful-mapping from X to ω. The phonological domain of T. S. I, which ranges from di-syllabic to quarto-syllabic, with penta-syllabic being accepted as well, signifies that a legitimate ω in Shaoxing dialect is di-, tri-, quarto- and penta-syllabic, rather than expanding indefinitely while the X grows longer through endless compounding. Hence, the phonological domain structure of T. S. I witnesses both matching and mismatching between a X and a ω on the dimension of constituent's size: a ω could be as long as, shorter than or longer than a X (Figure 3.14).

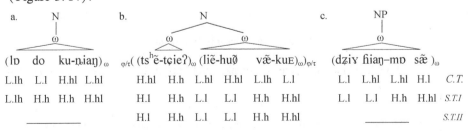

Figure 3.14 Prosodic parsing

In Figure 3.14 a, both the X-ω correspondence and the size constraint on ω are satisfied, so the entire compound mirrors into an independent phonological domain of T.S.I; in Figure 3.14 b, the hexa-syllabic compound [tsʰẽ-tɕie? li ẽ-huõ væ̃-ku ɛ] mirrors into two separate phonological domains of T.S.I resulting from the more restrictive requirement from ω structure well-formedness constraint at the expense of the isomorphism between X and ω; it is still due to the size effect that the M-N phrase [dʑiɤ ɦiaŋ mɒ sæ̃] in Figure 3.14 c maps into a single ω rather than two separate ωs (i.e. *(dʑiɤ)_ω and *(ɦiaŋ mɒ sæ̃)_ω) but not a Phonological Phrase / φ (i.e. *(dʑiɤ ɦiaŋ mɒ sæ̃)_φ) ①.

3.4.5 Phonetic Substance and Phonological Abstractness of the Size Effects

In the very last section we have introduced that the size constraint on ω is universal and has its roots in pure rhythmic patterns. Take Mandarin Chinese for concrete illustration. Wang (2000) argues that ω in Mandarin Chinese consists of either one foot (bi-syllabic or tri-syllabic) or two feet (bi-syllabic only). So, in Mandarin Chinese, a legitimate ω could be minimally bi-syllabic, tri-syllabic, and maximally quarto-syllabic, as shown in Figure 3.15 a – c. Wang's later research (2008) claims that in Mandarin Chinese, the speech rate has been accelerating, and the rhythmic unit has been enlarging; nevertheless, ω is still mainly di-, tri- and quarto-syllabic, and a penta-syllabic string still has to be decomposed into two separate ωs.

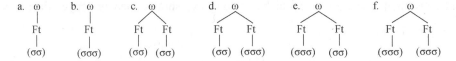

Figure 3.15 Organization of ω

Even though Mandarin-speakers speak much faster than before, their speech

---

① Sandhi changes to phrases are different from that of words, and φ does not compose a tone sandhi domain in Shaoxing dialect. This will be discussed in detail in Chapter 5.

rate is still not so fast as that of Shaoxing dialect. I assume that it is the typological differences in the finals of syllable that lie behind the distinction in speech rate between Mandarin Chinese and Shaoxing Chinese.

Zhang (2006) confirms that Shaoxing dialect has the same syllable types as that in Mandarin Chinese, as shown in Table 3.11:

Table 3.11 Syllable type in Mandarin and Shaoxing dialect

Syllable Structure	Shaoxing Chinese	Mandarin Chinese	Gloss
CV	[ɕi^{33}]	[ɕi^{51}]	opera
CVC	[ɕIŋ^{52}]	[ɕiən^{55}]	new
CGV	[ɕia^{35}]	[ɕiə^{35}]	write
CGVC	[ɕjaŋ^{35}]	[ɕjaŋ^{214}]	think
CGVV	[ɕjaŋ^{35}]	[ɕjau^{214}]	small

Actually it was claimed in traditional Chinese phonology that all Chinese dialects share the similar syllable patterns as are listed in the leftmost column in Table 3.11 above: A syllable maximally consists of an initial consonant, a pre-nuclear glide, a nucleus vowel, a final consonant or a post-nuclear glide (Chao 1968; Wang 1985).

With the same syllable templates to fill in, Shaoxing dialect's finals, in sharp contrast with those in Mandarin, are extremely impoverished in VV combinations and have glottal stops as coda (Zhang 2006). See the finals in Mandarin and Shaoxing dialect as shown in Table 3.12:

Table 3.12 Finals in Mandarin and Shaoxing dialect (Wang 2008; Zhang 2006)

	Ç	V (/Ṽ)	VV	GV(/Ṽ)	GVV	VC	GVC		
Mandarin		ï	ai	ia	iau	an	ian	uan	yan
		i	əi	iə	iəu	ən	iən	uən	yən
		u	au	ua	uai	aŋ	iaŋ	uaŋ	yəŋ
		y	əu	uə	uəi	əŋ	iəŋ	uəŋ	
		a		yə		ər			
		ə							

(continued)

	C	V (/Ṽ)	VV	GV(/Ṽ)	GVV	VC	GVC
SX	m̩ n̩ ŋ̍ l̩	ɿ I y e a ɤ o u	ẽ ɛ̃ θ̃	ɑɒ	ja je jo jɤ wa we wo	jɛ̃ jẽ ɥθ̃ wɛ̃ wθ̃	jɑɒ	I əŋ oŋ ɒŋ Iʔ əʔ oʔ ɛʔ	jaŋ joŋ waŋ woŋ wɒŋ	jaʔ joʔ waʔ woʔ

In the first place, in Shaoxing dialect, there is only one VV combination or diphthong, as defined by Trask (1996), i. e. /ɑɒ/, which could serve as the nucleus of a syllable, whereas Mandarin has a much richer diphthong inventory with four, namely /ai, əi, au, əu /. In the second place, while syllables with *ru* tones have already disappeared in Mandarin (Chao 1968; Wang 2008), glottal stop /ʔ/ as a coda still exists in Shaoxing dialect (Zhang 2006; Wang 2015). On the phonetic dimension, firstly, diphthongs have longer time duration than monophthongs; secondly, the checked syllables (i. e. syllables with glottal stops as coda) in Shaoxing dialect are of shorter time duration than the unchecked syllables (Qian 1992; Zhang 2006). Shaoxing dialect's poverty in nuclei with longer duration, but richness in syllables with shorter duration, immediately tells that a large portion of syllables in Shaoxing dialect take shorter time to be produced than their Mandarin counterparts do. This phonetic difference is fundamental in leading to different speech rates in Shaoxing dialect and Mandarin. If, in Shaoxing dialect, a syllable takes shorter time to be produced, then more syllables will be produced in a given period of time than in Mandarin. We believe this is the reason why in Shaoxing dialect not only di-, tri- and quarto-syllabic ωs (illustrated through Figure 3. 15 a – c) are legitimate, but penta-syllabic ωs composed of a bi-syllabic foot and a tri-syllabic foot (illustrated through Figure 3. 15 d and e), are also acceptable, for faster speech rate permits more syllables to be produced in a certain prosodic unit on a certain prosodic level, instantiated by ω here. Both phonologically-based (i. e. size effects reducible to natural rhythmic grouping) and phonetically-based (i. e. syllable duration) reasoning converge with our empirically-based proposal that in Shaoxing dialect qualified ω ranges from di-syllabic to penta-syllabic① and X-ω correspondence may be surpassed.

The phonological domain structure of T. S. I in Shaoxing dialect provides empirical evidence of the interaction between X-ω correspondence and prosodic structure well-formendness constraints.

T. S. I in Shaoxing dialect typically takes syntactic word X (X = N,A,V) as its phonological domain of application. The phonological domain structure of T. S. I possesses formal properties of prosodic structures distinct from that of syntactic structures. In Shaoxing dialect, the size effects on ω is more important than the faithful-mapping from X to ω. The phonological domain of T. S. I proves that a legitimate ω in Shaoxing dialect is di-, tri-, quarto- and penta-syllabic, which in consequence results in match / mismatch between a X and a ω on the dimension of constituent's size: A ω could be as long as, shorter than or longer than a X. ω in Shaoxing dialect is typologically different from that in Mandarin which is attributable to the differences in syllable-finals.

3.5 Tone Sandhi in Yuncheng Dialect

Tone sandhi of Tianjin dialect does not discriminate words from phrases. Its domain of application is restricted to di- and tri-syllabic strings. In a di- or tri-syllabic ω either mapped from a compound or a phrase, tone sandhi starts to work from exactly the right boundary of the ω. Tone sandhi of Yuncheng dialect which we are going to discuss in this section is compatible with that of Tianjin dialect in that:

---

① *Figure 3.15 f:Up to now, at normal speech rate, hexa-syllabic ω has not been proved yet from our empirical survey.

a) tone sandhi in Yuncheng dialect does not discriminate words from phrases, even short clauses as well;

b) tone sandhi in Yuncheng dialect operates from right to left as well;

c) the upper limit of the size of tone sandhi domain in Yuncheng dialect is quarto-syllabic.

However, tone sandhi in Yuncheng dialect differentiates from that in Tianjin dialect in that:

a) it is always sensitive to the internal morphosyntactic structure of the string it applies to;

b) it may not start to work from the very right edge of the string.

3.5.1 Phonology of Tone Sandhi in Yuncheng Dialect

3.5.1.1 Basics

Yuncheng dialect is a dialect of the Southern Jin family. Lü's (1989) description to tone sandhi in Yuncheng dialect is delicate and my analysis is chiefly based on Lü's data. All the data presented below are quoted from Lü (1989).

There are four citation tones in Yuncheng dialect, two falling tones in high register and low register respectively, one rising tone in low register, and one middle-registered level tone. We thus formalize them into L. hl, L. lh, H. hl, and H. l. See Table 3.13 for details:

Table 3.13 Citation tones in Yuncheng dialect

Tonal Category	*Yinping* Ia	*Yangping* Ib	*Shangsheng* II	*Qusheng* III
Tonal Features	L. hl	L. lh	H. hl	H. l

Exactly as in Tianjin dialect, the di-syllabic string is the minimal domain of application of tone sandhi in Yuncheng dialect which is typically constrained by OCP (Obligatory Contour Principle): Contour tones with identical tonal features cannot stand side-by-side, the first syllable will either change its register feature (i.e. H. hl + H. hl→L. hl – H. hl) *or its contour features* (i.e. L. hl + L. hl→

L. lh – L. lh), as a result. A new toneme, i. e. **H. lh**, emerges when two low rising tones are in juxtaposition. See Table 3.14 for di-syllabic tone sandhi patterns:

Table 3.14 Formal computation of di-syllabic tone sandhis in Yuncheng dialect

σ_1	σ_2			
	L. hl	L. lh	H. hl	H. l
L. hl	L. **lh** - L. lh			
L. lh		**H. lh** - L. lh		
H. hl			**L. hl** - H. hl	
H. l				

Di-syllabic sequence is the minimal domain of application of tone sandhi in Yuncheng dialect. In sequences with syllables more than three, resembling tone sandhi in Tianjin dialect, it applies from right to left, whereas distinct from that in Tianjin dialect, the right edge of its domain of application is sensitive to the string's morphsyntactic structure and thus may not align with the right boundary of the string.

But, recall that tone sandhi in Tianjin dialect does not discriminate phrases from words, it is the same situation in Yuncheng dialect where even a short clause could map into an independent domain of application of tone sandhi.

Viewing the basic facts presented above, it could primarily be seen that even though tone sandhi rules in Yuncheng dialect refer to morphsyntactic information, its phonological domain structure cannot be derived directly from syntactic constituency.

Lü (1989) states unequivocally that the domain of tone sandhi does not exceed four syllables. Limitation on size once again suggests a prosodic account of the definition of the phonological domain of tone sandhi in Yuncheng dialect. We propose that the interaction among prosodic structure well-formedness (size constraint, to be specific), phonological properties (leftwardness and Immediate Constituency Anchoring, to be specific), and syntactic-prosodic constituency correspondence shapes the phonological domain structure of tone sandhi in Yuncheng dialect.

3.5.1.2 Size Effects

3.5.1.2.1 Binarity

The di-syllablic string is the minimal phonological domain of application of tone sandhi in Yuncheng dialect. The undominance of Binarity is testified by tone sandhi of srtings with coordinate structure. In a tri-syllabic string ABC with coordinate structure, tone sandhi will take place if AB or BC in ABC satisfies the phonological environment, like [song zhu mei]① in Table 3.15 i, [mei ying fa] in Table 3.15 ii, while either A or B undergoes tone sandhi if both AB and BC meet the requirement. like [ri yue xing], [hu ma gou] in Table 3.15 iii.

Table 3.15 Binarity: Tone sandhi in Yuncheng dialect

Syntactic Structure	Context of Tone Sandhi	Sandhi Forms	Examples
A + B + C	i. A<u>BC</u>	A'BC	[**song** zhu mei] pine bamboo plum
	ii. <u>AB</u>C	AB'C	[mei **ying** fa] US GB Fr
	iii. <u>AB</u>C	A'BC / AB'C	[**ri** yue xing] sun moon star hu **ma** gou tiger horse dog
A + B + C + D	iv. A + B + <u>C + D</u>	A'BC'D	[**ri** yue **xing**-chen] sun moon star
	v. A + <u>B + C</u> + D	—	[gua guo jiu cai] melon fruit wine vegetable
[A + B] + [C + D]	vi. A + B + <u>C + D</u>	A'BC'D	[**da**-shui **xi**-cai] fetch water to wash vegetables [**zou**-ma **guan**-hua] glance over things hurriedly
	vii. A + <u>B + C</u> + D	—	[zhuan-xiu gang-guan] expertise in repairing steel pipe [duo-chi qing-cao] have more grasses

Note: X' = sandhi-formed X

---

① As the phonetic transcription of the examples making use of IPA is inadequate in Lü (1989), Pinyin, the system of romanization used to represent the phonetic notation of Mandarin Chinese, is used for representation.

Quarto-syllabic string ABCD, like [ri yue xing-chen] in Table 3.15 iv, is parsed into two independent di-syllabic units. These two units are independent from each other and tone sandhi applies to them separately, but no more sandhi activities take place between these two units even if the tonal contexts (i. e. identical contour tones in juxtaposition) permit BC or BC' to undergo tone sandhi changes. For instance, tone sandhi does not apply to [gua guo] in [gua guo jiu cai] (see Table 3.15). The power of Binarity is demonstrated by strings with structure of [A + B] + [C + D] as well. (See examples in Table 3.15) No matter how tone sandhi processes on AB and CD respectively (e. g. [zou-ma guan-hua] in Table 3.15), no tone sandhi changes are witnessed in BC or BC' (e. g. [zhuan-xiu gang-guan], [duo-chi qing-cao] in Table 3.15). (See Figure 3.16 for illustration)

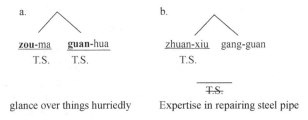

Figure 3.16 Binarity and tone sandhi in Yuncheng dialect

3.5.1.2.2 Span of Phonological Domain of Tone Sandhi

From Lü's (1989) data, we may find that the domain of tone sandhi in Yuncheng dialect is definitely larger than that of Tianjin dialect. Recall in Tianjin dialect, at a normal speech rate, the phonological domain of tone sandhi is generally di- or tri-syllabic, and a quarto-syllabic string will be cut into two separate tone sandhi domains, and rarely there is the case that the entire string maps into an independent tone sandhi domain, for example, "[mɤ-çi-kə tsʰuən] Mexico Village". Hence, the undominance of Binarity does not mean that tone sandhi in Yuncheng dialect is restricted to bi-syllabic strings. The domain of tone sandhi in Yuncheng dialect could extend as long as four syllables (Lü 1989) (Table 3.16).

Table 3.16 Tri- and quarto-syllabic tone sandhi in Yuncheng dialect

Syntactic Structure	Context of Tone Sandhi	Sandhi Forms	Examples
A + [B + C]	i. A<u>BC</u>	A'BC	[**gang** kai-yan] just start to perform [**liang** chang-duan] measure length
	ii. <u>ABC</u>	AB'C A'B'C	[jian **deng**-hua] cut papercut [xin **yu**-san] new umbrella [liang **kuan**-zhai] measure width
	iii. <u>AB</u>C	AB'C	[gang **kai**-gong] just start to work [zhi **yu**-san] paper umbrella [cheng **ren**-qing] owe favors
A + [B + [C + D]]	iv. A + [B + [C + D]]	Same as (i-iii)	
	v. A + [B + [<u>C + D</u>]]	A'B'CD AB'CD	[**zhi xiao** shou-tao] knit little gloves [**dang xiao** nü-xu] be a son-in-law [yan **xiao** nü-xu] act as son-in-law [kai **xin** ji-qi] operate a new machine
	vi. A + [<u>B + [C + D]</u>]	A'B'C'D AB'C'D A'BC'D	[chang **xin xiao**-mi] taste new millet [chi **xin xiao**-mi] eat new millet [qu xiao **jin**-bi] fetch the little golden pen

In Table 3.16 ii, the sandhi forms of [xin yu-san] and [liang kuan-zhai] indicate that tone sandhi rules apply to [yu-san] and [kuan-zhai] first, then sandhi formed [yü] and [kuan] create applicable contexts of tone sandhi for [xin] and [liang] which undergo sandhi process next accordingly as shown in Table 3.17 a, b. Contrastively, in Table 3.16 iii the sandhi forms of [kai], [zhi] and [cheng], bleed the application of tone sandhi to them as a consequence, as shown in Table 3.17 c – e.

Table 3.17 Feeding and bleeding

	Examples	Procedures of Tone Sandhi
a.	[xin yu-san] new umbrella	L. hl + **H. hl** + **H. hl**→**L. hl** + **L. hl** + H. hl → L. lh + L. hl + H. hl
b.	[liang kuan-zhai] measure the width	L. lh + **L. hl** + **L. hl**→ L. lh + L. lh + L. hl→H. lh + L. lh + L. hl
c.	[gang kai-gong] just start to work	L. hl + **L. hl** + **L. hl**→ L. hl + L. lh + L. hl
d.	[zhi yu-san] paper umbrella	H. hl + **H. hl** + **H. hl**→ H. hl + L. hl + H. hl
e.	[cheng ren-qing] owe favors	L. lh + L. lh + L. lh → L. lh + H. lh + L. lh

Either feeding or bleeding effects are involved in the sandhi processes, the examples exhibited above stand on the same ground: The entire tri-syllabic string constitutes an independent tone sandhi domain. The same thing holds in quarto-syllabic strings. Take typical examples [chang xin xiao-mi] and [chi xin xiao-mi] (both syntactically-structured as [A + [B + [C + D]]]) in Table 3.16 vi for illustration. Exactly the same as what we have seen in tri-syllabic strings, tone sandhi starts to work from the right side of strings and proceeds leftward cycle by cycle. By the cycle that [xin] changes into low rising tone L. lh, it consequently feeds [chang] (L. lh) but bleeds [chi] (L. hl) (see Table 3.18 for contrast).

Table 3.18 Directionality: Leftwardness

	Examples	Procedures of Tone Sandhi
a.	[chang [xin [xiao-mi]]] taste new millet	L. lh + L. hl + **H. hl** + **H. hl**→L. lh + L. hl + **L. hl** + H. hl →**L. lh** + **L. lh** + L. hl + H. hl → H. lh + L. lh + L. hl + H. hl
b.	[chi [xin [xiao-mi]]] eat new millet	L. hl + L. hl + **H. hl** + **H. hl**→L. hl + L. **hl** + **L. hl** + H. hl → L. hl + L. lh + L. hl + H. hl

According to Lü (1989), the upper limit of the size of the domain of application of tone sandhi in Yuncheng dialect is quarto-syllabic. Hence, the domain of tone sandhi of Yuncheng dialect ranges from di-syllabic to quarto-syllabic; nevertheless, the operation of tone sandhi is not restricted to a certain syntactic constituent as it freely applies to words, phrases and short clauses. From the analysis presented above we can also see that even though tone sandhi in Yuncheng dialect is indifferent to syntactic constituency, it is sensitive to the internal morphosyntactic structure of the string it applies to.

Analysis delivered up to now suggests that:

i. Syntactic constituency does not define the phonological domain structure of tone sandhi in Yuncheng dialect.

ii. The size effects require a prosodic account instead.

iii. The phonology of tone sandhi itself is sensitive to hence conditioned by the internal morphosyntactic structure of the string it operates on.

For the very last proposal, i. e. sensitivity to morphosyntactic structure, an immediate byproduct is the direction of application of tone sandhi: Tone sandhi in Yuncheng dialect applies cyclically leftward, which we have actually touched on in this section, and is one of the very important properties of the phonology of tone sandhi in Yuncheng dialect.

3.5.1.3 Directionality and Cyclic Application

3.5.1.3.1 Leftwardness

Tone sandhi of the sample strings shown above uniformly proceeds leftward, but examples like [qu xiao jin-bi] in Table 3.19 demonstrate no preference in directionality:

Table 3.19 The paradox of directionality

Examples	Tone Sandhi
[qu [xiao [jin-bi]]] fetch the little golden pen	**H. hl + H. hl + L. hl + L. hl**→ L. hl + H. hl + L. lh + L. hl

From Table 3.19 we see that [qu xiao] and [jin-bi] undergo tone sandhi changes respectively, and there is no crucial difference whether [qu xiao] or [jin-bi] proceeds first. The same situation can be seen in coordinate-structured strings, like [ri yue xing-chen] in Table 3.15, which undergo tone sandhi exactly the same as [qu xiao jin-bi] does. The situation is further complicated by the sandhi behavior of [gua guo jiu cai] in Table 3.15: though [guo jiu] satisfies the tonal context of tone sandhi rules, tone sandhi does not happen at all, namely, this quarto-syllabic coordinate-structured string apparently collapses into two independent tone sandhi domains. But this phenomenon is only restricted to coordinate-structured and 2 + 2-structured strings (e. g. [gua guo jiu cai] and [duo chi qing-cai] in Table 3. 15). We assume that this is uniquely constrained by Binarity. The undominance of Binarity tears a coordinate-structured quarto-syllabic string into two separate parts with equal size which then undergo tone sandhi independently. Since [ri yue xing-chen] maps into two separate minimal tone sandhi domains, it is pointless and unavailing to argue for directionality of tone sandhi with samples of this kind.

Actually, strings other than coordinate-structured ones do prove the directionality of tone sandhi. Examples in Table 3. 16 typically demonstrate that tone sandhi in Yuncheng dialect proceed cyclically leftward respecting the morphosyntactic structure of the string. Take [chang xin xiao-mi] and [chi xin xiao-mi] once again for illustration:

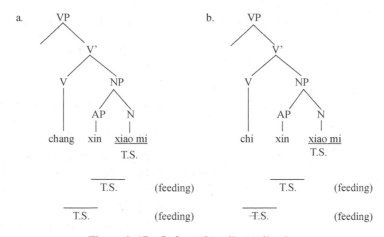

Figure 3. 17 Leftward cyclic application

In both cases in Figure 3. 17, tone sandhi starts to work from the rightmost syntactic terminal element N [xiao-mi]; [xin] undergoes sandhi change in the next step as long as sandhi-formed [xiao] and [xin] meet the tonal context of tone sandhi; as the tone sandhi rule continues to scan leftward, it goes on to change [chang] in Figure 3. 17 a with the sandhi tone for [chang] and sandhi-formed [xin] satisfies its requirement, but it stops to work on [chi] in Figure 3.17 b because the original tonal context (i.e. L. hl + L. hl) is ruined immediately when [xin] has put on the sandhi form.

Observing the syntactic structure of the sample string, tone sandhi operates leftward cycle by cycle. Nevertheless, cyclic application complicates the situation by introducing phonological opacity (Gussenhoven 2011), specifically feeding and bleeding effects as far as tone sandhi in Yuncheng dialect is concerned here.

3.5.1.3.2 Feeding Effects

Suppose there is a string "$\sigma_1 \ldots \sigma_{n-j-1}\sigma_{n-j} \ldots \sigma_n$", as long as tone sandhi in Yuncheng dialect proceeds leftward and scans the string leftward syllable by syllable, the sandhi-formed syllable σ_{n-j} may create permissible tonal environment that enables σ_{n-j-1} to undertake the sandhi form. See Table 3.20 for examples:

Table 3.20 Feeding effects

	Morphosyntactic Structure	Examples	Procedures of Tone Sandhi
a.	[A + [B + C]]	[xin yu-san] new umbrella	L. hl + H. hl + H. hl→L. hl + L. hl + H. hl→ L. lh + L. hl + H. hl
b.		[liang kuan-zhai] measure width	L. lh + L. hl + L. hl→L. lh + L. lh + L. hl→ H. lh + L. lh + L. hl
c.	[A + [B + [C + D]]]	[chang xin xiao-mi] taste new millet	L. lh + L. hl + H. hl + H. hl→L. lh + L. hl + L. hl + H. hl→ L. lh + L. lh + L. hl + H. hl→H. lh + L. lh + L. hl + H. hl
d.		[zhi xiao shou-tao] knit little gloves	L. hl + H. hl + H. hl + H. 1→L. hl + L. hl + H. hl + H. 1→ L. lh + L. hl + H. hl + H. 1

In Table 3.20, feeding effects come into existence immediately when the first cycle of tone sandhi is done, and last throughout the entire sandhi process. Take [chang xin xiao-mi] once again as an example (see the operation of tone sandhi in Figure 3.17). [xiao] in sandhi form enables [xin] to undergo sandhi change, then the sandhi-formed [xin] enables [chang] to surface with sandhi form.

In Table 3.20, the example in d different from those in a – c in that tone sandhi applies vacuously on the rightmost di-syllabic noun, hence the effects of tone sandhi settle into shape in the second cycle, namely the tonal context of [xiao shou] (also [xiao nü]) meets the requirement of tone sandhi rules, and [xiao] undergoes tone sandhi changes. Sandhi-formed [xiao] then feeds [zhi] and [tao] which put on the sandhi forms as a consequence. This is exactly what we have seen in Tianjin dialect in the sense that there are feeding, also bleeding effects in strings that undergo chained-up tone sandhi.

3.5.1.3.3 Bleeding Effects

In the string "$\sigma_1 \ldots \sigma_{n-j-1} \sigma_{n-j} \ldots \sigma_n$", the application of tone sandhi on σ_{n-j} may feed its application on σ_{n-j-1}, but there are also possibilities that the tonal context for σ_{n-j-1} to undergo tone sandhi is destroyed as soon as σ_{n-j} puts on the sandhi form, which is labeled as bleeding effects. See Table 3.21 for examples:

Table 3.21 Bleeding effects

	Morphosyntactic Structure	Examples	Procedures of Tone Sandhi
a.	[A + [B + C]]	[gang kai-gong] just start to work	i. L. hl + **L. hl** + L. hl→ L. hl + L. lh + L. hl ii. * **L. hl** + **L. hl** + L. hl → L. lh + **L. hl** + **L. hl**→ L. lh + L. lh + L. hl
b.		[zhi yu-san] paper umbrella	i. H. hl + H. hl + H. hl→ H. hl + L. hl + L. hl ii. * **H. hl** + **H. hl** + H. hl→ L. hl + **H. hl** + **H. hl**→ L. hl + L. hl + H. hl
c.		[cheng ren-qing] owe favors	i. L. lh + L. lh + L. lh→ L. lh + H. lh + L. lh ii. * **L. lh** + **L. lh** + L. lh→ H. lh + **L. lh** + **L. lh**→ H. lh + H. lh + L. lh

(continued)

	Morphosyntactic Structure	Examples	Procedures of Tone Sandhi	
d.		[chi xin xiao-mi] eat new millet	i.	L. hl + L. hl + **H. hl** + **H. hl**→ L. hl + **L. hl** + **L. hl** + H. hl → L. hl + L. lh + L. hl + H. hl
			ii.	* **L. hl** + **L. hl** + H. hl + H. hl→ L. lh + L. hl + **H. hl** + **H. hl**→ L. lh + L. hl + L. hl + H. hl
e.	[A + [B + [C + D]]]	[kai xin ji-qi] operate new machine	i.	L. hl + **L. hl** + **L. hl** + H. 1 → L. hl + L. lh + L. hl + H. 1
			ii.	* **L. hl** + **L. hl** + L. hl + H. 1 → L. lh + **L. hl** + **L. hl** + H. 1 → L. lh + L. lh + L. hl + H. 1
f.		[yan xiao nü-xu] Act new son-in-law	i.	H. hl + **H. hl** + **H. hl** + H. 1 → L. hl + L. hl + H. hl + H. 1
			ii.	* **H. hl** + **H. hl** + H. hl + H. 1 → L. hl + **H. hl** + **H. hl** + H. 1 → L. hl + L. hl + H. hl + H. 1

Setting aside the fact of leftward-application, tone sandhi could proceed from both directions as far as the tonal contexts are concerned. If tone sandhi of the sample strings listed in Table 3.21 all proceeds rightward from the very left boundaries, then the first syllables (σ_1s) of each string will surface with sandhi forms for σ_1 and σ_2, with citation tones in juxtaposition meeting the tonal requirements of tone sandhi (demonstrated by Table 3.21). However, in fact, patterns of tone sandhi in all the sample strings reveal that tone sandhi starts to work from the right boundaries of the strings and proceeds cyclically leftward. As σ_2s turn into sandhi forms in the last cycle but one, σ_1s with citation tones and σ_2s with sandhi tones no longer satisfy tonal contexts of tone sandhi; in consequence, σ_1s fail to undergo sandhi changes in the last cycle and surface with citation tones (demonstrated by Table 3.21). Figure 3.18 illustrates that the phonological procedures of a and b crucially deviate from each other in that the sandhi-formed non-periphery syllable bleeds tone sandhi of the string-initial syllable in "[cheng ren-qing] owe favors" but feeds that in [liang kuan-zhai].

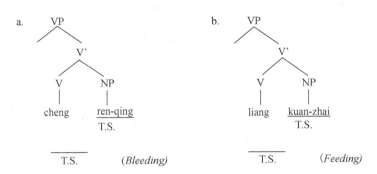

Figure 3.18 Bleeding and feeding effects

3.5.1.3.4 Cyclic Application

Let us review the examples presented in Tables 3.15, 3.16, 3.21 once again, but this time from the perspective of syntactic structure. Tone sandhi of all the sample strings uniformly starts to work from the right most, syntactically most embedded, di-syllabic immediate constituent, and proceeds leftward syllable by syllable perfectly observing the strings' syntactic structure. But, what if the right most morphosyntactic constituent is mono-syllabic? What if the di-syllabic morphosyntactic constituent, whether most embedded or not, is not in string-final position, for example, [B + C] in the structures of [A + [[B + C] + D]] and [[A + [B + C]] + D]? Is it just coincidence that the procedure of tone sandhi mirrors the morphosyntactic structure of the sample strings discussed so far, since after all, all the examples are inevitably structured as [A + [[B + C] + D]] or[A + [B + [C + D]]], which tallies with the assumption that tone sandhi operates cyclically leftward? More explorations on tone sandhis are required to clarify how syntax, prosody and phonology are balanced and thus hold each other in check.

3.5.1.4 Binarity, Immediate Constituency and Directionality of Tone Sandhi

3.5.1.4.1 Binarity and Immediate Constituency

Discussion in this section is built on the phenomenon that, in sharp contrast with the sandhi processes presented above, there is the frequent case that tone sandhis do not initiate from the very right edge of the string. See the examples listed in Table 3.22 below.

Table 3.22 Binarity and Immeidate Constituency

	Morpsyntactic Structure	Examples	Procedures of Tone Sandhi
a.	[A + [B + [C + D]]]	[chang xin xiao-mi] taste new millet	L. lh + L. hl + **H. hl** + **H. hl**→ L. lh + **L. hl** + **L. hl** + H. hl → **L. lh** + **L. lh** + L. hl + H. hl → H. lh + L. lh + L. hl + H. hl
b.	[A + [[B + C] + D]]	[duan xi-lian shui] carry wash water	i. L. hl + **H. hl** + **H. hl** + H. hl→ **L. hl** + **L. hl** + H. hl + H. hl→ L. lh + L. hl + H. hl + H. hl ii. *L. hl + H. hl + **H. hl** + **H. hl**→ L. hl + H. hl + L. hl + H. hl
c.	[[A + [B + C]] + D]	[xin pin-zhong hao] The new product is good.	i. L. hl + **H. hl** + **H. hl** + H. hl→ **L. hl** + **L. hl** + H. hl + H. hl→ L. lh + L. hl + H. hl + H. hl ii. *L. hl + H. hl + **H. hl** + **H. hl**→ L. hl + H. hl + L. hl + H. hl

We have repeatedly demonstrated in the previous sections that tone sandhi of [chang xin xiao-mi] proceeds from the very right boundary of the string and operates cyclically leftward (procedure of tone sandhi shown once again in Table 3.22 for the sake of clarity). If we simply focus on the tonal contexts of tone sandhi, then tone sandhi of [duan xi-lian shui] in Table 3.22 b and [xin pin-zhong hao] in Table 3.22 c should start to work from the right boundaries of both strings as it does in Table 3.22 a (i.e. procedure of tone sandhi illustrated in Table 3.22). Nevertheless, surprisingly enough, in both cases, tone sandhi starts to work from the penultimate syllables with the final syllables being stranded from the process. Why are the final syllables invalidated during the course of tone sandhi? The combined effects from Binarity and morphosyntactic structure are assumed here to take the responsibility.

Despite the differences in morphosyntactic structures of [chang xin xiao-mi], [duan xi-lian shui] and [xin pin-zhong hao], it is of crucial importance that the first cycle of tone sandhi applies to the rightmost di-syllabic morphosyntactic constituent in all three cases, namely, nouns [xiao-mi], [xi-lian] and [pin-zhong] in [chang xin xiao-mi], [duan xi-lian shui] and [xin pin-zhong hao] respectively as shown in Table 3.22 a – c.

Since [xiao-mi] in Figure 3.19 a is located by the right edge of verbal phrase, it is the most natural situation that the right boundary of tone sandhi coincides with the right edge of this VP; on the other hand, the compound-stem [xi-lian] in Figure 3.19 b and NP-head [pin-zhong] in Figure 3.19 c activate tone sandhi processes respectively, with the string-final mono-syllabic morpheme [shui] and the mono-syllabic adjective [xiao] stranded even though both single-syllables with the penultimate syllables satisfy the tonal requirements of tone sandhi. Tone sandhi then continues to scan leftward, and the sandhi-formed [xi] and [pin] feed the initial syllables VP-head [duan] and NP-adjunct [xin] which surface with sandhi forms respectively.

Tone sandhi of [chang xin xiao-mi] and that of [duan xi-lian shui] and [xin pin-zhong hao] are different in that the latter does not start from the very right edges of the strings, but agrees with each other in that it is the rightmost di-syllabic immediate morphosyntactic constituent that initiates the operation of tone sandhi (Figure 3.19).

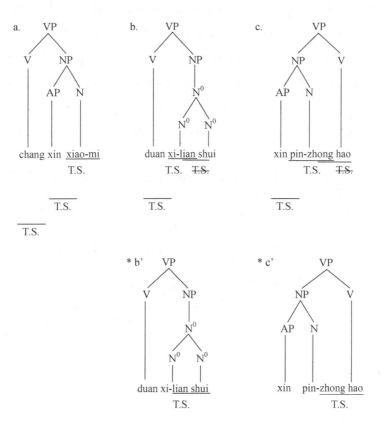

Figure 3.19 Binarity and Immeidate Constituency

Analysis presented up to now enables us to draw a comparatively complete but still-rough picture about the phonology of tone sandhi in Yuncheng dialect: purely tonologically speaking, tone sandhi in Yuncheng dialect is motivated by OCP; whereas, as soon as the carriers of tones, i. e. syllables, are involved, prosody and syntax will show their influences on tone sandhi through various ways. Prosodically speaking, the size of the phonological domain structure of tone sandhi has lower (i. e. minimally di-syllabic) and upper (i. e. maximally quarto-syllabic) limits. Morphosyntactically speaking, although the phonological domain of application of tone sandhi is insensitive to the distinction between different syntactic constituents, it is sensitive to the internal morphosyntactic structure of the string it applies to, which, at the same time, is crucially conditioned by prosody, i. e. Binarity once again.

Actually, Lü (1989) has already insightfully pointed out that it is a general and primary rule that the most unmarked tone sandhi domain is built on a di-syllabic immediate morphosyntactic constituent. So even if σ_{n-j-1} and σ_{n-j} in juxtaposition fulfill the requirements of tonal contexts of tone sandhi, for example, [ti hao] with H. hl + H. hl in [shen-ti hao] in Table 3.23 a, [ping men] with H. lh + H. lh in [he-ping men] in Table 3.23 c ii, tone sandhi will not take place if σ_{n-j-1} and σ_{n-j} connect to different morphosyntactic terminal nodes.

Table 3.23 Binarity and Immeidate Constituency (I)

	Syntactic Structure	Examples	Procedures of Tone Sandhi
a.	[[A+B]+C]	[shen-ti hao] in good health	L. hl + **H. hl** + **H. hl**→L. hl + L. hl + H. hl
b.		[tian-an men] Gate of Tian'an	**L. hl** + **L. hl** + L. lh→L. lh + L. hl + L. lh
c.		[he-ping men] Gate of Peace	i.　**L. lh** + **L. lh** + L. lh→H. lh + L. lh + L. lh ii.　*L. lh + **L. lh** + **L. lh**→L. lh + H. lh + L. lh

(continued)

	Syntactic Structure	Examples	Procedures of Tone Sandhi
d.	[A+[B+C]]	[jian deng-hua] cut papercuts	H. hl + **L. hl** + **L. hl**→H. hl + L. lh + L. hl
e.		[gang kai-gong] just start to work	i. L. hl + **L. hl** + **L. hl**→L. hl + L. lh + L. hl ii. * **L. hl** + **L. hl** + L. hl→L. lh + **L. hl** + **L. hl** →L. lh + L. lh + L. hl
f.		[gang kai-yan] Performance just starts.	**L. hl** + **L. hl** + H. hl→L. lh + L. hl + H. hl

Tone sandhi applies to the di-syllabic immediate morphosyntactic constituents compound-stems [tian-an] and [he-ping], but not to [ti hao] and [ping men] which do not connect to the same morphosyntactic terminal nodes thus immediate constituency fails them (see Figure 3.20 for illustration).

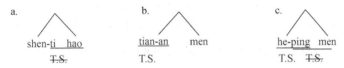

a. shen-ti hao   T.S.
b. tian-an men   T.S.
c. he-ping men   T.S. T.S.

Figure 3.20 Binarity & Immeidate Constituency (Ⅰ)

Analysis of examples in Figure 3.20 significantly reveals that Binarity and Immediate Constituency are of equal prevailing importance in initiating the operation of tone sandhi; meanwhile, the phonology of tone sandhi itself locates the rightmost di-syllabic immediate morphosyntactic constituent to activate its application. Once tone sandhi starts to work, it marches leftward without looking back, and this explains why [ping men] is excluded from the sandhi process as [he-ping] initiates tone sandhi which then patrols leftward and ignores [ping men] to the right of sandhi trigger [he-ping] in Figure 3.20 c.

3.5.1.4.2 Leftward Cyclic Application

In the very last subsection, we have reasoned that string final mono-syllabic morphosyntactic constituent is not qualified to initiate tone sandhi processes (see Table 3.23 and Figure 3.20) under the pressure of Binarity and Immediate Constituency. It is also the case in longer strings.

Table 3.24 Binarity and Immeidate Constituency (II)

	Syntactic Structure	Examples	Procedures of Tone Sandhi
a.	[[[A + B] + C] + D]	[gang-tie chang yuan] The iron factory is far away.	i. **L. hl + L. hl** + H. hl + H. hl → L. lh + L. hl + H. hl + H. hl ii. *L. hl + L. hl + **H. hl + H. hl**→ L. hl + **L. hl + L. hl** + H. hl → L. hl + L. lh + L. hl + H. hl
b.	[A + [[B + C] + D]]	[ai qing-hai sheng] next to Qinghai Province	i. **L. hl + L. hl** + H. hl + H. hl → L. lh + L. hl + H. hl + H. hl ii. *L. hl + L. hl + **H. hl + H. hl**→ L. hl + **L. hl + L. hl** + H. hl→ L. hl + L. lh + L. hl + H. hl
c.	[[A + [B + C]] + D]	[yuan pin-zhong hao] The original product is good.	i. L. lh + **H. hl + H. hl** + H. hl → L. lh + L. hl + H. hl + H. hl ii. *L. lh + H. hl + **H. hl + H. hl**→ L. lh + H. hl + L. hl + H. hl

In [gang-tie chang yuan] in Table 3.24 a, the mono-syllabic compound-root [chang] and the predicate [yuan] both surface with their citation forms even though they meet the phonological requirement of tone sandhi, i. e. high falling tones (H. hl) in juxtaposition. Contrastively, tone sandhi operates on [gang-tie] smoothly (i. e. L. hl in juxtaposition). This Paradox is exactly due to Binarity and Immediate Constituency. [Gang-tie], as a di-syllabic morphological immediate constituent, initiates the application of tone sandhi. [chang yuan], though di-syllabic and sits on the right edge of the phrase, is not an immediatate constituent at all, as [chang] and [yuan] connect to separate morphosyntactic terminal nodes, thus it loses to [gang-tie] in triggering tone sandhi processes. (See Figure 3.21 for illustration.)

In spite of the difference in morphosyntactic structure, in Table 3.24 [ai qing-hai sheng] and [yuan pin-zhong hao] resemble the sandhi behavior of [gang-tie chang yuan]. It is demonstrated in Figure 3.21 a – c that tone sandhi does not happen to [hai sheng] and [zhong hao], because [hai] and [sheng] connect to separate morphological nodes, similarly, [zhong] and [hao] connect to syntactic nodes independent to each other. Tone sandhi, being blind to them, continues to scan leftward for di-syllabic immediate constituent, di-syllabic compound-stems [qing-hai] and [pin-zhong] are targeted then. [pin-zhong] undergoes tone sandhi right away as it meets the phonological requirement of tone sandhi on the other hand, while [qing-hai] keeps the citation tones as OCP is not violated at all. Tone sandhis of [yuan pin-zhong hao] stops at [pin-zhong] as no more adjacent syllables with identical contour tones are found, but goes on to work in [ai qing-hai sheng] as citation-formed [ai] and [qing] meet the tonal requirements of tone sandhi.

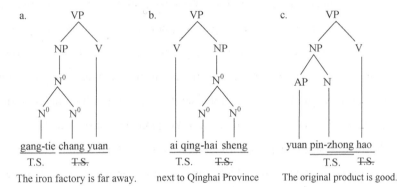

Note: Superscript 0 refers to morphological category.

Figure 3.21 Binarity and Immeidate Constituency (Ⅱ)

From the tone sandhis of [ai qing-hai sheng] and [yuan pin-zhong hao] it can be clearly seen the asymmetrical sandhi behavior between the mono-syllabic pre-di-syllabic-immediate-constituents, for example, [ai] and [yuan] in Figure 3.21 b, c, and the mono-syllabic post-di-syllabic-immediate-constituents, for example, [sheng] and [hao] in Figure 3.21 b and c. While [sheng] and [hao] fail to activate the process of tone sandhi, they are then deprived of the privilege of participating in this phonological activity. In contrast, [ai] and [yuan] enter the processing of tone sandhi as it scans leftward cyclically. An immediate consequence of this phenomenon is that—the right boundary of the domain of tone sandhi, apparently, may not always align with the right edge of the string that tone sandhi operates on. ①

The undominance of Binarity and Immediate Constituency endows the di-syllabic immediate morphosyntactic constituent to form a tone sandhi domain on its own. As soon as the di-syllabic immediate morphosyntactic constituent initiates the application of tone sandhi, tone sandhi may continue to apply cyclically leftward by observing the morphosyntactic computation of the string. Constrained by prosodic requirements, the domain of tone sandhi will however not exceed four syllables.

3.5.1.5 Summary of the Phonology of Tone Sandhi in Yuncheng Dialect

In the first place, tone sandhi in Yuncheng dialect does not distinguish words from phrases or shorts clauses, whose phonological domain of application has lower and upper limits. Binarity is undoubtedly dominant and controls two major aspects of tone sandhi: i) a di-syllabic string can map into the minimal independent phonological domain of tone sandhi; ii) in a poly-syllabic string, it is the rightmost di-syllabic immediate morphosyntactic constituent that initiates tone sandhi of this string. The phonological domain of tone sandhi can extend to as large as quarto-syllabic, to which tone sandhi applies cyclically leftward, conditioned by the syntactic structure. Hence, we can also see that in a poly-syllabic string, the phonology of tone sandhi in Yuncheng dialect endows the rightmost binary syntactic terminal element, but not the syllable by the right edge of the string with the privilege to initiate the application of tone sandhi. In short, tone sandhi in Yuncheng dialect is:

i. sensitive to the length of the string it applies to;
ii. insensitive to the distinction between different syntactic constituents;
iii. sensitive to the internal morphosyntactic structure of the string it applies to.

Analysis up to now reveals that tone sandhi in Yuncheng dialect presents

---

① The mismatch between phonological domain structure and syntactic structure as far as boundary alignment concerned is also exemplified by H-spreading Nonfinality in Xitsonga which will be discussed in detail in Section 3.5.2.2 in comparison with tone sandhi in Yuncheng dialect.

complicated interactions between prosody and syntax, prosody and phonological rules, and syntax and phonological rules. On the one hand, the size of the domain of tone sandhi is constrained by prosody; on the other hand, temporarily speaking, the application of tone sandhi is conditioned by the internal morphosyntactic structure of the string. The phonological domain structure of tone sandhi is then vital in formalizing the relationship among morphosyntactic structuring, prosodic-oriented size effects, and the application of phonological rules.

3.5.2 Phonological Domain Structure of Tone Sandhi in Yuncheng Dialect

3.5.2.1 Mismatch Between Syntactic Constituency and Prosodic Constituency

As early as in Section 3.2.2, we have reasoned that in Mandarin a ω is minimally di-syllabic and maximally quarto-syllabic, which is testified to by Tianjin dialect, a Mandarin-based dialect, and the construction of tone sandhi domain in Tianjin dialect is seriously taken as the diagnosis. Yuncheng dialect falls into the same type with Mandarin and Tianjin dialect, because in Yuncheng dialect the domain of application of tone sandhi also ranges from di-syllabic to quarto-syllabic which is obviously prosodically constrained. The size effects tell that a legitimate phonological domain of tone sandhi in Yuncheng dialect has to be a legitimate prosodic constituent, i.e. ω. So, the same as in Tianjin dialect and Shaoxing dialect, the domain of application of tone sandhi in Yuncheng dialect is also defined through ω.

Still similar to Tianjin dialect, the phonology of tone sandhi in Yuncheng dialect is not sensitive to syntactic constituency. A legitimate tone sandhi domain could possibly be a syntactic word, a phrase or even a short clause on the condition that its length does not exceed four syllables, which severely undermines the correspondence between syntactic constituency and prosodic constituency.

The strict restriction to four or fewer syllables and tremendous indifference to morphosyntactic constituency suggests the outranking of prosodic structure well-formedness constraints over isomorphism between syntactic constituents and prosodic constituents.

3.5.2.2 Prosodic Structure Well-formedness Constraints

In Section 3.5.1.2 we have introduced that the prosodic structure well-formedness constraint—Binarity is so powerful that it splits strings structured as [A + B + C + D] or [A + B] + [C + D] like "[ri yue xing-cheng] sun, moon, star" and "[zou ma guan hua] glance over things hurriedly" into two separate domains of tone sandi which are two unmarked independent ωs in essence (illustrated in Figure 3.22). It could then be predictable that on the sentence level, the maximal domains of tone sandhi (ranging from di-syllabic to tri-syllabic in length) will be iteratively built from the right edge of the sentence to the left edge of the sentence.

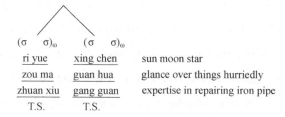

Figure 3.22 Sentence-level iterative-building of tone sandhi domains

Hence, a di-syllabic immediate morphosyntactic constituent enjoys the privilege to be first parsed into an independent tone sandhi domiain as Binarity ensures its prosodic status, namely, a ω.

3.5.2.3 Binarity, Immediate Constituency and Directionality of Tone Sandhi

Just as with what we have argued and reasoned for in Tianjin dialect and Mandarin, mono-syllabic morphosyntactic constituents resort to adjunction to gain legal prosodic status. In Yuncheng dialect, as long as a di-syllabic morphosyntactic immediate constituent can stand on its own prosodically, a mono-syllabic morphosyntactic constituent adjoins to the di-syllabic one to which it most closely relates so as to participate in prosodic computation. In consequence, morphosyntactic structure will be mirrored into the prosodic constituent, which is essentially diagnosed by tone sandhi. See Figure 3.23 a:

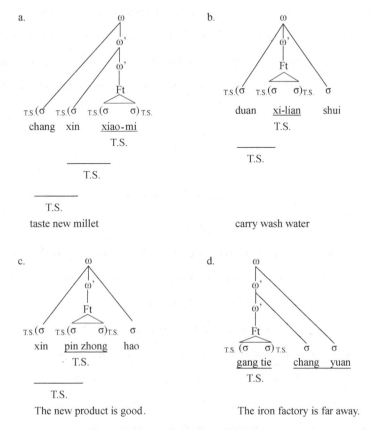

Figure 3.23 Cyclic application of tone sandhi within ω

In Figure 3.23 a, c, mono-syllabic syntactic constituents [xin] and [chang] adjoin to the minimal ω [xiao-mi] in succession, thus finally resulting in a recursively-built ω. Recursion of this ω is testified to by how tone sandhi processes in this string: [xiao-mi] undergo tone sandhi in the first place, then [xin] and [chang] turn up with sandhi forms one by one.

In Section 3.2.3, we introduced Selkirk's (2011) proposal that besides the interaction between morph-syntax and prosody, phonological rules on their own may refer to syntactic or prosodic information as well. Selkirk supports her proposal with H-tone spreading in Xitsonga. H-tone spreading is a sentence-level phonology (Kisseberth 1994; Cassimjee & Kissberth 1998). Though its phonological domain structure is defined through the prosodic constituent Phonological Phrase (PPh / φ), H-tone spreading itself is also sensitive to prosodic structures (Selkirk 2011: 443): "A lexical high tone spreads rightward from its underlying position, but it is (i) blocked from spreading onto the final, rightmost, syllable of a φ-domain, as illustrated in Figure 3.24 a, and (ii) blocked from spreading across the left edge of a φ-domain, as illustrated by Figure 3.24 b".

Figure 3.24 Prosodic domain of H-tone spreading (Selkirk 2011)

Sensitivity to prosodic boundaries is the property of H-tone spreading. Tone sandhi in Yuncheng dialect is analogous to H-tone spreading in Xitsonga in that leftward application, as an intrinsic property of tone sandhi, is alert to the internal structure of ω. See Figure 3.23 b – d.

As mono-syllabic morphosyntactic constituents adjoin to the di-syllabic one that they morphosyntactically intimately relate to, an "extended" ω is then constructed. When the application of tone sandhi is initiated by the minimal ω, it immediately proceeds leftward and the pre-minimal-ω mono-syllabic constituents (if there were any) are fortunate enough to enter the procedure of tone sandhi in the same way that they enter into this "extended" ω; consequently, a recursively-structured phonological domain of tone sandhi is born, exemplified by Figure 3.23 a – c. But, the post-minimal-ω mono-syllabic constituents (if there were any) do not have the fortune to participate in the process of tone sandhi which marches leftward without looking back as soon as is initiated by the minimal ω, exemplified by Figure 3.23 b – d.

Both H-tone spreading in Xitsonga and tone sandhi in Yuncheng dialect are sensitive to prosodic information. The former is sensitive to the boundaries of φs, while the latter is sensitive to the internal structure of "extended" ωs. Tone sandhi in Yuncheng dialect crucially differs from Tone Sandhi I in Shaoxing dialect on this point.

In Shaoxing dialect, the domain of application of Tone Sandi I is also defined through ω, prosodic structure well-formedness constraints realized as size effects also dominate syntactic-prosodic constituency correspondence, but the phonology of tone sandhi in Shaoxing dialect itself does not refer to any prosodic nor morphosyntactic information. In Yuncheng dialect, on the one hand, prosodic constituents are built with reference to morphosyntactic structure; on the other hand, though ω defines tone sandhi domain, tone sandhi itself is also sensitive to the internal structure of ω, which is actually inherited from the morphosyntactic structure.

The domain of tone sandhi in Yuncheng dialect ranges from di-syllabic to quarto-syllabic strings irrespective of syntactic constituency proves that prosodic structure well-formedness constraint—Binarity outranks X-ω correspondence. A significant difference from Tianjin dialect and Shaoxing dialect is that the phonological rules of tone sandhi in Yuncheng dialect refer to domain information. Together with Binarity and morphosyntactic structuring, cyclic application of tone sandhi explains recursion in ω is inherited from morphosyntactic structure, and leftward processing explains the mismatch between the right edge of domain of tone sandhi and the right boundary of ω.

3.6 Summary

In this chapter we have mainly discussed syntactic-prosodic constituency correspondence on the ω-level diagnosed by phonological domain structure of tone sandhi in Chinese dialects. We have examined three dialects, i.e. Tianjin dialect—Mandarin-based dialect, Shaoxing dialect—North Wu dialect, and Yuncheng dialect—South Jin dialect. Besides data collected from literature, we have also conducted social investigations on tone sandhi in Tianjin dialect and Shaoxing dialect.

It is the frequent case that ω fails to match with X empirically supported cross-linguistically (Nespor & Vogel 2007) , while there are also cases that empirical evidence testifies that morphosyntactic structure mirrors into ω (Kabak & Revithiadou 2007; Selkirk 2011). All three dialects discussed here testify to the mismatch between ω and X due to the high ranking of the size constraints on ω. Yuncheng dialect and Tianjin dialect also testify to the influence on prosodic structure from morphosyntax because the phonology of tone sandhi in Yuncheng dialect and that of a subgroup in Tianjin dialect are sensitive to the morphosyntactic structures.

The prosodic size effects are common across languages at all three levels of prosodic constituents, namely, ω, φ and ι, and this may interact with syntactic-prosodic constituency correspondence constraints with the ranking between them varying from language to language (Ghini 1993; Inkelas and Zec 1995; Selkirk 2011). In all the three dialects we examined in this chapter, the phonological domain structure of tone sandhi suggests that the size effects on ω override X-ω correspondence. Like what Booij (1983) predicts, a ω may be larger, smaller than or equal to an X. No matter how small (i. e. mono-syllabic) or how large (e. g. poly-syllabic compound) an X is, the size of ω always has lower and upper limits which are inherent properties of prosodic constituents. All the three dialects prove that a ω is minimally di-syllabic, which can be formalized through the markedness constraint Binarity requiring a ω minimally consist of one di-syllabic foot. The phonological domain structure of tone sandhi diagnoses that the upper limits of ω vary from dialect to dialect: Tianjin dialect allows for di- and tri-syllabic ω, in Shaoxing dialect a ω could extend to as long as penta-syllabic, while Yuncheng dialect sits in between, permitting quarto-syllabic ω. Variation on upper limits of ω suggests typological differences on the prosodic organization of ω. For instance, Tianjin dialect sharply contrasts with Shaoxing dialect in that Tianjin dialect permits a ω being composed of a one di-syllabic or a tri-syllabic foot, while Shaoxing dialect permits a ω being composed of a di-syllabic foot and a tri-syllabic foot. In the face of strong requirements on the size of prosodic constituent, syntactic-prosodic constituency correspondence is demoted in all these three dialects.

On the syntax-phonology interface, Selkirk (2011: 448 – 449) proposes that there are three sources that may influence the match and mismatch between prosodic constituents and syntactic constituents: prosodic structure well-formedness constraints, language-specific syntactic structure, and phonology. Both phonologies of tone sandhi in Tianjin dialect and Shaoxing dialect are insensitive to the morphosyntactic structures of the domain that they apply to, so the phonological domain structure of tone sandhi in both dialects is the product of interaction between prosodic structure well-formedness constraints and syntactic-prosodic constituency correspondence. The phonology of tone sandhi in Yuncheng dialect, typologically differs from Tianjin dialect and Shaoxing dialect in that it is sensitive to its domain structure. As long as prosodic structure well-formedness constraints defeat syntactic-prosodic constituency correspondence and restrict the domain of application of tone sandhi to within four syllables, the phonology of tone sandhi itself probes the rightmost di-syllabic immediate morphosyntactic constituent within the domain of its application to activate itself.

Reference to morphosyntactic structure in the processing of phonology explains recursion in ω in Yuncheng dialect. In Tianjin dialect, the phonology of tone sandhi makes no reference to morphosyntactic structure, so it is the phonology of the neutral tone that takes the responsibility of triggering the mapping of recursion in morphosyntactic structures into ω.

Chapter 4

Correspondence Between XP and PPh

In Selkirk's (2011) version of the prosodic hierarchy, PPh / φ is the prosodic constituent immediately above the prosodic constituent PWd / ω, and immediatey below the prosodic constituent IP / ι. The Match Theory of syntactic-prosodic constituency correspondence (Selkirk 2011: 439) proposes that φ interacts with phrasal level syntactic constituents: A phrase in syntactic constituent structure must be matched by a corresponding prosodic constituent, call it φ, in phonological representation.

The Match Theory asserts the general principle that XP matches with φ during the mapping from syntactic constituents to prosodic constituents. In the prosodic hierarchy, the Strict Layer Hypothesis expresses the idea that all the ωs included in a phrase join to form an n-ary branching φ which defines the prosodic domain of the phrase (Nespor & Vogel 2007). The notion of φ is promoted on the grounds that syntactic phrasing is inadequate in computing the application of phonological rules, and systematic prosodic properties play a crucial role in defining the domain structure of phonological rules. The phonological domain structure of tone sandhis in Xiamen dialect, representative of South Min dialects, is proposed to be defined through φ, since syntactic constituency alone cannot explicitly predict the application of tone sandhis in these dialects.

Chapter 4　Correspondence Between XP and PPh

According to Zhang (1985), the distribution of South Min dialects is rather broad, covering the vast south part of Fujian, most part of Taiwan and the east part of Guangdong. Despite the differences in the phonetic realization of pitch values of tones, the phonology of tone sandhis of the South Min dialects is highly unified, at least testified to by Xiamen dialect, Zhangzhou dialect of Fujian and Chenghai dialect of Guangdong. Xiamen dialect, the representative dialect of the South Min dialects inside Fujian, has received great attention from linguists and is one of the best described the South Min dialects ever since Luo (1931), Li (1962), Yuan (2001). Successive works, like Zhang (1983), Chen & Li (2008), Chen (2008), Yang (2010), etc., have enlarged the research scope to other South Min dialects inside Fujian, and have clearly pointed out that tone sandhis in other South Min dialects operate the same way as those in Xiamen dialect do, irrespective of the variations in the pitch values of tones. The South Min dialects in the east part of Guangdong have also received extensive study. Tone sandhis of the South Min dialects in east Guangdong are documented in Zhang (1979), Lin (1995, 1996), Shi (2011) and others, though research has unfortunately mostly remained confined to the word level. In order to establish a relatively thorough understanding of the operation of tone sandhis in the South Min dialects in eastern Guangdong, we then selected Chenghai dialect, and conducted investigations on its tone sandhis ranging from words to sentences. Both phonetic analysis and perceptive denotation reveal that tone sandhi in Chenghai dialect processes in the same way as that in Xiamen dialect does. All the facts listed above drive us to preliminarily assume that tone sandhis in the South Min dialects, either inside southern Fujian or inside eastern Guangdong, share the same module of operation. So in this chapter, we will discuss the correspondence between XP and φ mainly based on data of tone sandhis in the South Min dialects. Xiamen dialect, the most well documented dialect of the South Min family, is selected as the carrier of analysis, whose working model is by no means unique nor unusual, as demonstrated at least with circumstantial evidence provided by Zhangzhou dialect and Chenghai dialect.

Data on Xiamen dialect is selected from Chen (2000) and Lin (1994), data on Zhangzhou dialect is cited from Yang (2010), and data on Chenghai dialect is collected by the author. ①

4.1 Promoting PPh

4.1.1 Raddopiamento Sintattico in Italian

Nespor & Vogel (2007) has discussed the domain of application of Raddopiamento Sintattico (RS) of Italian (spoken by educated speakers from Florence). Through this phonological phenomenon, we can clearly see that the domain of application of RS cannot be predicted directly from syntactic constituency, rather, a phonological phrase (φ), constructed on the base of XP has to be introduced to account for the issue at hand.

(4.1) Raddopiamento Sintattico (RS) (Nespor & Vogel 2007: 165 – 166)

RS applies in a sequence of two ωs (ω_1 and ω_2) to lengthen the initial consonant of ω_2 if a) the consonant to be lengthened is followed by a sonorant, specifically a vowel or other non-nasal sonorant, and b) if ω_1 ends in a vowel which is the DTE (i.e. main stress syllable) of ω … RS is a rule that applies across words and that its domain of application cannot be identified with any syntactic constituent since syntactic constituents of the same type may behave differently with respect to the rule.

See the examples below of RS in Italian:

---

① Lin (1995, 1996) has described tone sandhi rules in Chenghai dialect in detail. We established a corpus of tone sandhi on sentence level based on Lin (1995, 1996). My deep gratitude goes to Chen Jie, a native speaker of Chenghai pursuing MA study in the Chinese Department of China Normal University, without whom the research on tone sandhis in Chenghai dialect would be impossible. He helped to conduct field work and provided perceptive denotation. Phonetic and statistical analysis were conducted by the author. Research results were doubled checked by Chen Jie and the author.

Chapter 4 Correspondence Between XP and PPh

(4.2) a. Perché Carlo non é venuto? → Perché [k:]arlo

Why didn't Carlo come?

b. Che c' é un perché Carlo lo sa. → ... perché [k]arlo

Carlo knows that there is a reason.

In (4.2)a, RS applies to *perché Carlo*, but it fails in (4.2)b. What conditions the application of RS is the key issue. To be more specific, the main concern for RS is how the domain of the application of RS is defined. Examples below show the contexts in which RS does in (4.3) and does not in (4.4) apply.

(4.3) a. Avrá t:rovato il pescecane.

He must have found the shark.

b. La gabbia ég:iá c:aduta.

The cage has already fallen.

c. È appena passato con tre c:ani.

He has just passed by with three dogs.

d. Era venuto con tre p:iccolo cobra.

He came with three small cobras.

e. Il tuo pappagallo ép:iú l:oquace del mio.

Your parrot is more talkative than mine.

(4.4) a. Devi comprare delle mappe di cittámolto vecchie.

You must buy some very old city maps.

b. La gabbia era dipinta di giácompletamente.

The cage was already completely painted.

c. Ne aveva soltanto tre **di** bassotti.

He had only three dachshunds.

d. L'entrata allo zoo costa di piú **per** i turisti che per i locali.

The entrance to the zoo is more expensive for tourists than for locals.

e. Guardó **piú** attentamente e vide che era un pitone.

He looked more carefully and saw it was a python.

It can be seen that in (4.3) a that RS applies between an auxiliary and a verb, and in (4.3) b that it applies between an auxiliary and a preverbal adverb, and between a preverbal adverb and a verb. In (4.3) c and (4.3) d, examples of RS are given between a quantifier and a noun, and between a quantifier and a prenominal adjective, respectively. Finally, (4.3) e shows that RS applies both between a copula and the comparative particle *piú*, and between *piú* and an adjective. The example in (4.4), on the other hand, shows contexts in which RS is blocked, that is, between an NP and an AP in (4.4) a, between two adverbs in (4.4) b, between a quantifier and a PP in (4.4) c, between an adverb and a PP in (4.4) d, and between a verb and a comparative adverb.

"From such data it can be seen that RS applies to the left of the head of a phrase, within its maximal projection, but not to its right ... The fact that the environment for RS is the left rather than the right side of the head is not a language specific property of Italian, but instead is due to the fact that the left side of the head is the nonrecursive side of a phrase in Italian." (Nespor & Vogel 2007: 168) The domain of RS extends beyond syntactic terminal elements, i.e. syntactic words, but does not extend leftward beyond the maximal projection of a lexical element. Following the Match Theory, which proposes that the prosodic constituent φ corresponds to syntactic phrase, the phonological domain structure of RS in Italian is defined through prosodic constituent φ. However, the isomorphism between XP and φ is not guaranteed because RS applies to the head of a phrase and what precedes it, but the constituents to the right of the head are excluded from mapping into the same φ. (see Figure 4.1 for illustration)

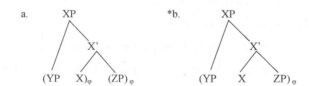

Figure 4.1 Parsing of φ in Italian based on RS

The domain of application of RS can be clearly seen when the syntactic constituents map into prosodic constituents. (4.5) and (4.6) are the sentences we have seen above in (4.3) and (4.4), which are presented in their φ structures.

(4.5) a. (Avrát:rovato)$_φ$ (il pescecane)$_φ$.
He must have found the shark.
b. (La gabbia)$_φ$ (ég:iá c:aduta)$_φ$.
The cage has already fallen.
c. (È appena passato)$_φ$ (con tre c:ani)$_φ$.
He has just passed by with three dogs.
d. (Era venuto)$_φ$ (con tre p:iccolo cobra)$_φ$.
He came with three small cobras.
e. (Il tuo pappagallo)$_φ$ (ép:iú l:oquace)$_φ$ (del mio)$_φ$.
Your parrot is more talkative than mine.

(4.6) a. (Devi comprare)$_φ$ (delle mappe)$_φ$ (di città)$_φ$ (**m**olto vecchie)$_φ$.
You must buy some very old city maps.
b. (La gabbia)$_φ$ (era dipinta)$_φ$ (di giá)$_φ$ (completamente)$_φ$.
The cage was already completely painted.
c. (Ne aveva soltanto tre)$_φ$ (**d**i bassotti)$_φ$.
He had only three dachshunds.
d. (L'entrata)$_φ$ (allo zoo)$_φ$ (costa di piú)$_φ$ (**p**er i turisti)$_φ$ (che per i locali)$_φ$.
The entrance to the zoo is more ecpensive for tourists than for locals.
e. (Guardó)$_φ$ (piú attentamente)$_φ$ (e vide)$_φ$ (che era un pitone)$_φ$.
He looked more carefully and saw it was a python.

From the examples above we see that the phonological phrase φ is not isomorphic to the syntactic phrase, and RS is a ω juncture rule which is obligatory within a φ but not between the φs. See the example below:

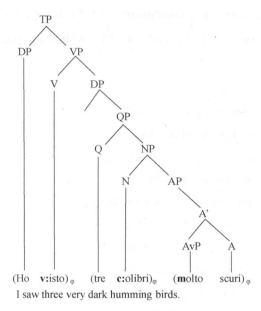

(Ho v:isto)_φ (tre c:olibri)_φ (molto scuri)_φ
I saw three very dark humming birds.

Figure 4.2 Prosodic domain of RS in Italian

4.1.2 XP-φ Correspondence

Analysis of the domain structure of RS in Italian testifies to the existence of the prosodic constituent φ. The domain of application of RS cannot be told through the syntactic structures directly, but the φs mapped from the syntactic constituents actually define the RS application domain. Further, as with ω, it is not necessarily the case that φ is always isomorphic to XP (X = lexical category). It is assumed (Nespor & Vogel 2007: 168) that the non-isomorphic mapping of PPh / φ may relate to the direction of branching of the syntactic phrase. Italian spoken in Florence is a right-branching language, thus the mapping of φ is sensitive to the right edge of the lexical head, and extends regressively to the un-recursive side of the syntactic phrase concerned. The contexts of tone sandhi in Xiamen dialect, very similar to RS in Italian, can be defined through φ. It is assumed here that a major difference between Xiamen dialect and Italian is that the right boundary of the phonological changes (tone sandhi of the former, RS of the latter) are sensitive to the right boundary of XPs (X = lexical category) and that of Xs (X = lexical category), respectively.

4.1.3 φ Restructuring in Raddopiamento Sintattico

Since it is not as stable as ω, φ is comparatively flexible; therefore, restructuring of φ may take place instantiated by RS in Italian. See the two sets of examples of application of RS below:

(4.7) a. (Porterá)_φ(due tigri)_φ(fuori dalla gabbia)_φ
He will take two tigers out of the cage.
b. (Vaccineró)_φ(tutte le scimmie)_φ(entro due giorni)_φ
I will vaccinate all the monkeys within two days.
c. (Venderá)_φ(questo leopardo)_φ(in dicembre)_φ
He will seel this leopard in December.
d. (Hanno)_φ(dei caribú)_φ(molto piccoli)_φ
They have some very small caribous.

(4.8) a. (I caribú)_φ(n:ani)_φ(sono estinti)_φ
Dwarf caribous are extinct.
b. (Se prenderá)_φ(qu:alcosa)_φ(prenderá)_φ(t:ordi)_φ
If he catches something, he will catch thrushes.
c. (Ho visto)_φ(qualche fagiano)_φ(blu)_φ(ch:iaro)_φ
I've seen a few light-blue pheasants.

Examples in (4.7) show that application of RS is strictly confined within φ, and will not happen across φ-boundaries even if the segmental contexts are met. However, counter examples listed in (4.8) seemingly undermine the conclusion that arrived at just now: Since the RS rule is a φ-span phonological process, why can it operate crossing φ-boundaries?

Nespor & Vogel (2007: 172 – 173) argues that it is not irregular application of RS across φ-boundaries, but prosodic parsing of φ is reorganized as the cases of (4.8) are concerned. Since the domain of φ is supposed to be composed of a lexical head X and all the constituents proceeds the head X within the maximal projection of X, the application of RS between the head X and the constituent locating on the recursive side of XP as the cases shown in (4.8) indicates restructuring of φ has taken place between *I caribú* and *nani* in (4.8) a, between *Se prenderá* and *qualcosa*, *prenderá* and *tordi* in (4.8) b, between *blu* and *chiaro* in (4.8) c. So, the examples shown in (4.8) should have prosodic structures as follows:

(4.9) a. (I caribú **n**:ani)$_φ$(sono estinti)$_φ$
b. (Se prenderá **qu**:alcosa)$_φ$(prenderá **t**:ordi)$_φ$
c. (Ho visto)$_φ$(qualche fagiano)$_φ$(blu **ch**:iaro)$_φ$

However, inspecting the examples in (4.7), (4.8) and (4.9) again, it should be made clear that restructuring of φ is conditioned by the syntactic structure of the complement to the right side of the phrase head X (which is the recursive side of the phrase). According to Nespor & Vogel (2007: 172 – 173), if the first complement to the right of phrase head X maps into two or more separate φs, for example, (*due tigri*)$_φ$(*fuori dalla gabbia*)$_φ$ in (4.7) a, (*tutte le scimmie*)$_φ$(*entro due giorni*)$_φ$ in (4.7) b, (*dei caribú*)$_φ$(*molto piccoli*)$_φ$ in (4.7) c, (*dei caribú*)$_φ$(*molto piccoli*)$_φ$ in (4.7) e, φ restructuring will not take place; if the first complement to the right of phrase head X maps into a single φ, φ may take place, namely the complement will be regrouped into the φ initiated by the head X just as with the cases in (4.9).

From RS in Italian we can find that factors like length, rate of speech, etc. may lead to φ restructuring, which is not random in any sense, since syntactic, prosodic, phonological or even phonetic conditions may set restrictions on it. Conditioned φ restructuring is also witnessed in the South Min dialects and will be discussed in detail.

From RS it can be seen that the correspondence between syntactic constituents and prosodic constituents is rather complicated on the level of φ in light of the facts that: 1) a φ may not align with an XP (X = lexical cateogry) on both edges; 2) conditioned restructuring of φ may arise. The South Min family offers clearer pictures.

4.2 Tone Sandhi in Xiamen Dialect

It is reported in Li (1962), Yuan (2001) and others that there are both regressive and progressive tone sandhis in Xiamen dialect, a representative dialect of the South Min family. The regressive one is the tone sandhi in the common sense, while the progressive one resembles the neutral tone in Mandarin, according to Li (1962). Progressive tone sandhi in Xiamen dialect is the focus of discussion in this chapter. So in the analysis below, "tone sandhi of Xiamen dialect" refers to "regressive tone sandhi of Xiamen dialect". Chen (1987) is the pioneer work on the phonological study of tone sandhi in Xiamen dialect, and Lin (1994) pushes the understanding of tone sandhi of this dialect further. Our discussion here will be based on their contributions, hence, we will begin with introducing Chen's (1987) and Lin's (1994) analysis. Tone sandhi in Chenghai dialect and Zhangzhou dialect will supply supporting evidence.

4.2.1 Basics

There are seven citation tones in Xiamen dialect, which are labelled as *yinping / Ia*, *yangping / Ib*, *shang / II*, *yinqu / IIIa*, *yangqu / IIIb*, *yinru / IVa* and *yangru / IVb* in the traditional Chinese literature, and it can be seen that tonal categories *yinshang /IIa* and *yangshang / IIb* are no longer distinguishable from each other (Li 1962; Yuan 2001; Li 2004). In spite of trivial phonetic differences in terms of pitch values between different versions, these seven citation tones in Xiamen dialect can be formalized as follows (Table 4.1):

Table 4.1 Phonological representation of citation tones in Xiamen dialect (Chen 2000)

	I	II	III	IV
a	HH	HM	ML	ML
b	MH	HM	MM	H

The phonological representations of the citation tones listed above are given following Chen's (2000) configuration. Tone sandhi of Xiamen dialect is rather complicated. Preliminarily, tone sandhis can be divided into two independent sets conditioned by whether it is checked-toned syllable or not. Regulations of tone sandhi in Xiamen dialect is shown in Figure 4.3. Though not the focus in my study here, it has to be noted that the sandhi form of an unchecked syllable is identical to another citation tone, or in other words, tone sandhi of Xiamen dialect is in fact using one citation tone to substitute another citation tone. Very interestingly, the substitutions are chained up into a circle as is shown in Figure 4.3 a.

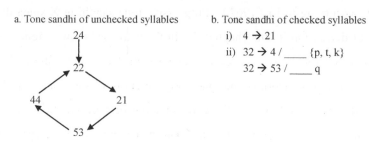

Figure 4.3 Sandhi changes in Xiamen dialect (Chen 1987, 2000)

Another noticeable characteristic of tone sandhi in Xiamen dialect which is very important to our research here is that, in a poly-syllabic tone sandhi domain, while the final syllable keeps its citation form, all the previous syllables undergo sandhi changes, from right to left, one by one.① So in Xiamen dialect, in a certain string, the syllable that keeps its citation tone, which is consequently addressed as nucleus syllable, marks the right boundary of the domain of application of tone sandhi. Tone sandhi in Zhangzhou dialect and Chenghai dialect operates in the same way as that in Xiamen dialect does, only tone sandhi in Xiamen dialect is extraordinary in that the substitution of one citation tone with another happens to form a "perfect circuit of substitution" (demonstrated in Figure 4.3 a).

Now a crucial question arises: What sort of syllables are qualified to become the nuclei? Since the phonology of tone sandhi gives no information on

---

① To a certain extent, phonology of tone sandhi in Xiamen dialect is context-free, because once the domain of tone sandhi is confirmed, non-final syllables within the domain will undergo sandhi changes automatically and the sandhi forms are entirely self-conditioned, as can be seen from Figure 4.3.

the structure of its domain of application, it is supposed that either syntax or prosody is responsible for this.

4.2.2 Sentential AdvP vs. Verbal AdvP—Chen's (1987) Analysis

Chen (1987) has very insightfully detected that tone sandhi in Xiamen dialect is by no means mere phonetic changes, but is highly correlated with syntax. From the examples① listed below, it can be seen that tone sandhi targets the rightmost syllable of lexical categories (i.e. nouns, verbs, and adjectives) as its "nucleus syllable":

(4.10) a.   A-ying]$_N$# lai   a]$_V$#
           A-ying come ASP
           A-ying has come.
     *a'. A-ying m]$_{Neg}$# lai
           A-ying not come
           A-ying hasn't come.
      b.   yi dui A-ying]$_N$# tsin ho]$_V$#
           he to A-ying very kind
           He is very kind to A-ying.
     *b'. yi dui]$_P$#A-ying tsin ho
           he to A-ying very kind
           He is very kind to A-ying.
      c.   sang tsit p'ih liok-yah-p'ih]$_N$# hoo A-ying]$_N$#
           give one CL   video film   to A-ying
           Give one video film to A-ying.
     *c'. sang tsit p'ih]$_{CL}$# liok-yah-p'ihhoo]$_{Prep}$# A-ying
           give one CL   video film to A-ying
           Give one video film to A-ying.

The examples in (4.10) exclude functional categories from marking the

---

① All the sample sentences of Xiamen dialect are cited from Chen (1987, 2000) and Lin (1994).

right boundary of domain of tone sandhi, as typical as the example shown in (4.11), it is actually the rightmost syllable of XP (X = noun, verb and adverb) (Figure 4.4 a) rather than that of V, N and A (Figure 4.4 b) that mark the right boundary of tone sandhi domain in Xiamen dialect.

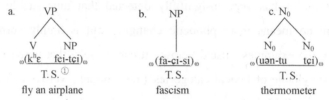

Figure 4.4　Chen's (1987) proposal on domain parsing of tone sandhi in Xiamen dialect

(4.11)　a.　lao tsin-a-po # m xiong-sin ying-ko # e kong-we# .
　　　*b.　lao tsin-a-po # m# xiong-sin # ying-ko # e#kong-we# .
　　　　　Old lady　　not believe　　parrot　can　talk
　　　　　The old lady doesn't believe that parrots can talk.

In (4.11) a, domain parsing is significantly different from that in b in (4.11) that, as a matter of fact, the lexical head "[xiong-sin] believe" does not initiate an independent domain of application of tone sandhi. It is the right edge of XP (i. e. "[lao tsin-a-po]_NP old lady", "[ying-ko]_NP parrot", "[kong-we]_VP talk"). that coincides with the right boundaries of tone sandhi domains (Chen 1987, 2000: 438) (irrelevant syntactic details are omitted) (Figure 4.5):

Chapter 4　Correspondence Between XP and PPh　　129

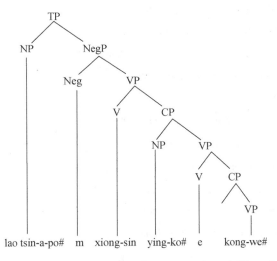

Figure 4.5　Alignment between the right edge of XP and the right boundary of tone sandhi domain

It is obvious that the right boundaries of tone sandhi domains appear after NPs (i.e. "[lao tsin-a-po]$_{NP}$ old lady", "[ying-ko]$_{NP}$ parrot") and VP (i.e. "[kong-we]$_{VP}$ talk"), but they are not found after syntactic terminal elements regardless of whether they belong to lexical categories or functional categories (i.e. "[m] not", "[xiong-sin] believe", "[e] can"). However, it is too early to assert that XPs attract tone sandhi boundaries. Chen (1987: 125) pointed out a problem exhibited by sentential-adjunct AdvP and verbal-adjunct AdvP: While there is always a boundary of tone sandhi found to the right of sentential-adjunct AdvP, we fail to observe one after verbal-adjunct AdvP. See the examples in (4.12) and (4.13) below:

(4.12) a. Ting sio-tsia]$_{NP}$# kai-tsai]$_{AdvP}$# tse　tsit pan ki]$_{NP}$#]$_{VP}$
　　　　Ting Miss　fortunately　take this CL flight
　　　　Fortunately, Miss Ting took this flight.
　　b. li te-it-tsio]$_{AdvP}$# ma tioq　pue-siong]$_{VP}$#
　　　　you at-least　also must　pay-for-damage
　　　　At least, you must pay for the damage.

(4.13) a. tsĩ]$_{NP}$# tioq k'iam-k'iam-a]$_{AdvP}$ ying]$_{VP}$#

Money must sparkingly use

One must use money wisely.

b. Ting sio-tsia]_NP# luan-tsu]_AdvP kong]_VP#

Ting Miss mindlessly talk

She talks mindlessly.

c. k'uã tsit pai]_FreP dian-yã]_NP#]_VP

watch one time movie

watch the movie once

d. t'ak puã tiam-tsing ku]_AdvP ts'eq̃]_NP#]_VP

read half hour long book

read a book for half an hour

Both adverbs are adjuncts in nature, but while sentential AdvP triggers tone sandhi boundaries (see "[kai-tsai] fortunately", "[te-it-tsio] at least") in (4.12), verbal AdvP (i.e. "[k'iam-k'iam-a] sparklingly", "[luan-tsu] mindlessly", "[tsit pai] one time", "[puã tiam-tsing ku] half hour long") in (4.13) seems blind to this.

4.2.3 Lexical-Government—Lin's (1994) Analysis

Lin (1994), inspired by Hale & Selkirk's (1987) analysis of Papago, also assumes that tone sandhi in Xiamen dialect is directly syntactically-conditioned, and the different behaviors between sentential AdvPs and verbal AdvPs are due to the categorical distinctions of the heads that govern① them. To make it concrete, if an XP is governed by a lexical category, then there will not be a tone sandhi boundary to its right; if a XP is governed by a functional category, then there will be a tone sandhi boundary to its right. See the syntactic derivation of (4.13) b and (4.12) a below for demonstration:

---

① In generative grammar, government expresses abstract syntactic relation. In the most general sense, in a syntactic phrase, the head governs its dependents, for example, a verb governs its object. (Xu 2009)

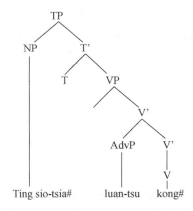

Figure 4.6 Lexical-governed AdvP

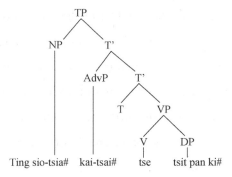

Figure 4.7 Functional-governed AdvP

In Figure 4.6 we can see that AdvP [kai-tsai] is governed by the functional head complementizer (C); a tone sandhi boundary is then motivated to its right. Contrastively, in Figure 4.6, AdvP [luan-tsu] is governed by lexical head V and tone sandhi is then blind to it. Lin's proposal of lexical-government on the parsing of domain of application of tone sandhi in Xiamen dialect is distinct from that of Chen (1987) in the following two crucial aspects:

i. It is still the right edge of XP that aligns with the right boundary of a domain of application of tone sandhi, but it no longer matters, in Lin's framework, whether this X belongs to lexical categories or functional categories. (see Figure 4.8 for illustration)

ii. Whether an XP is capable of marking the right boundary of the domain of tone sandhi depends on whether it is functional-governed. If this XP is functional-governed, then it will attract the right boundary of a domain of application of tone sandhi. (see Figure 4.8 for illustration)

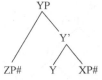

X = lexical category, functional category
Y = functional category

Figure 4.8 Lexical-government and parsing of domain of tone sandhi in Xiamen dialect

Despite the technical differences, both Chen's (1987) and Lin's (1994) proposals endeavor to explain the building of the domain of application of tone sandhi through syntax directly and both have insightfully pointed out that lexical-functional distinction is vital in computing the working domain of tone sandhi in Xiamen dialect. However, Lin (1994) is still inadequate in solving the problem brought about by functional-governed AdvP and lexical-governed AdvP, typically exemplified by "BA" sentence and "BEI" sentences. See the example of a "BA" sentence below[①]:

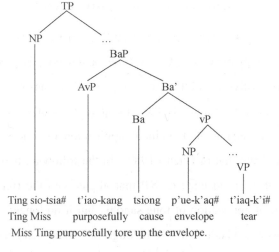

Ting sio-tsia#　t'iao-kang　tsiong　p'ue-k'aq#　t'iaq-k'i#
Ting Miss　　　purposefully　cause　 envelope　　tear
Miss Ting purposefully tore up the envelope.

Figure 4.9 Tone sandhi in "BA" sentence

---

① The phrases that "BA" and "BEI" connect to are labelled as "BaP" and "BeiP" for the sake of salience and clarity.

Chapter 4 Correspondence Between XP and PPh

Huang, Li & Li (2004), Tang (2010) and others are explicit that "BA" does not belong to lexical category as it does not assign θ-roles, but connects to the matrix light verb "v"① which belongs to a functional category, hence the adverb "[t'iao-kang] purposefully" is functional-governed. Domain parsing in this sentence sharply conflicts with Lin's proposal that "functional-governed XP marks the right boundary of the phonological domain of tone sandhi". The light verb "BA" together with its adjunct [t'iao-kang] is included in the same domain of tone sandhi initiated by NP "[p'ue-k'aq] envelope". But following Lin's line, the functional-governed AdvP [t'iao-kang] should have activated an independent domain of tone sandhi as "[kai-tsai] fortunately" does shown in Figure 4.7. This paradox is witnessed in "BEI" sentences as well.

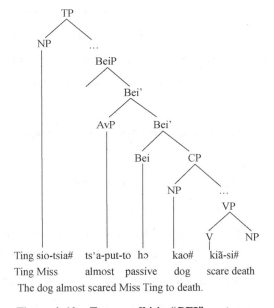

Figure 4.10 Tone sandhi in "BEI" sentence

In the sentence shown in Figure 4.10, the NP "[kao] dog" initiates a domain of application of tone sandhi which extends leftward with "BEI" and includes its adjunct AdvP "[ts'a-put-to] almost".

---

① Light verb has little sematic meaning on its own but behaves as eventuality predicate (Tang 2010).

Tone sandhi of sentences shown in Figure 4.9 and Figure 4.10 strongly challenges Lin's proposal of lexical-government. Actually, if we go back and check Chen's (1987) analysis again, his gist that the phonology of tone sandhi is sensitive to XP (X = lexical category) tells the condition how the domain of tone sandhi is constructed. However, direct reference to syntactic structure cripples his argument in the face of the asymetric sandhi behaviours between the functional-governed AdvP and the lexical-governed AdvP. Nonetheless, the sensitivity to XP-boundaries of the phonology of tone sandhi in Xiamen dialect reminds us of RS in Italian: Both are phonological processes operating on the phrasal level and the domain structures of both are regularly constructed but not directly syntactically predictable. The similarities between these two phonological activities invite us to propose a prosodic account of the parsing of phonological domain of application of tone sandhi in Xiamen dialect as what we have seen in RS in Italian. What's more, the conditioned restructuring of the prosodic domain of tone sandhi will explain the asymmetry between functional-governed AdvP and lexical-governed AdvP.

4.3 Phonological Domain Structure of Tone Sandhis

Chen (1987) and Lin (1994) try to account for the construction of tone sandhi domain in Xiamen dialect through syntax only, which is successful in describing the fundamental contexts in which tone sandhi applies but fails in predicting precisely when and how tone sandhi applies. The resemblance between tone sandhi in Xiamen dialect and RS in Italian inspires us to take prosody into account, with syntactic information being observed while examining the domain structure of tone sandhi in Xiamen dialect. As long as it is certain that the right edge of XP aligns with the right boundary of tone sandhi domain, according to the Match Theory, the phonological domain of tone sandhi in Xiamen dialect has the prosodic status of PPh / φ. So, the example in (4.11) would have the parsing of the phonological domain of application of tone sandhi as follows:

(4.14) (lao tsin-a-po)$_\varphi$(m xiong-sin ying-ko)$_\varphi$(e kong-we)$_\varphi$.
The old lady doesn't believe that parrots can talk.

Parsing of the domain of tone sandhi in Xiamen dialect reveals that the construction of φ confirms to the prediction made by Nespor & Vogel (2007: 168) that " ... in languages whose recursive side is to the right of the head, the φ will extend to its left." Indeed, in sentences with various kinds of syntactic structures in Xiamen dialect, the phonological domain structure of tone sandhi indicates leftward-extension of φ. See the examples listed below (Table 4.2):

Table 4.2 Leftward-extension of φ

	Application of Tone Sandhi	Prosodic Parsing
a.	[peq [lu kuã i]$_{AP}$]$_{VP}$# [puaq [lu t'iam]$_{AP}$]$_{VP}$# climb more high fall more hard The higher you climb, the harder you fall.	(peq lu kuã i)$_\varphi$(puaq lu t'iam)$_\varphi$
b.	[t'ak [puã tiam-tsing ku]$_{AP}$[ts'eq̃]$_{NP}$]$_{VP}$# read half hour long book read a book for half an hour	(t'ak puã tiam-tsing ku ts'eq̃)$_\varphi$
c.	[tsĩ]$_{NP}$#[tioq [[k'iam-k'iam-a]$_{AP}$ying]$_{VP}$]$_{VP}$# money must sparkingly use One must use money wisely.	(tsĩ)$_\varphi$(tioq k'iam-k'iam-a ying)$_\varphi$
d.	[sang [tang-oq]$_{NP}$# [[tsit pun ts'eq]$_{NP}$]$_{VP}$]$_{VP}$# give schoolmate one Cl book give a schoolmate one book	(sang tang-oq̃)$_\varphi$(tsit pun ts'eq̃)$_\varphi$
e.	[sang [[tsit pun ts'eq]$_{NP}$# [hɔ [tang-oq]$_{NP}$]$_{PP}$] $_{VP}$]$_{VP}$# give one Cl book to schoolmate give one book to a schoolmate.	(sang tsit pun ts'eq)$_\varphi$(hɔ tang-oq)$_\varphi$
f.	[sang [lang-k'e]$_{NP}$# [kau [mng-k'ao]$_{NP}$] $_{PP}$]$_{VP}$# accompany guests to door send guests to the door	(sang lang-k'e)$_\varphi$(kau mng-k'ao)$_\varphi$

	Application of Tone Sandhi	**Prosodic Parsing**
g.	[tso [tsit ts'ut]$_{AP}$[liok-yã-p'ĩ]$_{NP}$#[[lai k'uã] $_{VP}$]$_{CP}$]$_{vP}$# rent a/one Cl video-movie to watch rent a/one video movie to watch	(tso tsit ts'ut liok-yã-p'ĩ)$_\varphi$ (lai k'uã)$_\varphi$

From Table 4.2 a, it can be seen that the tone sandhi domain may be a VP which contains a verb and postverbal adjunct, hence the entire VP maps into a φ. In Table 4.2 b, it is either the object NP or the VP itself that initiates a tone sandhi domain extending leftward with the postverbal adverb phrase and the verb included in, hence the entire VP maps into a φ. In Table 4.2 c, the VP initiates a tone sandhi domain which has preverbal adverb and modal verb included in, and the sentence initial subject NP forms another tone sandhi domain, hence this clause maps into two φs. Table 4.2 d,e show the application of tone sandhi in double object structure and its dative counterpart. Irrespective of head movement, NPs [tang-oq] and [tsit pun ts'eq] respectively mark the right boundary of domain of tone sandhi. The PPhs extend leftward, with preceding syntactic terminal segments (i. e. the verb [sang] and the preposition [hɔ]) included. Hence, regardless of the difference in syntactic derivation, it is the same situation that NP marks the right boundary of the tone sandhi domain which proves the construction of φ. In close connection to Table 4.2 e, in Table 4.2 f, the NP [mng-k'ao], functional-governed by a preposition also marks the right boundary of the tone sandhi domain. Similarly, in Table 4.2 g, even though VP [lai k'uã] is wrapped by CP and vP, it still activates a tone sandhi domain. However, this domain of tone sandhi only contains the VP itself, because the NP [liok-yã-p'ĩ] immediately in front of the VP initiates another tone sandhi domain.

From the analysis of examples in (4.15), it is detectable that:

i. The right boundary of a domain of tone sandhi always aligns with an XP (X = lexical category) no matter how deeply it is wrapped in, which coincides with Chen's (1987) idea.

ii. As long as the right edge of a domain of tone sandhi aligns with the right edge of XP, it is not necessarily the case as the left edge of a domain of tone sandhi is concerned. This implies that the tone sandhi domain is not identical with any syntactic constituents. This is why it fails to compute the domain structure of tone sandhi solely from syntax.

Hence, I assume that the domain of application of tone sandhi in Xiamen dialect is constructed on the base of prosodic constituency:

(4.15) φ-Defined Domain of Application of Tone Sandhi in Xiamen Dialect

φ_{n-1}'s right boundary aligns with the right boundary of XP (X = lexical category) and it extends leftward with all the syntactic terminal segments to the left of XP until YP (Y = lexical category) comes into sight which initiates the mapping of φ_n.

Both RS in Italian and tone sandhi in Xiamen dialect reveal that XP-φ correspondence is hardly guaranteed, which Nespor & Vogel (2007) attributes to the direction of syntactic branching. In Chapter 3, we have proved, through the analysis of Tianjin dialect and Shaoxing dialect, that on the ω level, syntactic-prosodic constituency correspondence is undermined due to the high pressure of prosodic structure well-formedness constraints, and through Yuncheng dialect, that phonology itself may introduce intervening factors. On φ-level, syntactic-prosodic constituency correspondence still cannot be guaranteed with pressure regardless of whether or not it originates from syntax, as far as Xiamen dialect is concerned. See the example below for how semantic ambiguity is distinguished from the construction of domain of tone sandhi, or to be straightforward, from the parsing of prosodic constituent φ, which reflects the differences in syntactic structuring initiating the semantic ambiguity.

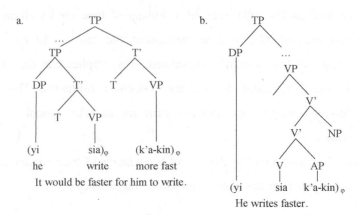

Figure 4.11 Mismatch between XP and φ, as influenced by syntactic structure

Figure 4.11 demonstrates the mapping from syntactic constituents to prosodic constituents evidenced by the domain grouping of tone sandhi. In Figure 4.11 a, the TP-specifier is also a TP itself, so its terminal element VP [sia] marks the right boundary of a φ with the pronoun subject① included, which is prosodically weak and dependent. TP-complement VP [k'a-kin] initiates another φ in the same way. In Figure 4.11 b, rather than a VP as in Figure 4.11 a, [k'a-kin] adjoins to verb [sia] as an adverb, hence VP [sia k'a-kin] mirrors into a φ with the pronoun subject included; therefore, the entire TP corresponds to a φ as a consequence.

All the examples discussed above tell us that in Xiamen dialect nonisomorphism between XP and φ is produced while the domain of application of tone sandhi extend leftward, but the rule that the right edge of a φ aligns with the right edge of an XP (X = lexical category), irrespective of what kind of

---

① Subject pronouns fail to initiate a φ. According to Abney's (1987) DP Theory, pronouns are determiners in essence, and project into DPs, for example, [you]_{DP}. Extensive cross-linguistic research shows that, as a functional category, a pronoun, phonologically speaking, behaves significantly differently from the members of lexical categories. In Xiamen dialect, despite the phrasal status, a pronoun is incapable of mapping into a φ on its own like a NP does. In Figure 4.11 a, we see that the mono-syllabic VP [sia] marks a φ boundary, whereas the subject DP [yi], also mono-syllabic, fails in initiating a φ on its own, instead, it is invited into the φ initiated by [sia]. It is the same situation in Figure 4.11 b. Pronoun DP incorporates into the φ whose right boundary aligns with the right edge of VP [sia k'a-kin].

head (i. e. lexical or functional) governs it, is never violated. Focus NP and Topic NP add supporting evidence.

(4.16) (Ting sio-tsia)$_\varphi$ (liam ts'iu-sik)$_\varphi$ (ke t'eng ø hɔ ts'at-a)$_\varphi$
Ting Miss even jewelry also remove trace to burglar
Miss Ting removed even her jewelry and gave it to the burglar.

The result of application of tone sandhi reveals that focalized NP [ts'iu-sik] in (4.16) introduces a φ boundary. PP complement NP [ts'at-a] activates another φ with its governor Preposition [hɔ] included. Because the complement of V [t'eng], namely the NP [ts'iu-sik], is focalized and has moved upward, whereas phrasal head V is incapable of initiating φ, consequently, the verb V [t'eng] and preverbal adjunct AP [ke] are covered by the same φ initiated by NP [ts'at-a].

(4.17) (Ting sio-tsia)$_\varphi$ (p'ue)$_\varphi$ (sia liao lɔ)$_\varphi$
Ting Miss letter write ASP Prt
As for the letter, Miss Ting has written it.

Topics mark φ boundaries too. In (4.17) NP [p'ue] which is originally the object of [sia liao lɔ], becomes topicalized through movement. The preposed NP [p'ue] naturally activates a φ, while VP [sia liao lɔ], without a complement, marks another φ boundary on its own. ①

---

① For the example of (4.17) we hold that the topic structure is formed through A'-movement (non-argument movement, to be exact). However, in the syntactic literature, whether topics concern movement or not is in contention (Xu & Langendoen 1985; Aoun & Li 2003). Huang et al. (2009) argue that some topics are derived from movement and related to a gap in the comment clause, while some others are base-generated and can be interpreted according to an aboutness relation which means there is no gap in the comment clause but the comment clause talks about the topics. Setting aside the rather complicated and delicate syntactic justification (those who are interested may refer to Huang et al. 2009 for discussion in detail), tone sandhis of Xiamen dialect confirm Huang et al.'s (2009) assumption empirically.

4.4 Phonetically-Conditioned PPh Restructuring

In the previous section, I postulated that domain structure of tone sandhi in Xiamen dialect is defined through the prosodic constituent φ, discussed in depth how prosody and syntax interacts in Xiamen dialect on the φ-level, and evidenced by the construction of domain of tone sandhi in various kinds of syntactic structure. We arrived at an important proposal that predicts the formation of the phonological domain structure of tone sandhi in Xiamen dialect: the right edge of an XP (X = lexical category) aligns with the right edge of a tone sandhi domain which extends leftward, because Xiamen dialect is a right-branching language, until another XP (X = lexical category) comes into sight, which then will initiate another domain of tone sandhi. However, the problem posed in Chen (1987) and Lin (1994) still remains untouched: Why can a functionally-governed adjunct initiate a tone sandhi domain, (4.18) a for instance, while a lexical-governed adjunct cannot, (4.18) b for instance?

(4.18) a. Ting sio-tsia]$_{NP}$# **kai-tsai**]$_{AdvP}$# tse   tsit pan ki]$_{NP}$#]$_{VP}$
 Ting Miss   fortunately   take this CL flight
 Fortunately, Miss Ting took this flight.
 b. Ting sio-tsia]$_{NP}$# **luan-tsu**]$_{AdvP}$ kong]$_{VP}$#
 Ting Miss   mindlessly   talk
 She talks mindlessly.
 c. Ting sio-tsia]$_{NP}$# **t'iao-kang**]$_{AdvP}$ tsiong p'ue-k'aq]$_{NP}$# t'iaq-k'i]$_{VP}$#
 Ting Miss   purposefully   cause envelope   tear
 Miss Ting purposefully tore up the envelope.

Apparently adjuncts in (4.18) a and b distinguish from each other in that the former initiates a domain of tone sandhi while the latter fails to do so, which Lin (1994) attributes to the functional-lexical distinction of the head that governs the adjunct. (4.18) c falsifies this interpretation right away in the sense that the adjunct is governed by a functional head but fails in activating a tone sandhi domain. Examining (4.18) a – c again, we can see that in (4.18) a the head (i.e. Complimentizer) governing the adjunct [kai-tsai] has no overt phonetic form, while in (4.18) c the head that the adjunct [t^{h}iao-kang] adjoins to has overt phonetic form [tsiong]; meanwhile, the head that governs the adjunct [luan-tsu] also has overt phonetic form [kong]. Setting aside the functional-lexical distinction between the heads to which adjuncts adjoin, if the head has overt phonetic value, like [tsiong] and [kong] in (4.18) b and c, its adjunct will not initiate a tone sandhi domain; contrastively, if the head has no overt phonetic value, like the case in (4.18) a, its adjunct is endowed with the opportunity to initiate a tone sandhi domain. I thus propose a rule of restructuring φ which applies when certain phonetic and syntactic conditions are met:

(4.19) φ Restructuring in Xiamen Dialect

    If the head to which an adjunct adjoins has no overt phonetic value, the adjunct will be endowed with the privilege of initiating a domain of application of tone sandhi on its own.

Phonetic covertness of the head indicates its adjuncts lose close juncture with the syntactic constituents to the right of the head, and this loose conjunction provides the possibility of restructuring a φ into two separate ones. This is reminiscent of tone sandhi in Shaoxing dialect. In Chapter 3 I have introduced that ω-level tone sandhi can take place in phrases if the terminal elements of a phrase are closely connected, otherwise those terminal elements will map into ω separately. Both cases in Xiamen dialect and Shaoxing dialect imply the reflection of syntactic intimacy in the constituting of prosodic constituents. See the examples below:

(4.20) a. (tsit-e gin-a)$_φ$ (k'un-lat tak-ts'eq)$_φ$
    This boy   diligent study
    This boy studies hard.

b. (pin-tua (gin-a)$_\varphi$

   lazy boy

   lazy boy

In (4.20) a, the verb adjunct [k'un-lat] is located in the same φ with the verb [tak-ts'eq] as predicted by (4.15), analogously, in (4.20) b the adjunct AP [pin-tua] and the head noun [gin-a] map into a single tone sandhi domain①:

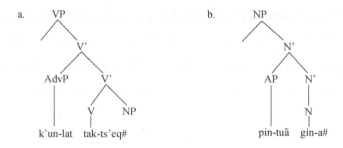

Figure 4.12

The breaking of syntactic intimacy can be reflected through the parsing of prosodic constituents as well. See examples below:

(4.21) a. [m-t'ang [tsiaq [hit liap [**ts'i-sik**]$_{AP}$[p'iang-ko]$_{NP}$#]$_{DP}$]$_{VP}$]$_{CP}$

  don't eat that CL green apple

  don't eat that green apple

b. [m-t'ang [tsiaq [[**ts'i-sik**]$_{AP}$# [hit liap [p'iang-ko]$_{NP}$]$_{DP}$]$_{FocP}$]$_{VP}$]$_{CP}$

Syntactically, (4.21) a contrasts with (4.21) b in the position of NP-adjunct AP [ts'i-sik]. In (4.21) b, AP [ts'i-sik] is focalized and is promoted to the spec-FocP position. Since the head Foc governing it has no overt phonetic value, AP [ts'i-sik] initiates a domain of tone sandhi on its own as predicted by φ restructuring rule in (4.19). Whereas, in (4.21) a, this AP [ts'i-sik]

---

① An adjunct does not change the phrasal type of a NP and a VP, both of which follow the same pattern in their internal structures (Huang, Li & Li 2009).

remains in-situ, and the lexical head [p'iang-ko] governing it is phonetically overt, hence, the right edge of NP [ts'i-sik p'iang-ko] introduces in the right boundary of domain of tone sandhi, which extends onto the nonrecursive side of the string and eventually includes all the syntactic constituents to its left. ① The structure of tone sandhi domain thus demonstrates that this long embedded phrase maps into a single φ which obviously leads to severe violation of XP-φ correspondence. (See Figure 4.13 for illustration)

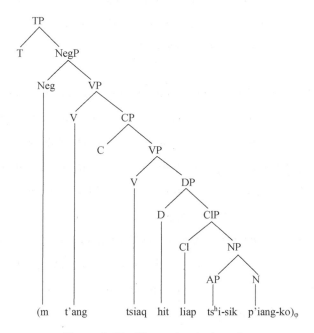

Figure 4.13 The restructuring of φ

I have just given several pages to argue for a phonetic-conditioned φ restructuring based on phonological facts of the construction of domain of tone sandhi. However, the φ restructuring rule in (4.19) is also explicit about the distinction between arguments and adjuncts are which maintained in Chen (1987). The recognition of adjunct-status of an XP is vital in interpreting the

---

① Besides pronoun DPs, all NPs are assumed to project into DPs in Abney's (1987) DP Theory, like what we see in Figure 4.13: [hit$_D$ [liap$_{Cl}$ [[ts'i-sik]$_{AP}$ p'iang-ko$_N$]$_{NP}$]$_{ClP}$]$_{DP}$ that one Cl green apple. This DP entirely maps into the φ initiated by the right-most noun phrase [ts'i-sik p'iang-ko$_N$].

processing of tone sandhi in Xiamen dialect.

(4.22) a.　pin-tuã] # e　gin-a] #

　　　　lazy　Comp boy

　　　　lazy boy

　　b.　ts'ong-bing] # k'un-lat] #　e　gin-a] #

　　　　smart　hard-working　E　boy

　　　　a smart and hard-working boy

　　c.　yi　tong-lian]$_{AdvP}$ # tia　yin bo]$_{NP}$ # e　we]$_{NP}$ #

　　　　he　of-course　listen　his wife　E　talk

　　　　Of course, he listens to his wife.

Si (2004), Lu (2003) and Xiong (2005) argue that, the Chinese De ("e" in Xiamen dialect) deserves the status of functional head as a D (determiner) does, and Si (2004) proposes that De will project into a DeP which internally resembles the structure of VP in the sense that both have the specifier and the complement. Following Si's (2004) syntactic model of De phrase, [pin-tuã e gin-a] has the syntactic derivation as shown in Figure 4.14 b. Similar to a VP, the right edge of DeP-complement (i.e. NP [gin-a]) marks a φ boundary, and the head [e] is included into this φ. AP [pin-tuã] in spec-DeP (no longer an AP adjunct as in [pin-tuã gin-a] marks the right boundary of another φ on its own.

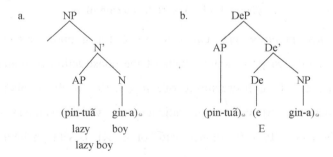

Figure 4.14　DeP (I)

In longer sentences, for example (4.22) c, the specifier of DeP marks a φ boundary as well: The right edge of NP [yin bo] aligns with the right boundary of a φ, the syntactic terminal segment verb [tia] is included in this φ. The CP adjunct AP initiates another φ because the head C governing it has no overt phonetic value as predicted by (4.19), and the pronoun [yi] gains prosodic status by entering into this φ. (see Figure 4.15 for illustration)

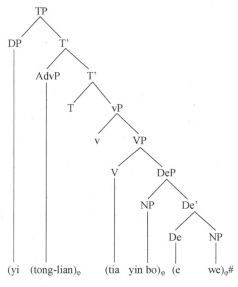

Figure 4.15 DeP (II)

Promoting De to head status and subscribing NPs to DP-complements facilitates a unified analysis and avoids awkward syntactic manipulation. In (4.23), there is a tone sandhi boundary after [mua-a] in (4.23) a, but not in (4.23) b, suggesting different phrasal statuses of [mua-a]. Lin (1994) assumes that NP [mua-a] in (4.23) a is a DP-complement. Because it is governed by non-lexical head D, a tone sandhi boundary is triggered to its right edge. But [mua-a] is just an NP and it is lexically governed by predicate [dua], hence no tone sandhi boundary is motivated. Lin (1994) attributes the different syntactic computations of [mua-a] to a different semantic interpretation—referentiality. [Mua-a] in (30b) is non-referential, so it will not project into a DP.

(4.23) a. mua-a# tua# e sio-piã #

Sesame-seed big E bun

buns on which the sesame-seeds are small

b. mua-a tua# e sio-pia#

Sesame-seed big E bun

buns as big as sesame-seed

But, if we resort to the prosodic account, things become simple and straightforward. First of all, De-complement NP [sio-p'iă] initiates a domain of tone sandhi, i. e. a φ, with DeP head [e] included in (see Figure 4. 16 a and b for illustration). Then, setting aside the internal structure, [mua-a tua] serves as Specifier-De in both cases. In (4. 23) a, [mua-a tua] is a CP, so [tua] being the predicate initiates a tone sandhi domain, i. e. a φ, the subject NP [mua-a] then initiates another tone sandhi domain, i. e. a φ, on its own (see Figure 4. 16 a). In (4. 23) b, [mua-a tua] is an AP, so the adjective head [tua] initiates a domain of tone sandhi, i. e. a φ, with its adjunct [mua-a] included in.

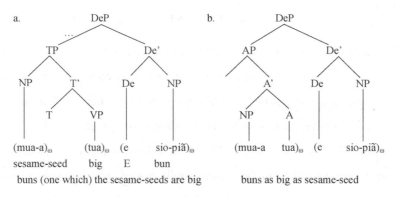

Figure 4.16 Prosodic parsing

4.5 Summary

In this chapter we have demonstrated that the domain of application of certain phonological rules is expressed through prosodic constituent φ. The notion of φ is promoted on the grounds that syntactic phrasing is inadequate in computing the application of phonological rules. The Match Theory asserts the general principle that XP maps into φ during the mapping from syntactic constituents to prosodic constituents. From the computation of the phonological domain structure of tone sandhi in Xiamen dialect, a representative dialect of the South Min family, we can see that φ refers more generally to syntactic constituency in its construction resulting in severe demotion of XP-φ correspondence. Besides syntax-prosody interface constraints, syntactic information also asserts influence on the construction of φ. The pressure from syntax on the parsing of φ varying from language to language needs to be understood from two separate perspectives: First, as Nespor & Vogel (2007: 185) found, the mapping rule for φ is not random but refers to phrase internal syntactic notions like the word categories (i. e. lexical or functional) of syntactic phrasal heads (e. g. RS in Italian) or syntactic phrases (e. g. tone sandhi in Xiamen dialect), the distinction between adjunct and argument (e. g. tone sandhi in Xiamen dialect), etc. Second, as Selkirk (2011: 449) argued, language-particular syntactic structure, like the syntactic locus of displaced constituents (e. g. Xiamen dialect), the direction of phrasal branching (e. g. right-branching Xiamen dialect, left-branching Japanese), etc. can have consequences for the construction of prosodic structure. The construction of φ is characterized by the facts that tone sandhi domain is sensitive to specific syntactic constituents but indifferent to the other types of syntactic constituents; the general syntactic structural relation is observed during the construction of tone sandhi domain. Since φ treats certain syntactic constituents quite differently from the others, and since the relative positions between syntactic constituents are determined by the direction of recursion of syntactic phrase, nonisomorphism between φ and syntactic phrase is a natural consequence.

In addition to the general properties of φ formation summarized above, application of phonological rules also indicates φ restructuring rules, which result in either splitting (e. g. tone sandhi in Xiamen dialect, conditioned by the phonetic covertness of phrase head) or merging (e. g. RS in Italian, conditioned by the branching of phrase complement) of φ, another cause of XP-φ nonisomorphism. φ restructuring rules make distinctions among the same syntactic constituents while no such criteria can be detected from syntax at all, which explains the facts that the same type of syntactic constituents may behave differently during the application of φ formation rules. Nespor & Vogel (2007) points out that sensitivity to certain syntactic notions constitutes factors leading to φ restructuring, based on RS in Italian and Iambic Reversal in English. In Xiamen dialect, we find that syntactic intimacy resulting from phonetic covertness plays a role in the reconstruction of prosodic structures.

Xiamen dialect, the representative dialect of the South Min family inside Fujian, was selected in this chapter to illustrate the interaction between syntax and prosody on φ. Tone sandhis in Chenghai dialect were also examined and were proved to operate in the same model as tone sandhi in Xiamen dialect does. Empirically-based evidence reveals that the working model of tone sandhi in Xiamen dialect is by no means unique nor unusual, as circumstantial evidence from Zhangzhou dialect and Chenghai dialect demonstrates. As the primary bearer of research in this chapter, tone sandhi in Xiamen dialect is characterized by:

i. Tone sandhi in Xiamen dialect is a phonological activity conducts on the prosodic level, and φ is its working unit.

ii. The same as Italian, φ in Xiamen dialect extends leftward as it is syntactic structure is right-branching.

iii. Theoretically, φ is mapped from the syntactic phrase, but in Xiamen dialect φ may not be isomorphic with the syntactic phrase: The right boundary of a φ always aligns with the right edge of a XP, and it extends leftward until it meets another XP which is supposed not to be an adjunct.

iv. If the head (belonging to either the lexical category or the functional category) that the adjunct adjoins to has no overt phonetic form, then the adjunct itself will initiate a domain of tone sandhi, otherwise, it joins into the same domain of tone sandhi which has the head to which it adjoins included in.

Based on the properties of phonology of tone sandhi in Xiamen dialect, I have proposed a φ mapping rule and a φ restructuring rule.

The φ mapping rule postulates that the right edge of a XP (X = lexical category) aligns with the right edge of a φ which extends leftward (because Xiamen dialect is a right-branching language) until another XP (X = lexical category) comes into sight which then maps into another φ. Because prosodic constituent φ in Xiamen dialect treats syntactic constituent XP (X = lexical category) differently from other syntactic constituents in the spirit that the right edge of a φ always aligns with the right edge of a XP (X = lexical category); meanwhile, syntactic phrase in Xiamen dialect is left-headed (namely rightward recursion), requirements from prosody-syntax interface constraints, prosodic structure well-formedness constraints and syntactic structuring combine to formulate the φ which may not be isomorphic with the syntactic phrase.

The φ restructuring rule predicts that if the head (either lexical or functional) to which an adjunct adjoins has no overt phonetic value, the adjunct will be endowed with the privilege of mapping into a φ on its own. Phonetic covertness of the head indicates its adjuncts lose close juncture with the syntactic constituents to the right of the head, and this loose conjunction provides the possibility of restructuring one φ into two separate ones. This behavior is by no means restricted to the South Min farnily, or at least to Xiamen dialect. ω-level tone sandhi in Shaoxing dialect can take place in phrases if the terminal elements of a phrase are closely connected, otherwise those terminal elements will map into ω separately. Based on large amount of cross-linguistic data, Nespor & Vogel (2007) claims that the larger the prosodic constituent is, the more likely it is to be restructured due to various factors, like length, rate of speech, style, etc. In Chapter 5, it will be demonstrated that restructuring is rather common in Intonational Phrase / ι.

Selkirk (2011) proposes that there are three sources of cross-linguistic variation in phonological domain structure: prosodic structure formation, syntactic structure and phonology proper. I have proved, on the ω level, in Tianjin dialect and Shaoxing dialect, prosodic structure well-formedness constraints are dominant in shaping the phonological domain structure, with syntactic-prosodic constituency correspondence being undermined; in Yuncheng dialect, while prosodic structure well-formedness constraints are observed, the phonology of tone sandhi introduces intervening factors. In Xiamen dialect, on the φ level, both prosodic structure well-formedness constraint and syntactic structuring contribute to the parsing of tone sandhi domains. XP-φ (X = lexical category) constituency correspondence is not guaranteed.

Chapter 5

Correspondence Between CP and IP

In the Match Theory of syntactic-prosodic constituency correspondence (Selkirk 2011: 439), ι is the largest prosodic constituent that interacts with syntactic constituents. It is proposed that: A clause in syntactic constituent structure must be matched by a corresponding prosodic constituent, call it ι, in phonological representation.

The Match Theory asserts the general principle that CP matches with ι during the mapping from syntactic constituents to prosodic constituents. In the prosodic hierarchy, the Strict Layer Hypothesis expresses the idea that all the φs included in a string join to form an n-ary branching ι which defines the prosodic domain of the string (Nespor & Vogel 2007). Based on cross-language data, Nespor & Vogel (2007) points out that ι is a quite flexible prosodic constituent, because various factors, like syntactic structure, speech rate, style, size effects on prosodic constituents and so on, may influence its construction, which in consequence may lead to mismatch between CP and ι. It is also owed to Nespor & Vogel (2007) that intonation contour across a ι and pauses by the ends of ιs, together with ι-level phonological rules (both segmental and tonal) diagnose the correspondence between ι and CP.

The same as in the previous two chapters, the phonological domain structure of tone sandhi and tone sandhi rules themselves are taken into account to compute the formation of ι. Tone sandhi from three Chinese dialects, namely, Zhengjiang dialect, Shaoxing dialect and Wenzhou dialect, will be examined in detail.

5.1 Promoting IP

In the prosodic hierarchy, ωs compose a phonological phrase φ, then φs compose a larger prosodic constituent, i. e. ι. Each of these prosodic constituents is mapped from a certain syntactic constituent. Cross language studies show that there are phonological rules that take ιs as the domains of application. Nasal Assimilation (NA) in Spanish is a typical example. In Spanish, nasals are homorganic to a following consonant within and across words (Nespor & Vogel 2007: 44):

(5.1) a. ga[m] ba   shrimp
     b. co[m] piedad   with pity
     c. elefa[n] te   elephant
     d. si[n] tardar   without delaying
     e. la[ŋ] gosta   lobster
     f. come[ŋ] carne   (they) eat meat

But NA does not always happen across words, and the contexts of the application of NA cannot be predicted from syntactic constituency. Nespor & Vogel (2007: 211) propose that it is appropriate to represent the domain of application for the rule of NA with the prosodic constituent ι. See the examples below (bold letter means NA applied, bold and italicized letter means NA failed to apply):

(5.2) a. [ι Las plumas de faisàn cuestan tantísimo hoy dia ι]
         Pheasant feathers are very expensive nowadays.
     b. [ι Un gran balcón*ι*] [ι como saben*ι*] [ι puede ofrecer mucho placer ι]
         A large balcony, as they know, can offer much pleasure.

Chapter 5 Correspondence Between CP and IP

Within an ι, NA applies both within words and across words as is shown in (5.2) a; contrastively, NA does not apply across words if they do not belong to the same ι as is shown in (5.2) b.

If the mapping from clause to ι exactly follows the Match Theory, or to be more specific, an ι is always isomorphic to a CP, then the domain of application of NA could be supposed to be directly understood from the syntactic constituent. But non-syntactic factors, such as length, rate of speech, style of speech, semantic prominence, etc., may lead to restructuring of ιs. The variations in the parsing of the ιs result in the variations in the application of NA. Nespor & Vogel (2007: 212) demonstrates the impacts of length and rate of speech on the structuring of ιs in Spanish with the examples below:

(5.3) a. [ι Mi faisán come tres veces por dia ι]
My pheasant eats three time a day.
b. [ι Muchos estudios sobre el comportamiento del delfin ι]
[ι concluyen que algunos dipos de delfines son más inteligentes que otros ι]
Many studies about the behavior of dolphins
conclude that some type of dolphins are more intelligent than others
c. [ι Muchos estudios sobre el comportamiento del delfinconcluyen que algunos dipos de delfines son más inteligentes que otros ι]

The ι is isomorphic with the CP in (5.3) a; however, if a CP is too long, a long ι is broken down into several shorter ιs like the case of (5.3) b. This may be due to "... physiological reasons having to do with breath capacity and ... reasons related to the optimal chunks for linguistic processing..." (Nespor & Vogel 2007: 194). Nevertheless, if the sentence in (5.3) b is uttered more quickly and more colloquially, an ι isomorphic with the CP, as is shown in (5.3) c, will be constructed. It is also noteworthy that ι restructuring is not random at all for it always occurs at the end of an XP, but not after a X within a XP as demonstrated by examples in (5.3).

Similar to NA in Spanish, the notion of ι is also well motivated in Chinese.

As we will see later in this chapter, domains of tone sandhis in Zhenjiang dialect, Shaoxing dialect, and Wenzhou dialect can only be detected through the prosodic constituent—ι.

❈ 5.2　Quick-Tempo Tone Sandhi in Zhenjiang Dialect

Zhenjiang dialect is a dialect of South Mandarin. Bordering on Wu dialect, Zhenjiang dialect shares a lot with Wu dialect. For instance, like Wu dialect, Zhenjiang dialect also distinguishes two kinds of tone sandhi patterns, which are conditioned by rate of speech. Zhang (1985) has delivered a thorough description of the phonology of tone sandhi in Zhenjiang dialect. Our discussion will chiefly be based on Zhang's (1985) data.

5.2.1　Phonology of Tone Sandhi

In comparison with Wu dialect, Zhenjiang dialect is impoverished in tonal inventory, with just five citation tones; on the other hand, it resembles Wu dialect in that *ru* tone / *IV is* still preserved. See Table 5.1 for formal account of the citation tones in Zhenjiang dialect:

Table 5.1　Citation tones of Zhenjiang dialect

Yinping Ia	Yangping Ib	Shang II	Qu III	Ru IV
H. hl	H. lh	L. hl	H. h	

The duration of *ru* tone / *IV* is shorter than the other four tones, and it ends with glottal stop. Zhang (1985) states that *rusheng* / *IV* has the same pitch contour and pitch height with *qu* tone / *III*, and it cannot be discriminated from *qu* tone /*III* in terms of tone sandhi behavior; therefore, Zhang (1985) subscribes them to the same toneme. We follow Zhang's (1985) proposal, and formalize these two tones with the same tonal feature H. h.

The minimal domain of application of tone sandhi in Zhenjiang dialect is also di-syllabic. Resembling Mandarin, tone sandhi in Zhenjiang dialect is right-

Chapter 5   Correspondence Between CP and IP

dominant in the sense that the final syllable keeps its citation form and conditions the sandhi changes of the initial syllable. See Table 5.2 for di-syllabic sandhi patterns:

Table 5.2   Di-syllabic tone sandhi①

σ_1	σ_2		
	hl	lh	h
H. hl		H. l –	
L. hl	H. **lh** –	L. l –	
H. lh		H. lh –	
H. h		H. h –	

From Table 5.2 we can see that di-syllabic tone sandhi in Zhenjiang dialect is characterized by:

i. The tone of σ_2 does not undergo any changes (so it is omitted in the sandhi patterns in Table 5.2 for the sake of clarity).

ii. σ_1 neutralizes to rising tone lh or level tone l/h conditioned by the contour features of σ_2. The register of σ_2 is irrelevant to the sandhi changes of σ_1.

iii. σ_1 with level tone H. h keeps its citation form.

iv. σ_1 with tonal shapes other than level neutralize to high rising tone H. lh in front of falling tones hl.

v. σ_1 with falling tones H/L. hl neutralize to level tones l with the register feature kept when it is in front of rising lh or level l tones.

vi. σ_1 with rising tone lh neutralizs to low level tones L. l in front of level tones as well, but it keeps its citation form if σ_2 is a rising tone too.

Zhang (1985) also reports that, resembling Mandarin, Zhenjiang dialect has neutral tone. σ_2 in a di-syllabic word may lose its base tone and surface with neutral tone whose phonetic value is determined by the offset of σ_1. See examples below:

---

① Phonological representations are given based on the data from Zhang (1985).

Table 5.3 Neutral Tones in Zhenjiang dialect

	Examples			Sandhi Forms
a.	[pei tsə] cup suffix	[sẽn kə] three CL	[fuŋ tʰəu] wind suffix	42-1 H. hl-N
b.	[tʰɛ tsə] stick suffix	[tɕʰȳ kə] entire CL	[thĩ tʰəu] sweet suffix	33-5 H. l-N
c.	[ji tsə] chair suffix	[liaŋ kə] two CL	[tsən tʰəu] pillow suffix	22-1 L. l-N
d.	[mĩ tsə] face suffix	[sɿ kə] four CL	[u tʰəu] cloth suffix	55-5 H. h-N
e.	[tsuaʔ tsə] table suffix	[səʔ kə] ten CL	[moʔ tʰəu] wood suffix	5-5 H. h-N

As the concrete phonetic value of neutral tone does not matter for our discussion here, we will simply use "N" to represent syllables with neutral tone. It is worth noting that the high falling tone H. hl and the high level tone H. h keep their citation forms in front of neutral tones (see the examples in Table 5.3 a, d, e), while the high rising tone H. lh and the low falling tone L. hl will change into level tones in front of neutral tones, but with register features kept respectively (see the examples in Table 5.3 b, c). This minor characteristic of word with neutral tone will be mentioned again in the next section.

5.2.2 Domain Structure of Tone Sandhi

In Section 5.1 we have introduced that the application of NA in Spanish may be influenced by the rate of speech. If uttered in normal or slow tempo, resembling Tianjin dialect, poly-syllabic tone sandhi of Zhenjiang dialect applies leftward based on the di-syllabic ones (see examples in Table 5.4), and it will not stop until a prosodic pause is met; if uttered in quick tempo, Zhang (1985) tentatively proposes that the influence of Wu dialect emerges—while directionality remains impact, di-syllabic tone sandhi rules only apply to the final two syllables, all the preceding syllables will surface with middle level tone H. l (see examples in Table 5.5).

Chapter 5　Correspondence Between CP and IP　　157

Table 5.4　Tri-syllabic tone sandhi in normal/slow tempo

	Example	*Rightward Application	Leftward Application
a.	[hua-sən mi] peanut	**H. hl-H. hl**-L. hl → H. lh-**H. hl**-**L. hl**→ *H. lh-H. lh-L. hl	**H. hl**-**H. hl**-L. hl → **H. hl**-**H. lh**-L. hl → H. l-H. lh-L. hl
b.	[sʅ ɕiŋ-ɛ̃n] stubborn	**L. hl-H. hl**-L. hl → H. lh-**H. hl**-**L. hl**→ *H. lh-H. lh-L. hl	**L. hl-H. hl**-L. hl → **L. hl-H. lh**-L. hl → L. l-H. lh-L. hl
c.	[la [tɕiŋ-pɔ]] alarm the siren	**H. hl-L. hl**-H. h → H. lh-L. **hl**-**H. h** → *H. lh-L. l-H. h	**H. hl**-L. **hl-H. h** → H. hl-L. l-H. h

Table 5.5　Quick-tempo tone sandhi

a.	[hoŋ- ləu moŋ]ₙₚ H. l　L. l　H. h *The Story of the Stone*
a′.	[wo -mən [tu ɛ [kʰɛ̃n [hoŋ- ləu moŋ]]]]_CP H. l H. l　H. l　H. l　H. h　H. l　L. l　H. h We all love reading *The Story of the Stone*.
b.	[miŋ- pɔ tsəu -kʰɛ̃n]ₙₚ H. l　H. h　H. lh　H. hl *Ming Pao Weekly*
b′.	[tʰa ɕĩ - tsɛ [kən wo [tɕʰy [mɛ[miŋ -pɔ tsəu -kʰɛ̃n]]]]]_CP H. l　H. l H. l　H. l　H. l　H. l　H. l　H. l　H. h　H. lh　H. hl He is going to buy a piece of *Ming Pao Weekly* with me right now.

The examples in Table 5.4 and Table 5.5 reveal that tone sandhi in Zhenjiang dialect proceeds from right to left and the entire string is its working-domain, if there is no pause within this string. What arouses more of our interest is, in fact, the tone sandhi in quick tempo. This kind of tone sandhi can be witnessed from poly-syllabic compounds to sentences, as can easily be captured in Table 5.5. This is what exactly happens to NA in Spanish: nasals are homorganic to a following consonant both within and across words. As tone sandhi of Zhenjiang dialect in quick tempo may apply to a syntactic constituent as large as a clause, it is reasonable to propose that, the same as NA in Spanish, the domain of application of tone sandhi of Zhenjiang dialect in quick tempo is ι mapped from CP, too. Hence, tone sandhi of Zhenjiang dialect in quick tempo is for sure ι span tone sandhi.

The application of tone sandhi in Zhenjiang dialect on the sentential level in quick tempo is quite flexible, reflecting the restructuring of ι. This non-isomorphism between CP and ι may be due to non-syntactic factors, e. g. length, as we have seen is the case with NA in Spanish. In (5.3), a long CP may map into a single ι when it is uttered fast enough, as (5.3) c shows, but this ι could be restructured into a sequence of shorter ιs, as is shown in (5.3) b, whose boundaries are followed with detectable intonational pauses, but must respect the integrity of immediate syntactic constituent. So, with the rate of speech kept, because of the limitation of breath capacity, a long ι may be restructured into shorter ιs. However, as the control of breath is rather individualized, restructuring of ι is inevitably flexible which is manifested through the variabilities of sandhi readings. See a typical example offered in Zhang (1985):

Table 5.6 Variabilities in the parsing of the domain of tone sandhi

	[wo [tɕiŋ -ka tsɔ -saŋ[tsɔ -ji pa tʰa [sẽn kʰuɛ tɕʰĩ]]]] I today morning already BA him three CL money I have already given him three dollars this morning.									
Citation tone	L. hl	H. hl	N	L. hl	N	L. hl	L. hl	L. hl	H. hl	H. hl	H. h	H. lh
Fast reading i	L. hl#	H.1	N	L.1	N#	H.1	H.1	H. lh	H. hl#	H.1	H. h	H. lh#
Fast reading ii	H.1	H.1	N	L.1	N#	H.1	H.1	H. lh	H. hl#	H.1	H. h	H. lh#
Fast reading iii	H.1	H.1	N	H.1	N	H. lh	L. hl#	H.1	N	H.1	H. h	H. lh#
Fast reading iv	H.1	H.1	N	L.1	N#	H.1	H.1	H.1	N	H.1	H. h	H. lh#
Fast reading v	H.1	H.1	N	H.1	N	H.1	H.1	H.1	N	H.1	H. h	H. lh#
Note: 1) Phonological representation of tone sandhi patterns are given based on the data in Zhang (1985). 2) # marks the right boundaries of tone sandhi domains. 3) Neutral tones are exempt from tone sandhi in quick tempo.												

There are five possible readings to the same sentence in Table 5.6. Fast reading v differentiates from the other four readings in that the entire sentence maps into a single domain of application of tone sandhi in quick-tempo, while it has obviously been cut into smaller units in various ways as the parsing of domain of tone sandhi varies from fast reading i to reading iv. This virtually and vitally indicates the flexibility of ι-restructuring. (see Figure 5.1)

Chapter 5   Correspondence Between CP and IP   159

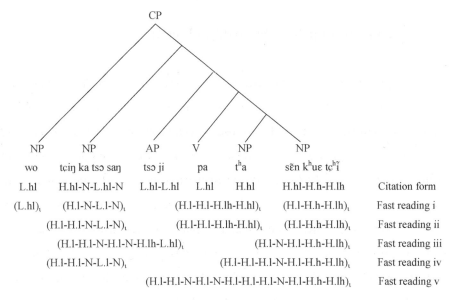

Figure 5.1   Prosodic parsing

From Figure 5.1 we clearly find that the right boundary of every XP (NP and AP in this case) but not X (V in this case) could align with the right boundary of a domain of tone sandhi. This reminds us of NA in Spanish again: restructuring of ι is flexible in that the possibility of the introduction of intonational pauses into the sentence is not invariable, but it is also not random in that the integrity of immediate syntactic constituents cannot be violated.

Quick-tempo tone sandhi in Zhenjiang dialect makes no reference to its domain information. However, the phonological domain structure of the application of tone sandhi diagnoses the mapping from CP to prosodic constituent ι, and the variabilities in it diagnoses ι restructuring in violation of CP-ι correspondence.

Greatly resembling the tone sandhi in Wu dialect, Zhenjiang dialect has two sets of tone sandhi rules, namely, a normal-tempo one and a quick-tempo one. Shaoxing dialect, as is typical of Wu dialect, also has two sets of tone sandhi rules. Complicated enough, these two sets of tone sandhi rules do not apply parallel, phonological opacity will arise as the result of successive application.

✻ 5.3　Tone Sandhi II in Shaoxing Dialect

In Chapter 3, we have introduced Tone Sandhi I (T. S. I) in Shaoxing dialect. In this section we will focus on Tone Sandhi II (T. S. II). While admitting the infusion of T. S. I to those so-called closely connected phrases, like Modifier-Noun phrases, or coordinate structured strings, the pitch contour of a string with T. S. II applied is clearly distinct from that of a string with T. S. I. [ɦuoŋ sɒ ɲiɣ ɲio?] is a very typical example. Prof. Wu Zihui, also a native speaker of Shaoxing dialect, says that if [ɦuoŋ sɒ ɲiɣ ɲio?] is used as a compound, which means "braised beef", then it is produced as L. l – H. h – H. h – H. hl (see Spectrogram 5.1); if it is a V-O structured phrase, which means "braise the beef", then it is produced as L. l – H. h – L. l – H. h (see Spectrogram 5.2).①

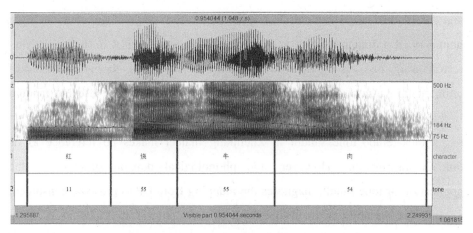

Spectrogram 5.1　Compound [ɦuoŋ sɒɲiɣɲio?]

---

① Special gratitude to my partner Gu Shengyun for sharing this piece of valuable information with me.

Chapter 5 Correspondence Between CP and IP

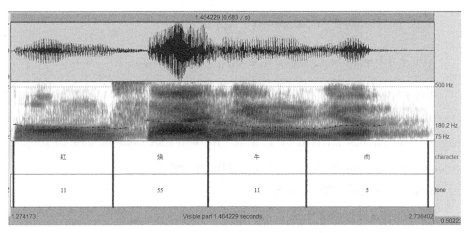

Spectrogram 5.2 Phrase [ɦuoŋ sɒɲiɣɲio?]

Apparently, the same string with two different grammatical structures accompanied by alternative readings gives the impression that tonal contours produced by tone sandhi rules are adjoint features of syntactic constituents. To put it more clearly, the case of [ɦuoŋ sɒ ɲiɣ ɲio?] elicits an assumption that tone sandhis in Shaoxing dialect directly refer to morphosyntactic constituents. As a matter of fact, in Wu (2007), Wang (2015) and others, tone sandhis in Shaoxing dialect are categorized as word-level tone sandhi (i.e. T. S. I) and phrasal-level tone sandhi (i.e. T. S. II). In Chapter 3 we have reasoned that phonology of T. S. I in Shaoxing dialect does not refer to any morphosyntactic information, but has its domain of application defined through the prosodic constituent ω. Analysis on T. S. II in this chapter will show that:

i. T. S. I in Shaoxing dialect does not directly refer to syntactic constituents either;
ii. T. S. I and T. S. II do not apply parallel, but in succession;
iii. T. S. I is a ω-span phonological rule, T. S. II is however ω-juncture phonological phenomenon;
iv. Domain of application of T. S. II is defined through ι;
v. Interaction between metrical stress, prosodic well-formedness constraint and phrasal stress shape the ι-level pitch contour.

5.3.1 Parallel or Successive Application

5.3.1.1 Tone Sandhis of S-V Structured Strings

Before examining factors regulating the operation of T. S. II, we first have to confirm how to identify T. S. II. Wang (2015) has described sandhi forms of two types of phrases affected by T. S. II. We will start from the case of subject-predicate (S-P) construction, and try to figure out:

1) the phonetic clue of T. S. II;

2) the domain of T. S. II;

3) the order of application between T. S. I and T. S. II.

According to Wang (2015), in a di-syllabic S-V structured string, σ_1, i. e. the mono-syllabic noun, changes into a high level tone or a rising tone, while σ_2, the mono-syllabic predicate keeps the citation form. Despite the differences in tonal contours, the register of all σ_1s will reach the highest level. (See Table 5.7)

Table 5.7 Tone sandhis of subject-predicate structured string

Citation Form of σ_1	Sandhi Form of σ_1	Examples
yinping 52 / yinqu 33 / yangqu 11	55-	[sæ̃ kɒ] The hill is high.
yangping 231/ yangshang 113	115-	[ɦa do] The shoes are big.
yinshang 335	335-	[kɤ tɕiɒ] The dog is barking.
yinru 45	5-	[tɕiaʔ ɕiɒ] The feet are small.
yangru 23	25-	[ɦa kʰu] The medicine is bitter.

Wang's (2015) data on S-V construction stops at the combination of 1 + 1 (i. e. both subject and predicate are mono-syllabic). Our investigations go forward along Wang's lines, therefore include the n + 1 (i. e. poly-syllabic subject + mono-syllabic predicate) and n + 2 (i. e. poly-syllabic subject + di-syllabic predicate) S-V structured strings. For the recordings collected, we annotated the tone sandhis and revision was delivered afterwards with reference to the phonetic index. Let us first talk about the S-V construction with the combination of n + 1.

Tone sandhis of S-V structured strings with the combination of n + 1 chiefly resemble those of 1 + 1 (check Table 5.8 for sample strings):

i. Exactly the same as the mono-syllabic predicates in Table 5.7, the ones in Table 5.8, for example, "[to] many", "[hɒ] good", "[do] great" surface with base tones as well.

ii. The tonal contour of the poly-syllabic subject is almost the same as the tonal contour of a string with T. S. I (see Table 3.7 and Table 3.8 for reference) applied, only differing on the final syllable: while the strings with T. S. I applied end in either falling tone or level tone, the poly-syllabic subjects of S-P structured strings uniformly end in high level tone, for example, in Table 5.8 [ɕiŋ fiɒ təŋ], [zE fiuE tɕy n̯i], [da tɕie? lie? du] and [iŋ ɕiaŋ lie?] all surface with H. h. This reminds us of the tone sandhi of di-syllabic S-V string. The mono-syllabic subject, whether it becomes a high level tone or not, its pitch contour will reach to the highest level (see Table 5.7).

Table 5.8 Tone sandhis of S-V structured string with the combination of n + 1

[[ɕiŋ-fiɒ-təŋ] to] There are many signal lamps.	Citation form	H. l – L. l – H. hl – H. hl
	Sandhi form	H. l – H. l – **H. h** – H. hl
[[zE-fiuE tɕy-n̯i] hɒ] Communism is good.	Citation form	L. lh – L. l – H. lh – L. l – H. lh
	Sandhi form	L. lh – H. h – H. h – **H. h** – H. lh
[[da-tɕie? lie?-du] do] The punishment is heavy.	Citation form	H. lh – H. h – L. h – L. l – L. l
	Sandhi form	H. lh – H. h – H. h – **H. h** – L. l
[[iŋ-ɕiaŋ-lie?] do] The impact is great.	Citation form	H. lh – H. lh – L. h – L. l
	Sandhi form	H. lh – H. h – **H. h** – L. l

Observation of the regularities of pitch contours of S-P structured strings in the combination of n + 1 prompts us to primarily propose that:

i. T. S. I and T. S. II applies in succession to the subject. After the application of T. S. I, T. S. II uniformly changes the final syllable of the subject into high level tone H. h;
ii. Subject and predicate form two separate units of tone sandhi. While T. S. I applies within each unit, T. S. II applies at the junction of these two units.

If our assumption is correct, then this two-step way of application of tone sandhis should be defended by the n + 2 cases. First check Table 5.9 for examples:

Table 5.9 Tone sandhis of S-V structured strings with the combination of n + 2

	Citation form	L. 1 – L. hl – H. hl – L. hl – L. hl
[[zɿ zẽ -tɕiŋ] bi-lɒ] The optic nerve is fatigued.	Sandhi form	L. 1 – H. h – **H. h** – L. 1 – H. hl
[[tɕiɒ-ɦiø̃ zɿ-ȵiø] foŋ-fu] Educational resources are ample.	Citation form	H. 1 – L. h – L. hl – H. hl – H. 1
	Sandhi form	H. 1 – H. h – H. h – **H. h** – H. 1 – H. h
[[dʑiŋ liɣ-kẽ] bɒ-fæʔ] Bird flu broke out.	Citation form	L. hl – L. hl – H. lh – H. 1 – H. h
	Sandhi form	L. 1 – H. h – **H. h** – L. 1 – L. 1

If we examine the tonal contours of the examples in Table 5.9 following the two-step way promoted just above, then the tone sandhis of S-V structured strings with the combination of n + 2 should process as follows:

i. Poly-syllabic subject and di-syllabic predicate establish the domain of application of T. S. I separately. Take [dʑiŋ liɣ kẽ bɒ fæʔ] in Table 5.9 for instance. "[dʑiŋ liɣ kẽ] bird flu" and "[bɒ fæʔ] broke out" undergo tri-syllabic and di-syllabic T. S. I respectively, and take the sandhi forms of L. 1 – H. h – H. hl and L. 1 – L. 1 (see Stage I in Figure 5.2 for illustration).

ii. In juxtaposition with the predicate, the tone of the final syllable of the subject continues to change, and surfaces with high level tone H. h (see tone sandhi on Stage II, as is shown in Figure 5.2).

Chapter 5   Correspondence Between CP and IP

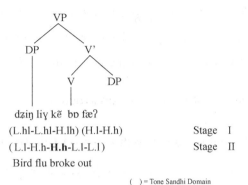

Figure 5.2   Tone sandhis of [dʑiŋ liɣ-kẽ bɒ-fæʔ] Bird flu broke out.

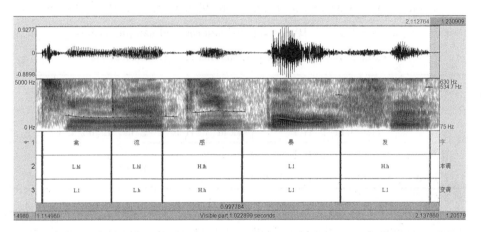

Spectrogram 5.3   [dʑiŋ liɣ-kẽ bɒ-fæʔ] Bird flu broke out.

Our computation made above converges with the pitch contour of [dʑiŋ liɣ-kẽ bɒ-fæʔ] in Spectrogram 5.3: The pitch contour of [dʑiŋ liɣ kẽ] rises to high register, then falls to low register which is kept through [bɒ fæʔ]. From the data in Wang (2015) and the data obtained from our investigation, the tone sandhi of a S-V-structured string operates on two levels: i) T. S. I applies, separately, to the subject and the verb; ii) T. S. II drives the right-most syllable of the subject to undergo further tonal changes and surfaces with high level tones as a result. Moreover, T. S. II as a juncture phonological rule is regressive in the sense that if there were two constituents in juxtaposition, it only affects the elements of the left one.

The same as strings with S-V structure, the tone sandhis of strings with

Verb-Object (V-O) structure also process in this two-step fashion, firstly within the syntactical terminal elements, then between them. We will examine the tone sandhis of the V-O structured cases in the upcoming section.

5.3.2 Tone Sandhis in V-O Construction

5.3.2.1 Di-syllabic Tone Sandhis in V-O Construction

From Wang (2015) we see that in a di-syllabic V-O structured string, σ_1 uniformly surfaces with level tone either registered H or l; σ_2, in general, keeps its citation form, except that it changes into high level tone H. h when its base tone is *yinqu*. See Table 5.10 for sandhi patterns and sample strings.

Table 5.10 Di-syllabic tone sandhis in V-O Construction

σ_1	σ_2				
	H Registered				L Registered
	H. hl	H. l	H. lh	H. h	L. hl / L. lh / L. l / L. h
H Registered	H. l –	H. l – H. h			H. h –
L Registered	L. l –	L. l – H. h			

It is hardly possible to confirm, simply with data collected from di-syllabic strings, whether or not the tone sandhis of V-O construction process in the two-step fashion just the same as we have seen in S-V construction. To put it more clearly—how is the tone sandhi domain of a V-O structured phrase built? We need to check the sandhi patterns of longer V-O structured strings before delivering an answer.

5.3.2.2 Tri-syllabic Tone Sandhi of V-O Construction in the Combination of 1+2

Let us talk about the tone sandhi in tri-syllabic strings first. All the strings are in the combination of 1 + 2 (i.e. mono-syllabic verb and di-syllabic object). More than 70 pieces of data were collected from Wang (2015). Though limited, it is sufficient enough for us to predict the sandhi patterns of tri-syllabic phrases with V-O construction in the combination of 1 + 2 (see Table 5.

Chapter 5   Correspondence Between CP and IP   167

11 for sandhi patterns and sample strings):

i. The mono-syllabic verbs overwhelmingly become high level tone H. h. (See the letters in bold in Table 5.11)

ii. The di-syllabic objects uniformly undergo T. S. I . For instance, the sandhi forms of [ɦia-fɒŋ] in [kʰE ɦia-fɒŋ] (H. h - L. l - H. hl), [laŋ-væ] in [tsʰɒ laŋ-væ̃] (H. h - L. lh - H. hl), [do-lE] in [taŋ do-lE] (H. h - L. l - L. l) are the same as they are in isolated forms (compare the sandhi form of the objects in Table 5.11 with patterns of di-syllabic T. S. I in Table 3.6).

Table 5.11   Tone sandhis of V-O structured phrases with the combination of 1 + 2

Tonal Contour	σ₂ Register	Sandhi Patterns	Examples
hl /h	H	**H. h** - H. l - H. hl / H. h	[dzəŋ fɒŋ-liaŋ] enjoy the cool
	L	**H. h** - L. l - H. hl / H. h	[kʰE ɦia-fɒŋ] prescribe medication
lh	H	**H. h** - H. lh - H. hl	[tso sɣ-tɕia?] play a trick
	L	**H. h** - L. lh - H. hl	[tsʰɒ laŋ-væ] lack of creativity
l	H	**H. h** - H. l - H. l	[kʰuẽ æ̃-kɒ] sleep at night
	L	**H. h** - L. l - L. l	[taŋ do-lE] to thunder

We left the question open in the previous section: How is the domain of application of V-O structured strings constructed? From the tri-syllabic string we are now observing, despite the various phonetic realizations, it is rather safe to arrive at the conclusion that the tone sandhi domain of a V-O-structured string is also built in the two-step fashion exactly the same as with the S-V structured case:

i. As long as the sandhi form of the object is in accord with the pattern of di-syllabic T. S. I, the verb and the object form domains of T. S. I separately. Take [fɒŋ-liaŋ] from Table 5.11 for illustration. [dzəŋ] and [fɒŋ-liaŋ] undergo T. S. I respectively. [dzəŋ] keeps its base tone L. hl as it is the only syllable in the domain of tone sandhi, while [fɒŋ-liaŋ] becomes H. l - H. hl. (see Stage I in Figure 5.3 for illustration).

ii. In juxtaposition with the object, the mono-syllabic subject changes into high level tone H.h (see the tone sandhi on Stage II, as is shown in Figure 5.3).

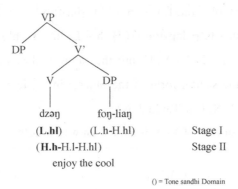

Figure 5.3 Tone sandhis of V-O phrase in the combination of 1 + 2

The building of tone sandhi domains of V-O structured tri-syllabic strings is exactly the same as that of the S-V structured strings we explored in the previous section: Syntactic terminal elements form tone sandhi domains separately first, then comes the tone sandhi between syntactic terminal elements.

To further confirm this conclusion, we conducted investigations on polysyllabic tone sandhi to V-O structured strings in the combination of 1 + n and 2 + n. Statistical analysis reveals that in spite of the trivial phonetic deviation, it is phonologically significant to assert that tone sandhis of V-O phrases, as well as the S-V structured ones, do not operate in a one-stop fashion, but are conducted firstly within syntactic terminal elements and then between them.

In Chapter 3 we have delivered a rather thorough analysis of T.S.I. Based on the phonetic clues we have reasoned that: 1) the T.S.I domain is defined through prosodic constituents, i.e. ω; 2) inherent properties of prosodic structure place restrictions on the span of T.S.I domain which may lead to mismatch between syntactic constituents and prosodic constituents. In this chapter, through observing sandhi patterns of S-V and V-O structured strings, we have set T.S.II apart from T.S.I, and have established a very rough idea about T. S. II:

    i.   it starts to work as soon as T. S. I finishes its job;

    ii.   it applies between domains of T. S. I;

    iii. if a string maps into two separate domains (say, D_1 and D_2,) of T. S. I, T. S. II will change the final syllable of D_1 into high level tone.

All these invaluable findings inspire us to further propose and ask:

    i.   what the phonetic diagnosis of patterns of T. S. II is;

    ii.   since T. S. II applies at the junction of T. S. I domains and since the T. S. I domain is a prosodic constituent ω, then the domain of application of T. S. II must be a prosodic constituent of higher level;

    iii. what the prosodic status of T. S. II domain is, φ or ι ;

    iv. what factors are involved in shaping T. S. II?

To answer these questions, we have to check more data on tone sandhis in Shaoxing dialect. Our investigations have extended to sentential level; however, let us continue with the analysis of V-O structured cases so as to draw a complete picture.

5.3.2.3   Tone Sandhis of V-O Construction in the Combination of 1 + n

Wang (2015) stops at quarto-syllabic strings. Nevertheless, just from the few V-O structured strings with the combination of 1 + n, we form a preliminary impression that T. S. I and T. S. II apply in succession, the tonal contour of the mono-syllabic verb is flattened out, and the objects undergo tone sandhi in accord with the sandhi patterns on the word level. To verify this assumption, V-O structured strings with the combination of 1 + n and 2 + n are added to our research list. The same as with the investigation we introduced in the previous sections, perceptive annotation and phonetic verification were done in sequence. See Table 5.12 for the V-O structured samples in the combination of 1 + n:

Table 5.12 Tone sandhis of V-O structured strings in the combination of 1 + n

	Citation form	H. hl – H. hl – H. l – L. l – L. lh – L. l
[kʰE [tsʰẽ-tɕi ɦiɤ̃-doŋ kuE]] hold the spring sports meeting	Sandhi form	**H. l** – H. l – H. h – L. l – L. l – L. l
[ma [tɕiŋ-tɕi seʔ-ɦioŋ vɒŋ]] buy affordable housing	Citation form	L. l – H. hl – H. l – H. h – L. l – L. hl
	Sandhi form	**H. l** – H. l – H. h – H. l – H. l – H. l
[kʰẽ [tsʰẽ-tɕieʔ liẽ-huɤ̃ væ̃-kuE]] enjoy the spring festival gala	Citation form	H. l – H. hl – H. h – L. hl – H. hl – L. lh – L. l
	Sandhi form	**H. l** – H. l – H. h – L. l – L. l – H. h – H. hl
[doʔ [pʰu-tʰoŋ ɕiŋ-li ɦioʔ]] take general psychology	Citation form	L. h – H. lh – H. hl – H. hl – L. lh – L. h
	Sandhi form	**H. l** – H. lh – H. h – H. l – H. h – H. hl

Let us examine the sandhi behaviors of the mono-syllabic verb first. Our investigation reveals that for the V-O structured phrases in the combination of 1 + n, mono-syllabic verbs overwhelmingly surface with mid-level tone (see the examples of sandhi forms of mono-syllabic verbs in Table 5.12) followed by perceivable pauses. Take "[doʔ [pʰu-tʰoŋ ɕiŋ-li ɦioʔ]] take general psychology" (see Spectrogram 5.4) for instance, [doʔ] appears as H. l, and a pause as long as 1/2 second between [doʔ] and [pʰu-tʰoŋɕiŋ-li ɦioʔ] is perceived. The pitch height of mono-syllabic verbs in our investigation is obviously not in accordance with that in Wang (2015). In Wang (2015), all the mono-syllabic verbs in V-O structured phrases are noted as H. h (see Table 5.11); meanwhile, whether there is a perceivable pause between the mono-syllabic verb and the poly-syllabic object is not mentioned in Wang (2015) either. In Chapter 3, we have introduced that mono-syllabic constituent can stand alone prosodically with their rhyme lengthened or with an empty beat inserted to their right (Feng 1996) which is verified by the [A + [B + C + D]] structured tone sandhi in Tianjin dialect. We propose it is the same situation here in Shaoxing dialect: the mono-syllabic verb is followed with an empty beat under the pressure of BINMIN and becomes prosodically independent. The realization of pitch height of the mono-syllabic verb is also metrically related which will be explained in Section 5.3.3.

Spectrogram 5.4 [doʔ [pʰu-tʰoŋ ɕiŋ-li ɦoʔ]] **take general psychology**

Second, for the object, by and large, the initial syllable is either level tone (e.g. [tsʰẽ] in [tsʰẽ-tɕi ɦiø̃-doŋ-kuE]) or rising tone ([pʰu] in [pʰu-tʰoŋ ɕiŋ-li-ɦoʔ]), the non-periphery syllables surface with level tones but pitch heights may differ (which is not trivial at all), and the final syllables neutralize to high falling tones ([vɒŋ] in [tɕiŋ-tɕi seʔ-ɦioŋ-vɒŋ]) or level tones (e.g. [kuE] in [tsʰẽ-tɕi ɦiø̃-doŋ-kuE]) (see Table 5.12).

Let us analyze the sandhi patterns of these poly-syllabic objects (attention: syllables no fewer than five) in detail. Take [doʔ pʰu-tʰoŋ ɕiŋ-li-ɦoʔ] as an example once again. In Spectrogram 5.4, a slight dip in the pitch contour of [pʰu] means that [pʰu] surfaces with rising tonal contour and a high level pitch contour is sustained throughout [tʰoŋ], then, there is a sudden drop of the pitch height from [pʰu-tʰoŋ] to [ɕiŋ-li-ɦoʔ]. Despite this downstep, the pitch contour of [ɕiŋ-li-ɦoʔ] is rather regular and accords with the sandhi patterns of T.S.I: within its pitch range, the pitch contour rises to the highest level from [ɕiŋ] to [li] then finishes with a falling end realized through [ɦoʔ]. Both phonetic and perceptive analyses indicate that the phonological representation of tone sandhi of [pʰu-tʰoŋ ɕiŋ-li-ɦo?] in [do? pʰu-tʰoŋ ɕiŋ-li-ɦo?] is H. lh – H. h – H. l – H. h – H. hl.

As a compound, according to patterns of T. S. I (check Table 3. 9 in Chapter 3), the tone sandhi pattern of [pʰu-tʰoŋ ɕiŋ-li-ɦo?] is supposed to be H. lh – H. h – H. h – H. h – H. hl. But, it actually reads as H. lh – H. h – **H. l** – H. h – H. hl (as per what we have discussed just now). This paradox reminds us of [ɦuoŋ-sᴅ ȵiɣ-ȵio?]—the same string with two different phonological spell-outs. (Spectrogram 5. 1 and Spectrogram 5. 2)

Recall that [ɦuoŋ sᴅ ȵiɣ ȵio?] spells out as L. l – H. h – H. h – H. hl when it is used as a compound. This sandhi form is in accord with the multi-syllabic tone sandhi patterns of words / compounds we summarized in Table 3. 9 in Chapter 3. That is to say, the entire compound is the T. S. I domain.

[ɦuoŋ sᴅ ȵiɣ ȵio?] has another reading L. l – H. h – **L. l** – h. hl. If [ȵiɣ ȵio?] is interpreted as the object of [ɦuoŋ sᴅ], i. e. the string is used as a VP phrase. As independent syntactic terminal elements, if [ɦuoŋ sᴅ] and [ȵiɣ ȵio?] undergo T. S. I separately, then [ɦuoŋ sᴅ] is supposed to surface as L. l – H. hl and [ȵiɣ ȵio?] is supposed to surface as L. l – H. hl. Compared with ᵥᴘ(ɦuoŋ sᴅ ȵiɣȵio?)ᵥᴘ(L. l – H. h – **L. l** – h. hl), it is obvious that T. S. II proceeds after T. S. I as [sᴅ] of [ɦuoŋ sᴅ] changes into high level tone H. h in front of the object [ȵiɣ ȵio?] (see Figure 5. 4 b for the processing of tone sandhis). [pʰu-tʰoŋ ɕiŋ-li-ɦo?] being a compound in nature and produced at normal tempo, undergoes tone sandhi changes, unexpectedly, like a phrase, just as [ɦuoŋ sᴅ ȵiɣ ȵio?] does:

1) T. S. I applies to [pʰu-tʰoŋ] and [ɕiŋ-li-ɦo?] respectively (Stage I in Figure 5. 4 c);
2) T. S. II applies between [pʰu-tʰoŋ] and [ɕiŋ-li-ɦo?], i. e. [tʰoŋ] surfaces as high level tone H. h (Stage II in Figure 5. 4 c).

Chapter 5 Correspondence Between CP and IP   173

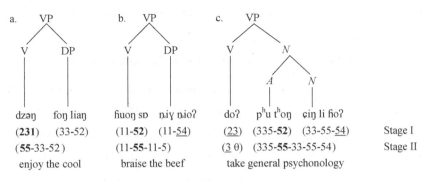

Figure 5.4 T. S. I and T. S. II in succession

The complex compound [pʰu tʰoŋ ɕiŋ li ɦoʔ] shows phonological changes as a phrase does, and it is not by chance that, a complex compound object, in a V-O structured phrase in the combination of 1 + n, is treated as a phrase when tone sandhi takes place (see Table 5.12 for instance). Analysis of the tone sandhis of V-O structured phrases in the combination of 1 + n vertifies an assumption we made in the previous section: T. S. II is a ω-juncture rule, which inevitably applies between ωs irrespective whether a ω corresponds to an entire syntactic terminal element X or a part of a syntactic terminal element X. However, another question then arises: Except that the mono-syllabic verbs in V-O structured phrases surface as mid-level tone H.l, all other data presented so far uniformly tell that the final syllable of ω_{n-1}, which is in juxtaposition with ω_n, surfaces with high level tone H. h. Where does this conflict come from? What if the verb is di-syllabic in V-O structured phrases?

5.3.2.4 V-O Construction in the Combination of 2 + n

In the very last subsection we delivered a detailed description of tone sandhi of V-O phrases in the combination of 1 + n. Comparing that with the data offered in Wang (2015), it can be found that the phonetic realization of mono-syllabic verbs have variations. In Wang (2015), the sandhi form of the mono-syllabic verb is annotated as a high level tone H. h, but in our investigation, it is the middle level tone H.l. The investigation on V-O structured phrases with di-syllabic verbs, however, reveals that almost all the di-syllabic verbs surface with the middle high level tone H. l too. See the tone sandhis of di-syllabic verbs of the sample strings listed in Table 5. 13.

Table 5.13   V-O construction with the combination of 2 + n

[tɕiẽ -sɒ [u-sɿ ba-fɒŋ]] reduce sewage discharge	Citation form	H. lh – H. lh – H. l – H. lh – L. hl – H. l
	Sandhi form	H. l – **H. l** – H. l – H. h – H. h – H. hl
[kʰẽ -tsẽ [ɦoʔ-zeʔ kɒ-liɣ]] launch academic exchange	Citation form	H. hl – H. lh – L. h – L. h – H. hl – L. hl
	Sandhi form	H. l – **H. l** – L. l – H. h – H. h – H. hl
[bæ̃-li [ɦiaŋ-lɒ pɒ-ɕiẽ]] apply for endowment insurance	Citation form	L. l – L. lh – L. lh – L. lh – H. lh – H. lh
	Sandhi form	H. l – **H. l** – L. lh – H. h – H. h – H. hl

Based on the understanding of the processing of tone sandhis established so far, regularities about the tone sandhis of V-O structured phrases in the combination of 2 + n are easily detected:

i. The di-syllabic verb and the object form separate the domains of T. S. I. T. S. I and T. S. II process in succession. Take [bæ̃-li [ɦiaŋ-lɒ pɒ-ɕiẽ]] in Table 5. 13 for illustration. In Spectrogram 5. 5, we see that the pitch contour of [bæ̃-li] is at the middle register which indicates that T. S. II further turns [bæ̃-li] into H. l – H. l after T. S. I changing it into L. l – L. l.

ii. For the poly-syllabic object, its phonological domain structure is built observing the constraints on ω. In Chapter 3 we have argued that speech rate and string length play a crucial role in shaping ω. Examples listed in Table 5. 12 and Table 5. 13 are deliberately selected to demonstrate once again the mapping of ω from poly-syllabic compounds constrained by BINMAX: compounds longer than penta-syllabic map into more than one ω, with the application of T. S. I and T. S. II occurring in succession (see examples in Table 5. 12), compounds no longer than penta-syllabic map into one independent ω with the application of T. S. I only (see examples in Table 5. 13).

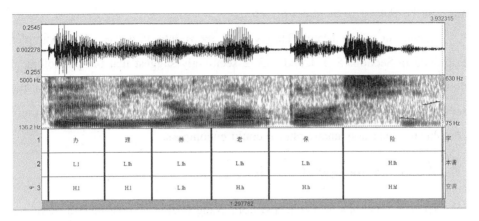

Spectrogram 5.5 [bæ̃-li [ɦiaŋ-lɒ pɒ-ɕiẽ]] apply for endowment insurance

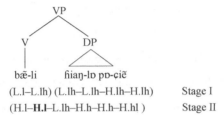

bæ̃-li   ɦiaŋ-lɒ pɒ-ɕiẽ
(L.l–L.lh) (L.lh–L.lh–H.lh–H.lh)   Stage I
(H.l–**H.l**–L.lh–H.h–H.h–H.hl)   Stage II

Figure 5.5 [bæ̃-li [ɦiaŋ-lɒ pɒ-ɕiẽ]] apply for endowment insurance

We have spared no effort in analyzing the tone sandhis of S-P and V-O structured phrases in the previous two sections. Table 5.8 and Table 5.9 have listed the tone sandhis of S-P structured strings, and Table 5.12 and Table 5.13 have listed the tone sandhis of V-O structured strings. In both structures, syntactic terminal elements (i.e. subject, predicate, verb, and object) constitute the domains of application of T.S. I separately, along with the regular cases that poly-syllabic subjects and objects map into more than one ω under the restriction of BINMAX. T.S. I first applies to every ω regularly, then the application of T.S. II follows between ωs without exception. The single deviation originates in the irregular phonetic realization of pitch height of both the mono- and di-syllabic verbs in V-O structured phrases in the sense that in a "… ω_{n-1} ω_n…" sequence, the final syllable of ω_{n-1}, which is mapped from the verb in a V-O structured phrase surfaces with the middle registered level tone H.l but the high level tone H.h elsewhere. This deviation is by no means sporadic and will be proved to be stress-driven.

According to the Match Theory, XP maps into PPh / φ. The examples examined in Sections 5.3.1 and 5.3.2 seemingly suggest that the phonological domain of T. S. II is defined through φ. Our investigation of tone sandhis on the sentence level reveals that the domain of application of T. S. II is far more complicated than a syntactic phrase could encompass.

5.3.3 Phonology of T. S. II

Through observing data collected from Wang (2015) and our investigation, we now have a much clearer picture about the phonology of T. S. II which applies after T. S. I between ωs. Morpho-syntactically speaking, the contexts of T. S. II rules are rather complicated. We can witness T. S. II applying in situations ranging from between ωs within a complex compound, to between terminal elements of a phrase. But CP is the largest syntactic constituent in which T. S. II can be observed. Following the Match Theory, if syntactic constituent CP matches with prosodic constituent ι, then T. S. II is a ω-juncture phonological phenomenon which has its domain of application defined through ι.

As T. S. II applies between adjacent ωs, the properties of a ω are still visible and shade T. S. II. Meanwhile, T. S. II is also sentential level phonological activity as it takes an ι mapped from CP as its working domain, hence the operation of T. S. II will for sure reflect properties of syntactic structuring and restrictions from ι structure well-formedness constraints.

5.3.3.1 Right-Prominence and Tone Sandhis

Wang (2015) claims that "in Shaoxing ... the final syllable of a polysyllabic compound and phrase carries stress". Zhang (2013) further argues that as syntactic words map into a ω which is composed of metrical feet, the final syllable of a syntactic word must be a stressed syllable if this language has iambic foot. The empirically-based argument "foot heads and higher tone have an affinity for each other" (Goldsmith 1987; de Lacy 2002) and the phonetically-based argument "the pitch contour of a rising tone cannot reach as high as the highest point of the pitch of a falling tone" (Hsu 2006; Wu 1982) enable Zhang (2013) to go on to assert that in Shaoxing dialect the metrically right-prominent stress pattern is realized through the choice of tone on stressed syllables. Zhang (2006, 2013) proposed that in Shaoxing dialect there is a hierarchy of tonal prominence:

(5.4) Hierarchy of Tonal Prominence in Shaoxing dialect (Zhang 2006, 2013)
   hl > lh ; h > l
   (">" = more prominent)

Among the eight citation tones, falling tones hl (i.e. *ping* tone) are more prominent than rising tones lh (i.e. *shang* tone); high level tones h (i.e. *ru* tone) are more prominent than low level tones l (i.e. *qu* tone). Hence, it is a natural consequence that stressed syllables choose falling tones or high level tones, while unstressed syllables prefer rising and low level tones. This elegantly explains why in Shaoxing dialect the sandhi patterns of a ω spell out as follows (as has already been illustrated by Figure 3.13 in Chapter 3):

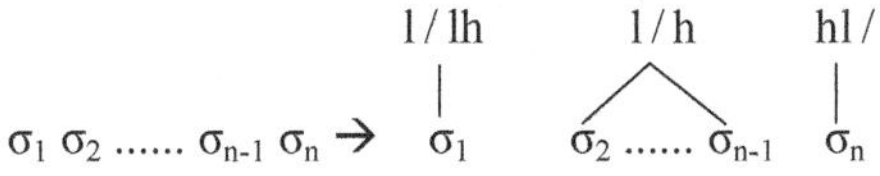

$$\sigma_1 \sigma_2 \ldots \sigma_{n-1} \sigma_n \rightarrow \underset{\sigma_1}{\overset{l/lh}{|}} \quad \underset{\sigma_2 \ldots \sigma_{n-1}}{\overset{l/h}{\wedge}} \quad \underset{\sigma_n}{\overset{hl/h}{|}}$$

Figure 5.6 ω-span tone sandhi in Shaoxing dialect

Figure 5.6 tells that within a poly-syllabic ω, the initial syllable can only carry rising tone (lh) or level tone (l) as an unstressed syllable; the final syllable carries falling tone (hl) or level tone (h) as a stressed syllable; the non-periphery syllables carry level tone conditioned such that the pitch height of σ_{n-j-1} cannot be lower than that of σ_{n-j} due to the pressure of right-prominence:

(5.5) *a.   H.h   H.l
              | |
          ω(… … σ_{n-j-1} σ_{n-j} … …)_ω

*b.   H.h   L.l
              | |
          ω(… … σ_{n-j-1} σ_{n-j} … …)_ω

Not only is T. S. I the phonetic realization of right-prominence on the ω level, but also T. S. II is the phonetic realization of metrical stress on the sentential level. Right-prominence requires that a ω end with falling tone (hl) or level tone (h); nonetheless, realization of the most unmarked falling tone (hl) in continuous speech is very difficult, hence, level tone (h) is chosen by the final syllables of non-periphery ωs, falling tone (hl) only being possible in the sentence final position. So, an entire pitch contour of T. S. II spells out as the pitch melody "mid-level / rising-high level" recurs until the melody "mid-level / rising-high level-falling" appears, as shown in Figure 5.7: ①

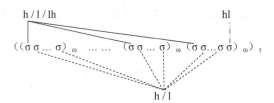

Figure 5.7 Phonetic diagnosis of T. S. II in Shaoxing dialect

5.3.3.2 BINMIN and T. S. II

In Section 5.3.2.3 we introduced that in V-O structured phrases, there is salient pause between the mono-syllabic verb and the poly-syllabic object which is in accordance with Feng's (1996) proposal that an empty beat is inserted after stranded single syllable to endow it with legitimate prosodic status. But in larger

---

① In Chapter 3 we have mentioned in footnote that in our investigation, phonetic analysis shows many sample compounds close with high level tone H. h, whereas the listeners perceive them as falling tone H. hl. This paradox is also closely related to metrical stress. First of all, both high falling tones and high level tones are candidates of stressed syllable. Articulation-oriented, a high level tone is the optimal choice regarding the Principle of Least Effort. Perception-oriented, a falling tone is a better choice for it best fits the requirement of right-prominence.

Chapter 5   Correspondence Between CP and IP *179*

syntactic constituents cliticization to adjacent constituents is a more unmarked resolution which can be verified in Shaoxing dialect as well as in Tianjin dialect (see Spectrogram 3.2 in Chapter 3 for reference).

Take the clause "[tɕia-lɒ-sɿ [ma [tɕiŋ-tɕi seʔ-ɦioŋ-vɒŋ]]] Teacher Jia bought the affordable housing." for illustration. From Spectrogram 5.6 we can find that from [tɕia] to [lɒ-sɿ-ma] the pitch contour rises to high register, then suddenly drops to middle register at [tɕiŋ]. Another drop of the pitch height is detected at [seʔ]. The downstepped realization of pitch contour from [tɕia-lɒ-sɿ ma] to [tɕiŋ-tɕi] then to [seʔ-ɦioŋ-vɒŋ] inspires us to inspect the pitch contour of this clause block by block: the melody "mid-level / rising-high level" is realized twice on [tɕia-lɒ-sɿ ma] and [tɕiŋ-tɕi] respectively, and the pitch contour on [seʔ-ɦioŋ-vɒŋ] spells out with the melody "mid-level / rising-high level-falling". Assembling these three pieces and reexamining them as a whole again, the pitch contour of this CP coincides with the sandhi pattern of T. S. II as demonstrated in Figure 5.7. Hence, phonetic clues render the prosodic parsing of this CP: [tɕia-lɒ-sɿ [ma [tɕiŋ-tɕi seʔ-ɦioŋ-vɒŋ]]] maps into three ωs, i.e. (tɕia-lɒ-sɿ ma)_ω, (tɕiŋ-tɕi)_ω and (seʔ-ɦioŋ-vɒŋ)_ω, with T. S. I and T. S. II proceeding successively (see Figure 5.8 for prosodic parsing and the processes of tone sandhis).

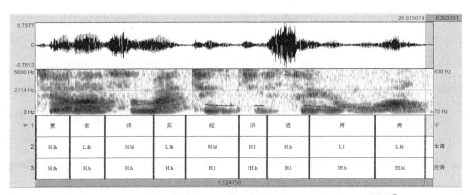

Spectrogram 5.6   [tɕia-lɒ-sɿ [ma [tɕiŋ-tɕi seʔ-ɦioŋ-vɒŋ]]]①
Teacher Jia buys affordable housing.

---

①   Decline is witnessed.

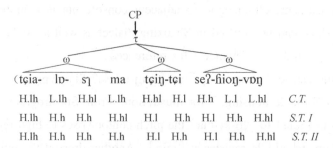

Figure 5.8 Tone sandhis and prosodic parsing on sentential level

However, what interests us about this sample is actually the prosodic parsing of the mono-syllabic verb [ma]. On the one hand, X-ω correspondence requires [ma] to map into a ω independently; on the other hand, BINMIN bans mono-syllabic ωs. As early as in Chapter 3, during the analysis of T. S. I, we reasoned that BINMIN outranks X-ω correspondence, namely, a ω has to be di-syllabic at least. Cliticization of [ma] to [tɕia-lɒ-sʅ] once again attests to the undominance of BINMIN on the sentential level (with BINMAX observed as well).

5.3.3.3 Right-Prominence and Information-Stress Principle

On the sentential level, mono-syllabic syntactic constituents, for example, the mono-syllabic verb [ma] we examined just now, incorporate into adjacent constituents to participate in prosodic activities. Di-syllabic verbs, without violation of BINMIN, being parsed into the most unmarked independent ω, behaves interestingly enough as far as tone sandhi is concerned. Take the clause "[tsaŋ kuɒŋ foŋ [sẽ-tɕiŋ [kʰo-ȵiẽ[tɕiŋ-fi]]] Zhang Guangfeng applies for research funds". for instance. From Spectrogram 5.7 we can see that the pitch contour is reset twice: The pitch height is downstepped first from [tsaŋ kuɒŋ foŋ] to [sẽ-tɕiŋ] then from [sẽ-tɕiŋ] to [kʰo-ȵiẽ tɕiŋ-fi]. This phonetic clue indicates that [tsaŋ kuɒŋ foŋ], [sẽ-tɕiŋ] and [kʰo-ȵiẽ tɕiŋ-fi] map into ωs separately, to which T. S. I and T. S. II apply in succession. As components of the ι, the sandhi forms of [tsaŋ kuɒŋ foŋ] and [kʰo-ȵiẽ tɕiŋ-fi] (H.1 – H. h – H. h and H. 1 – H. h – H. h – H. hl respectively) are in accord with the sandhi

Chapter 5 Correspondence Between CP and IP

patterns of T. S. II illustrated in Figure 5.7, but the sandhi changes of [sẽ-tɕiŋ] are irregular. According to Figure 5.6 and Figure 5.7, the process of tone sandhis of [sẽ-tɕiŋ] is supposed to be (5.6):

(5.6) * H. hl – H. lh → H. l – H. h → H. l – H. h

(5.6) predicts that [sẽ] changes into mid-level tone H. l, and [tɕiŋ] changes into high level tone H. h. But, as a matter of fact, pitch contour in Spectrogram 5.7 shows that both [sẽ] and [tɕiŋ] surface as mid-level tone H. l. Due to the restriction of right-prominence, the pitch height of [tɕiŋ] is not lower than that of [sẽ] as illustrated in (5.5), but there must be constraints other than IAMB regulating [tɕiŋ]'s tonal change since its pitch height has not risen to the height it was supposed to rise to.

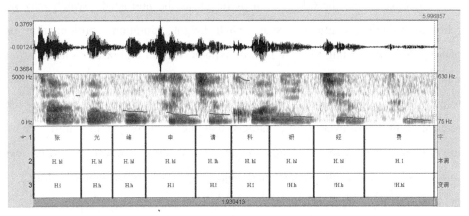

Spectrogram 5.7   [tsaŋ kuɒŋ foŋ [sẽ-tɕiŋ [kʰo-ɲie[tɕiŋ-fi]]]
Zhang Guangfeng applies for research funds.

Duanmu (2007) proposes that phrasal level stress should observe the Information-Stress Principle (5.7):

(5.7) The Information-Stress Principle (Duanmu 2007: 144)

      A word or phrase that carries more information than its neighbor(s) should be stressed.

Duanmu (2007) holds that constituents with more information load are stressed more, while constituents with less information load are stressed less. Taking the syntactic constituent XP for illustration, he continues to argue that the occurrence of a non-head is less predictable than the occurrence of a head. Therefore, the information load of XP is far greater than that of X, and the default phrasal stress goes to the non-head. This leads Duanmu (2007) to give a more subtle rule, Non-Head Stress in (5.8), which explains the regularity of phrasal stress assignment:

(5.8) Non-Head Stress (Duanmu 2007: 146)
    In the syntactic structure [X XP] (or [XP X]), where X is the syntactic head and XP the syntactic non-head, XP should be stressed.

(5.8) tells that the head is not as heavy as the non-head (which may be realized through constituent's size, pitch height, duration, prolongation or pause, etc). According to (5.8), a di-syllabic verb in a phrase or clause is not qualified to carry stress even though it can map into an independent ω. [sẽ-tɕiŋ] in [tsaŋ kuɒŋ foŋ [sẽ-tɕiŋ [kʰo-ɲ.iẽ[tɕiŋ-fi]]], though guaranteeing the realization of word-level stress, namely that the pitch height of [tɕiŋ] is no lower than that of [sẽ], it fails to get phrasal stress because it carries less information load than the subject and object do. As a consequence, [tɕiŋ] is demoted to middle register.

Therefore, [tsaŋ kuɒŋ foŋ [sẽ-tɕiŋ [kʰo-ɲ.iẽ[tɕiŋ-fi]]] embodies the control of tone sandhis from both word- and phrasal-level stress: Under the pressure of the right-prominent metrical stress pattern, (tsaŋ kuɒŋ foŋ)_ω, (sẽ-tɕiŋ)_ω and (kʰo-ɲ.iẽ tɕiŋ-fi)_ω all close with level tone h/l or falling tone hl, the Non-Head Stress Rule then asserts its strength through demoting the pitch register of the di-syllabic verb. (See Figure 5.9 for illustration)

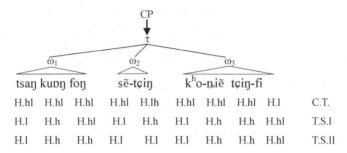

Figure 5.9 IAMB & the non-head stress rule

❋ 5.4 Tone Sandhi in Wenzhou Dialect

In the previous two sections, we have analyzed two ι-level phonological phenomena, namely quick-tempo tone sandhi in Zhenjiang dialect and T. S. II in Shaoxing dialect. Zhenjiang dialect has two sets of tone sandhi essentially conditioned by the rate of speech. The phonological domain of application of quick-tempo tone sandhi is defined through ι, which may be restructured due to the individualized control of breath resulting in mismatch between CP and ι. Restructuring of ι in Zhenjiang dialect is sensitive to syntactic integrity in the sense that it is always the case that the right boundary of a restructured ι aligns with the right boundary of an XP. T. S. II in Shaoxing dialect, which also applies at the ι-level, is a balance between phonetics, metrical stress, prosodic structure well-formedness constraints and phrasal prominence. Metrical stress patterns are still visible by the time T. S. II applies, as it is a ω-juncture rule in essence; a mono-syllabic morpho-syntactic constituent incorporates into an adjacent ω to gain legitimate prosodic status under the pressure of BINMIN; a sentential level stress pattern reshapes the pitch registers of certain ωs in regard to what syntactic constituents (i. e. phrase head or non-head) they map from.

We will close our discussion of ι-level phonological phenomena with tone sandhis in Wenzhou dialect, a representative dialect of the South Wu family. Wenzhou dialect, a typical Wu dialect, has tone sandhis comprising several sets of tone sandhi rules, whose domains of application are also morpho-syntactically grounded prosodic constituents, i.e. ω and ι. The sentential level stress patterns we have encountered in Shaoxing dialect restrict the processing of tone sandhis in Wenzhou dialect in a much more subtle way, and ι restructuring is witnessed in Wenzhou dialect as well.

Zheng-zhang (1964, 2007, 2008, etc.) has written a series of works on Wenzhou dialect which has offered a subtle description of the phonology of Wenzhou dialect. Chen (2000) is the first to advocate prosodic interpretations of tone sandhis in Wenzhou dialect, and the analysis we are going to deliver here is a refinement of Chen's (2000) prosodic-oriented computation based on the data collected from Zheng-zhang (1964, 1980, 2007, 2008, etc.) and Chen (2000).

5.4.1 ω-Span Tone Sandhi

5.4.1.1 Size Effects and ω-Span Tone Sandhi

Zheng-zhang (2008) reports that there are 8 citation tones in Wenzhou dialect. Like Shaoxing dialect, the 8 tones in Wenzhou dialect correspond to the four Middle Ancient Chinese tonal categories, i.e. *ping*, *shang*, *qu* and *ru*, evenly divided into two registers, i.e. *yin* and *yang*. Chen (2000) has reduced and formalized the tonal system of Wenzhou dialect to three pitch levels, namely H, M, and L. See Table 5.14 for the phonological representation of the citation tones in Wenzhou dialect given by Chen (2000: 477):

Table 5.14 Phonological representation of tone system

	Ping I	*Shang* II	*Qu* III	*Ru* IV
Yin a	M	MH	HM	Lq
Yang b	ML		L	

Chen (2000) claims that the difference between *II a* and *II b* can be reduced to the phonemic contrast between the voiced and voiceless onsets, hence he treats them as one toneme MH. It is the same situation with *IV a* and *IV b*.

He marks the checked toneme with "q" to discriminate it from *III b*.

Like all the other dialects we have discussed, the prosodic well-formedness constraint BINMIN is observed during the processing of tone sandhi in Wenzhou dialect, and the di-syllabic word is the minimal tone sandhi domain with both syllables undergoing sandhi changes. See the complicated di-syllabic sandhi patterns of Wenzhou dialect in Table 5.15:

Table 5.15 Patterns of di-syllabic tone sandhis in Wenzhou dialect (Chen 2000: 478)

σ_1	σ_2					
	M	ML	HM	L	MH	Lq
M	M. M	L. M	L. L	MLM. HM	HM. MH	HM. Lq
ML						
HM						
L	HM. M		HM. ML	HM. L		
MH						
Lq	Lq. M	L. L	Lq. HM	Lq. L	Lq. MH	Lq. Lq

Poly-syllabic tone sandhi is based on the di-syllabic one. In a tri-syllabic compound, the initial tone neutralizes to level tone, with opposite register feature to the final syllable. This behavior is labelled as Polarity in Chen (2000):

(5.9) Polarity: $\sigma \qquad \sigma \;\; \sigma]_{word}$
$\qquad\qquad\qquad |\qquad\quad\; |$
$\qquad\qquad\quad T \;\rightarrow\; L\;/\;\underline{\;\;}\;H$
$\qquad\qquad\qquad\qquad\; H\;/\;elsewhere$

If the compound is longer than tri-syllabic, all the syllables to the left of the antepenult will carry a default L by Default (Chen 2000):

(5.10) Default $\ldots \sigma \ldots \sigma\sigma\sigma]_{word}$
$\qquad\qquad\qquad\;\; |$
$\qquad\qquad\quad T \rightarrow L$

Still resembling Shaoxing dialect, the size of tone sandhi domain in Wenzhou dialect also has an upper limit. The longer a compound is, the less possible it is to map into an independent domain of application of tone sandhi. Compounds that undergo tone sandhi range from di-syllabic to penta-syllabic as documented in Zheng-zhang (2008) which also states that the domain of tone sandhi larger than penta-syllabic is rather rare, being highly restricted to translations of countries' names.

(5.11) Rule-Ordering of Tone Sandhi at ω-Level

a. [jyɔ z̩]   pine
   ML   L
   MLM HM
   ─────────
   ─────────

b. [[jyɔ z̩]   mɜ]   pine needles
    ML   L   ML   Citattion tone
         HM   ML   Di-syllabic T.S.
    H   HM   ML   Polarity
    ─────────   Default

c. [ɕi   siɛ]   doctor
   M   M
   M   M
   ─────
   ─────

d. [[ʔji ja]   ɕi   siɛ]   apothecary
    M   Lq   M   M   Citattion tone
               M   M   Di-syllabic T.S.
         H   M   M   Polarity
    L   H   M   M   Default

Typologically the same as T.S. I in Shaoxing dialect, the phonological domain structure of Wenzhou dialect shows a clear effect of syntactic constituency as well, in the sense that tone sandhi in Wenzhou dialect typically applies to syntactic words. Hence, according to the Match Theory, the domain of application of tone sandhi in Wenzhou dialect is also a ω mapped from syntactic word X.

(5.12) ω-Level Tone Sandhi

5.4.1.2 Diffusion into Phrases

However, X-ω correspondence is not the single strength regulating the phonological domain structure of tone sandhi in Wenzhou dialect. Like what we have seen in Shaoxing dialect, prosodic structure well-formedness constraints BINMIN and BINMAX assert that an unmarked domain of application of tone sandhi has to be minimally di-syllabic and maximally penta-syllabic. The undominance of BINMIN and BINMAX permits the application of tone sandhi rules to phrases on the condition that the phrase's syntactic terminal elements are of close juncture and the size of the phrase does not exceed penta-syllabic. See Table 5.16 for examples:

Table 5.16 Diffusion into phrases①

	Example	Citation Form	Sandhi Form
a.	[da zĩ] big tree	L + L	HM + L
b.	[lɜ [mɜ beŋ]] old illness	MH + ML + L	H + MLM + HM
c.	[[pʰa çi] liɜ ɲi] catch a cold	HM + M + MH + Lq	L + H + HM + Lq

Examples a and b in Table 5.16 are by nature syntactical phrases in the Modifier-Noun construction, yet exhibit phonological changes as a compound does. ω-level tone sandhi is indifferent to a string's internal syntactic structure but takes the entire phrase as its working domain. It is the same situation with c in Table 5.16. The boundaries between the subject and the predicate are blurred in the sense that ω-level tone sandhi treats this Subject-Predicate phrase as a compound which maps into a single ω. Difussion into phrases significantly reveals that prosodic structure well-formedness constraints, i. e. BINMIN and BINMAX outrank syntax-prosody interface constraint, i. e. X-ω correspondence, in Wenzhou dialect diagnosed by the phonological domain structure of ω-level tone sandhi. In this dimension, the North Wu dialect (Shaoxing dialect) and

---

① Data selected from Zheng-zhang (1964, 2008)

the South Wu dialect (Wenzhou dialect) fall into the same type.

5.4.2 Neutral Tone

Zheng-zhang (1964, 2007, 2008, etc) reported that there are two types of "neutral tone" in Wenzhou dialect. Allow us to address them as N. T. I and N. T. II temporarily for the sake of clarity. N. T. I only appears after stressed syllables and assimilates into the phonetic value of the stressed syllable it cliticizes to through Spreading (See Table 5.17 a for illustration) whether it is tonic or not in the lexicon. Along with the dependency of tone, syllables with N. T. I also exhibit segmental reduction instantiated by consonant lenition, vowel reduction, etc. (see Table 5.17 b – d for illustration) (Zheng-zhang 2007: 114):

Table 5.17 Phonological characteristics of a syllable with N. T. I

a.	Tonal Deletion and Spreading	MH HM MH H | | | | [ma ku] → [ma gu] already bought
b.	Voicing	[zo zๅ ta] → [zo zๅ da] sit here
c.	Spirantization	[tiɛ gei] → [tiɜ ɦe] beat him
d.	Monophthongization	[tiɛ gei] → [tiɛ ɦe] beat him

(5.13) Neutral Tone in Wenzhou Dialect

Both tonal and segmental changes taken place in a syllable with T. S. I in Wenzhou dialect resembling those taking place in Mandarin (Chao 1968; Lin & Yan 1980; Wang 2006). Actually Zheng-zhang (2007) is quite explicit about

the equivalence of T. S. I in Wenzhou dialect and neutral tone in Mandarin, which is further supported by evidence from the resemblance in the distributionin of their morpho-syntactic structures (Chao 1968; Zheng-zhang 2007):

Table 5.18 Distribution of neutral tones in Mandarin and N. T. I in Wenzhou Dialect

	Distribution	Mandarin	Wenzhou Dialect
a.	suffix	[tʂuə **tsï**] table	[zaŋ **ko**] kidney
b.	monomorpheme	[muə **li**] jasmine	[tɕoŋ **sʅ**] unavoidable in the long run
c.	verb particle	[mai **kuə**] already bought	[ma **gu**] already bought
d.	accusative pronoun	[ta **tʰa**] beat him	[tiɛ **ɦe**] beat him
Note: syllable in bold = neutral tone syllable			

From the examples listed in Table 5.18 we can see that neutral tone in Mandarin and N. T. I in Wenzhou dialect are uniformly enclitics of a full tone syllable, and distribute among suffixes, monomorphemes, verb-particles, accusative pronouns and so on. Both phonetic and morpho-syntactic clues drive Zheng-zhang (2007) to claim that N. T. I in Wenzhou dialect is equivalent to neutral tones in Mandarin. Further evidence nonetheless proves that the distribution of N. T. I in Wenzhou dialect is not entirely identical to that of neutral tone in Mandarin in the sense that N. Y. I in Wenzhou dialect covers not only morpho-syntactic enclitcs as shown in Table 5.18, but also prosodic enclitics, which will be introduced and discussed in Section 5.4.3.3.

5.4.3 ι-Span Tone Sandhi

The other type of "neutral tone", i.e. N. T. II, described in Zheng-zhang (2007), is by nature sentential level tone sandhi, for Zheng-zhang himself admits that this type of "neutral tone" equals to the "narrow sandhi" of other Wu dialects. We can see that he uses the term "neutral tone" to refer to this kind of tone sandhi simply because this sentential level phonological activity is a process of severe neutralization which will endow syllables uniformly with a tone (L). Whereas, you may immediately notice that, confusingly enough, neutralization to L also exists in ω-level tone sandhi. What is the distinction between the ω-level L and sentential level [L]?

In Section 5.4.1.1 we have demonstrated that on the ω-level, tone sandhi rule *Default* in (5.10) will turn all the syllables to the left of the antepenult to the default L. Both Zheng-zhang (1964, 2008) and Chen (2000) confirm that this ω-level phonological activity only refers to the neutralization of tones but the segmental qualities will remain intact. The situation for the sentential level L is not explicit enough. Zheng-zhang (2007) states that this sentential level L is low and short which indicates that there is segmental reduction (reduction in the rime to be specific) along with the demotion of tonal pitch value, but there are no supporting examples offered in Zheng-zhang (2007). Meanwhile, Chen (2000: 497) only refers to the tonal neutralization without mentioning segmental quality changes at all. So, with the data at hand, from the perspective of phonetics, it is not sufficient for us to assert that the sentential level tonal neutralization to L is different from the ω-level default L. In Wenzhou dialect, both ω-level and sentential level tone sandhis resort to the same phonetic vehicle, namely tonal demotion—*Default L*, to fulfill either prosodic or syntactic-prosodic interface requirements.

Now let us come to the crucial issue, the definition of the phonological domain structure of tone sandhi concerned in this subsection. Exactly the same as T.S. II in Shaoxing dialect, the domain of application of this kind of tone sandhi turns out to be a prosodic constituent ι, for it can be witnessed from phrases to clauses, and clause is the largest constituent it applies to, meanwhile restructuring of its domain "depending on the style and tempo of delivery" (Chen 2000: 497) can be witnessed as well. Therefore, according to the Match Theory—a syntactic clause corresponds to a prosodic constituent ι, the phonological domain structure of this kind of tone sandhi in Wenzhou dialect is defined through ι.

Simpler than T. S. II in Shaoxing dialect, restriction from metrical stress is not witnessed in ι-level tone sandhi in Wenzhou dialect. But more complicated than T. S. II in Shaoxing dialect, Information-Stress Principle is inadequate to explain the sandhi patterns of ι-level tone sandhi in Wenzhou dialect, because more syntactic information is involved so Stressability Hierarchy has to be introduced in.

5.4.3.1 Information-Stress Principle

Data from both Zheng-zhang (2007) and Chen (2000) show that in a string ω-span tone sandhi applies to all the ωs separately, then the ωs mapped from the head will be prosodically demoted and surface with L. It is noteworthy that the appearance of low level tone is by no means an accident, but prosodically motivated. During the discussion of sandhi patterns of T. S. II in Shaoxing dialect, it is argued that stressed syllables and higher tones have an affinity for each other, while unstressed syllables and low tones have an affinity for each other (de Lacy 2002). The di-syllabic syntactic head cannot surface with high registered tone because Non-Head Stress Rule (Duanmu 2007) deprives the head of carrying stress. Primarily, the Non-Head Stress Rule is also well observed in ι-span tone sandhi in Wenzhou dialect which also resorts to tonal changes to realize the phrasal level stress patterns. In Wenzhou dialect, in the case of ι-span tone sandhi, low tone L is chosen for an accentually demoted syllable.

5.4.3.1.1 ι-Span Tone Sandhi in $[X\ YP]_X$ Structured String

Let us begin with the most detectable case, the tone sandhis of [head + non-head] constructed strings, to illustrate the impact of Non-Head Stress Rule on ι-span tone sandhi. In a $[X\ YP]_{XP}$ phrase, the head X (= Noun, Verb, Adjective) will eventually surface with a low tone L under the pressure of the Non-Head Stress Rule becasue it is not qualified to carry a phrasal level stress. See the examples below in Figure 5.10:

a. [tsʰuo [mo   tɕi]ₙₚ]ᵥₚ   play majiang
   M   ML   HM   Citation tone
   (M)ω (MLM HM)ω   ω-span tone sandhi
   (L   MLM   HM)ι   ι-span tone sandhi

b. [sɿ   ɕy   [di   ʔjaŋ]ₙₚ]ᵥₚ   like movie
   MH   M   L   MH   Citation tone
   (HM   M)ω (HM   MH)ω   ω-span tone sandhi
   (L   L   HM   MH)ι   ι-span tone sandhi

c. [lai   [tɜ]ₐₚ]ᵥₚ   fall down
   L   MH   Citation tone
   (L)ω   (MH)ω   ω-span tone sandhi
   (L   MH)ι   ι-span tone sandhi

d. [kuɔ   [leŋ   tsʰeŋ]ₐₚ]ᵥₚ   state clearly
   MH   ML   M   Citation tone
   (MH)ω (L   M)ω   ω-span tone sandhi
   (L   L   M)ι   ι-span tone sandhi

Figure 5.10   ι-span tone sandhi in [X YP]$_X$ structured string

In verb-object phrases (a and b in Figure 5.10), syntactic terminal elements, i. e. the verbs ("[tsʰuo] play" and "[sɿ ɕy] like") and the object ("[mo tɕi] majiang" and "[di ʔjaŋ] movie") map into ω separately, after the application of ω-span tone sandhi to all the ωs one by one, Non-Head Stress Rule then turns the phrase head Vs ("[tsʰuo] play" and "[sɿ ɕy] like") into low tone L.

In Shaoxing dialect, size effects on a ω are still visible at the time that T. S. II starts to work because it is a ω-juncture phonological rule in nature. Wenzhou dialect differs from Shaoxing dialect on this point in that the former is blind to the length of syntactic terminal elements in the sense that once a constituent is located by the Non-Head Stress Rule, it will be accentually demoted and all syllables within it will turn up with L regardless how many ωs it maps into. From the examples in Figure 5.10 we can also find that in Wenzhou dialect Non-Head Stress Rule does not discriminate between the arguments (e. g. [mo tɕi] and [di ʔjaŋ], and the verbal complement (e. g. [tɜ] and [leŋ tsʰeŋ]), but is only alert to a constituent's head / non-head status.

5.4.3.1.2 ι-Level Tone Sandhi in [YP X]_X Structured String

The examples analyzed in the last subsection present the demotion of tones of syntactic heads in pretonic positions, it is also the case if the head constituent appears to the right of the non-heads. See the examples below in Figure 5.11.

a. [[dəu]_{NP} tʰoŋ]_{VP}		b. [[tsɜ]_{AP} tsau]_{VP}			
headache		leave early			
ML	HM	MH	MH		citation tone
(ML)_ω	(HM)_ω	(MH)_ω	(MH)_ω		ω-span tone sandhi
(ML	L)_ι	(MH	L)_ι		ι-span tone sandhi

c. [[tɕʰi kʰa]_{AP} kuɔ]_{VP}			d. [[mo ji]_{AP} huɔ fio]_{VP}			
state straightly			School is over right away.			
HM	HM	MH	MH	L	HM	Lq	citation tone
(L	L)_ω	(MH)_ω	(HM	L)_ω	(HM	Lq)_ω	ω-span tone sandhi
(L	L	L)_ι	(HM	L	L	L)_ι	ι-span tone sandhi

Figure 5.11 ι-span tone sandhi in [YP X]_X structured string

In a Subject-Predicate string in Figure 5.11, the predicate "[tʰoŋ] ache" is demoted to the low tone L under the pressure of the Non-Head Stress Rule. In the adjunct-head structured phrases in Figure 5.11 b – d, the heads ("[tsau] leave", "[kuɔ] state" and "[huɔ fio] school is over") are inevitably demoted to the low tone L as well, regardless the length of the adjuncts ("[tsɛ] early", "[tɕʰi kʰa] straightly" and "[mo ji] right away") or the length of the heads.

The analysis in the two subsections above reveals that once a constituent is located by the Non-Head Stress Rule, it will be accentually demoted and all the syllables within it will turn up with L. Secondly, we can also see that the Non-Head Stress Rule is sensitive to the distinction between head and non-head but does not discriminate adjuncts from arguments. Nonetheless, through observing the sandhi behaviors in longer strings, Chen (2000: 501) insightfully points out that in Wenzhou dialect, heads, arguments and adjuncts do differ from each other on the ability of carrying the sentential level stresses, in consequence, the Stressability Hierarchy is promoted.

5.4.3.2 Stressability Hierarchy

In the previous two subsections, we have demonstrated how the Non-Head

Stress Rule assigns sentential level stress to syntactic constituents with respect to tonal changes. For the sake of clarity, all the examples demonstrated above are verbal phrases. This does not mean that the Non-Head Stress Rule is restricted to phrasal level, rather it is visible in strings as large as a clause. The same as with T. S. II in Shaoxing dialect, this phonological phenomenon takes ι as its working domain as long as the Match Theory predicts that "a CP corresponds to an ι". But as far as we extend the research scope to sentential level, the Non-Head Stress Rule fails to explain the stress patterns when there are both arguments and adjuncts (both are non-heads) in the same clause. See the sample clause below:

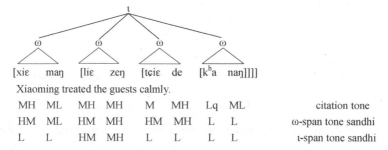

Figure 5.12   ι-span tone sandhi in CP

In this sentence, both the head ("[tɕiɛ de] treat") and its arguments, (i.e. the agent "[xiɛ maŋ] Xiaoming" and the theme "[kʰa naŋ] guests") are further demoted to the low tone L after the application of ω-span tone sandhi. Only the VP-adjunct (adverb "[liɛ zeŋ] calmly") sustains the sandhi form gained from the ω-level tone sandhi applied in the previous step. This example drives Chen (2000) to propose the Stressability Hierarchy as the backup for this sentential level phonological phenomenon:

(5.14) Stressability Hierarchy in Wenzhou Dialect①

    i) Non-Head > Head (Non-Head = Adjunct / Argument)

    ii) Adjunct > Argument

---

① This is a revised edition computed by the author based on Chen (2000: 500 – 501).
Based on English, Selkirk (1984) proposes a stressability hierarchy: argument > head > adjunct.

The Stressability Hierarchy directly conditions the application of ι-span tone sandhi in Wenzhou dialect:

(5.15) ι-Span Tone Sandhi in Wenzhou Dialect

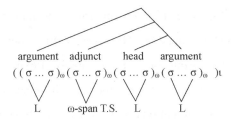

Up to now, a general image of tone sandhis in Wenzhou dialect has been well-established, which echoes tone sandhis in Shaoxing dialect in the following aspects:

i. Both Wenzhou dialect and Shaoxing dialect have two sets of tone sandhi rules;

ii. The phonological domain structures of the two sets of tone sandhis in both dialects are defined through the prosodic constituents ω and ι respectively;

iii. In both dialects, ω-span tone sandhi precedes ι-span tone sandhi;

iv. There are size effects on the domain structure of ω-span tone sandhi in both dialects;

v. In both dialects, phrasal level stress patterns constrain the operation of ι-span tone sandhi with reference to semantic-syntactic information.

Besides the characteristics shared with Shaoxing dialect listed above, ι-span tone sandhi in Wenzhou dialect resembles Zhenjiang dialect in that ι restructuring is witnessed in Wenzhou dialect as well.

5.4.3.3 ι Restructuring and Recursion in ω

At the very beginning of this chapter we have introduced that ι is a quite flexible prosodic constituent, for restructuring of ι is rather common due to various factors, like syntactic structure, speech rate, style, size effects on prosodic constituents and so on, resulting in mismatch between CP and ι (Nespor & Vogel 2007). NA in Spanish and quick-tempo tone sandhi in Zhenjiang dialect instantiate a long (NA)ι being broken down into several shorter ιs. Both cases reveal that if a CP is too long, like the case of (5.3) b and the one demonstrated in Figure 5.1, ι restructuring will take place due to physiological limitations on breath capacity. However, as the control of breath is rather individualized, restructuring of ι is inevitably flexible, which is manifested through various readings shown by the case in Zhenjiang dialect. Phonetically speaking, detectable intonational pauses mark the boundaries of the ιs within a string; phonologically speaking, the domains of application ι-span phonological processes diagnose ι boundaries, to be straightforward, the phonological domain structure of ι-span phonology reflects the organization of the ι. Despite the physiological limitation on breath capacity, it is frequently attested that prosodic structure regrouping is sensitive to syntactic constituency. For example, in both Spanish and Zhenjiang dialect, the right edge of the domain of application of NA and quick-tempo tone sandhi always align with the right boundary of an XP. In contrast to Spanish and Zhenjiang dialect, the construction of ι in Wenzhou dialect is sensitive to the prosodic grouping of functional categories (= determiners, prepositions, auxiliaries, modals, complementizers, conjunctions and other particles) (Chen 2000: 487).

Chapter 5 Correspondence Between CP and IP

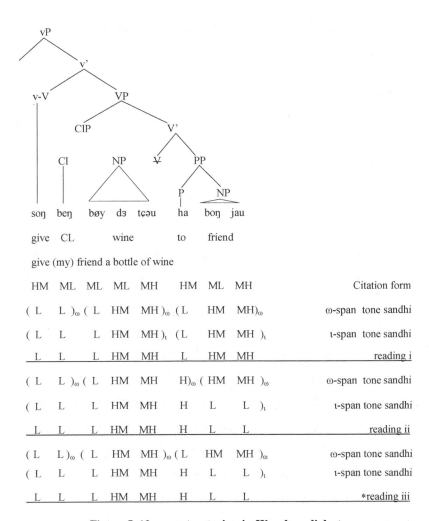

soŋ	beŋ	bøy	dɜ	tɕəu	ha	boŋ	jau	
give	CL		wine		to	friend		

give (my) friend a bottle of wine

HM	ML	ML	ML	MH	HM	ML	MH	Citation form
(L	L)ω	(L	HM	MH)ω	(L	HM	MH)ω	ω-span tone sandhi
(L	L	L	HM	MH)ι	(L	HM	MH)ι	ι-span tone sandhi
L	L	L	HM	MH	L	HM	MH	reading i
(L	L)ω	(L	HM	MH	H)ω	(HM	MH)ω	ω-span tone sandhi
(L	L	L	HM	MH	H	L	L)ι	ι-span tone sandhi
L	L	L	HM	MH	H	L	L	reading ii
(L	L)ω	(L	HM	MH)ω	(L	HM	MH)ω	ω-span tone sandhi
(L	L	L	HM	MH	H	L	L)ι	ι-span tone sandhi
L	L	L	HM	MH	H	L	L	*reading iii

Figure 5.13 ι restructuring in Wenzhou dialect

For the three possible readings of the clause demonstrated in Figure 5.13, reading i crucially differs from readings ii – iii on the construction of ι: reading i breaks the clause into two separate ιs, while CP-ι correspondence is well observed in readings ii – iii. For reading ii and *reading iii, according to Chen (2000: 498), the grammaticality lies in the prosodic grouping of the preposition "[ha] to".

Chen (2000: 494 – 495) proposes that when a functional word cliticizes to a lexical word to be prosodically parsed, in a [X [c X]] string, among the four potential ways of cliticization, only three are permissible in Wenzhou dialect:

(5.16)   [X [c X]]
   i. $((X\ c)_\omega)_\iota ((X)_\omega)_\iota$
   ii. $((X)_\omega)_\iota ((c\ X)_\omega)_\iota$
   iii. $((X\ c)_\omega (X)_\omega)_\iota$
   iv. $*((X)_\omega (c\ X)_\omega)_\iota$

   X = lexical category; c = functional category

ι boundaries tolerate both encliticization and procliticization as shown by (5.16) i – ii. Inside an ι, while encliticization is still permissible, procliticiztion is not accepted as shown by (5.16) iv. This condition on cliticization is then attested to by the case shown in Figure 5.13. When the entire clause maps into a single ι, the preposition "[ha] to" can only cliticize to the NP "[bøy dʒ tçəu] grape wine" and get pitch value H through Spreading which behaves like a neutral tone, and the ι surfaces with reading ii. Contrastively, reading iii is not favored, because "[ha] to" becomes enclitics to NP "[boŋ jau] friend" resulting in a marked parsing just as (5.16) iv does. Still, for the enclitics of "[boŋ jau] friend", reading i is well accepted as long as "[ha] to" stands in the ι-initial position, which is predicted by (5.16) i.

As early as in Section 5.4.2 we have introduced the neutral tone in Wenzhou dialect. Prosodic parsing in reading ii significantly proves that the neutral tone in Wenzhou dialect entails more than the neutral tone in Mandarin does. The neutral tone in Wenzhou dialect covers not only morpho-syntactic enclitcs as shown in Table 5.17, but also prosodic enclitics instantiated by the case of reading ii in Figure 5.13. The phonological domain structure of ι-span tone sandhi in Wenzhou dialect is sensitive to the distinction between lexical categories and functional categories thus producing ω enclitics. Being of functional category, this post-ω syllable is prosodicaly weak by nature (Selkirk 1996), hence it is not qualified to participate in ω-span tone sandhi, but only affiliates to its lexical host in the form of neutral tone, resulting in a recursively-built ω:①

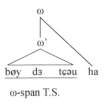

ω-span T.S.

N.T. / Spreading

Figure 5.14 Recursion in ω

NP [bøy dʒ tɕəu] maps into a ω and undergoes ω-span tone sandhi, then the preposition [ha] adjoins in and forms an extended ω ((bøy dʒ tɕəu)_ω ha)_ω. [ha] assimilates to the H of its host (bøy dʒ tɕəu)_ω through Spreading. This recursively-built ω obviously violates syntactic-prosodic constituency correspondence at least in the sense that the preposition does not constitute an immediate syntactic constituent with [bøy dʒ tɕəu] as long as it actually heads NP [boŋ jau].

It is not random that a functional head encliticizes to a preceding constituent which is not contained in the phrase this functional word heads, like the case of ω-restructuring in Wenzhou dialect. At the very beginning of this book I have introduced that it is reported in Shanghai dialect (Selkirk & Shen 1990: 321 – 322; Zhu 2006) that a functional word which appears to the right of verb but is not governed by the verb may be included in a ω initiated by this verb:

---

① It might be argued that this ω-enclitic group constitute a CG which is proposed in Nespor & Vogel's (2007) model of Prosodic Hierarchy, i. e. ((bøy dʒ tɕəu)_ω ha)_CG. We insist that this ω-enclitic group is a recursively-built ω. Because the prototype of the prosodic constituent of a neutral tone syllable together with its host syllable in Wenzhou dialect is ω which has already been confirmed in Section 5.4.2. Moreover, there is no more independent evidence on the promotion of CG in Wenzhou dialect.

(5.17) a. [z [laq [zawŋ-he]$_{NP}$]$_{PP}$]$_{VP}$
　　　　　live in　Shanghai
　　　　　live in Shanghai
　　　　　(LH　LM)$_\omega$　(LH　MH)$_\omega$　　Citation tone
　　　　　(L　　H)$_\omega$　(L　　H)$_\omega$　　Sandhi tone
　　　b. [tsou [taw [noe-tsiŋ]$_{NP}$]$_{PP}$]$_{VP}$
　　　　　walk　to　　Nanjing
　　　　　walk to Nanjing
　　　　　(MH　MH)$_\omega$　(LH　HL)$_\omega$　　Citation tone
　　　　　(M　　H)$_\omega$　(L　　H)$_\omega$　　Sandhi tone

Following Selkirk (2011:453), the Match Theory theoretically permits this cross-boundary-reprosodicalization. Correspondence constraint MATCH-XP-φ requires that the syntactic structure [V [Fnc [N]$_{NP}$]$_{FncP}$]$_{VP}$ map into a φ-domain structure (V Fnc (NP)$_\varphi$)$_\varphi$. This embedded structure provides the verb and functional head with opportunities of being parsed into an independent prosodic constituent: a ω in the case of Shanghai dialect, a recursive ω in the case of Wenzhou dialect.

�֍ 5.5　Summary

In this chapter we chiefly discussed the phonological activities of the largest prosodic constituent, namely ι. Three dialects, Zhenjiang dialect, Shaoxing dialect and Wenzhou dialect fall into the research scope of this chapter in examining the correspondence between the syntactic constituent CP and the prosodic constituent ι. Both Shaoxing dialect and Wenzhou dialect are Wu dialects; even though Zhenjiang dialect is Mandarin-based literally defined in Chinese dialectology, it is tremendously colored by the Wu dialects at least as far as tone sandhi is concerned.

Zhenjiang dialect has two sets of tone sandhi rules essentially conditioned by the rate of speech. In normal or slow tempo, poly-syllabic tone sandhi of Zhenjiang dialect applies leftward based on the di-syllabic ones, and it will not stop until a prosodic pause is met. In quick tempo, the rightmost two syllables undergo di-syllabic tone sandhi changes, while all the syllables to the left of the antepenult will surface with the middle level tone H. l.

As the tone sandhi of Zhenjiang dialect in quick tempo may apply to a syntactic constituent as large as a clause, the phonological domain of quick-tempo tone sandhi is defined through ι. Hence, the tone sandhi of Zhenjiang dialect in quick tempo is an ι-span phonological activity.

The quick-tempo tone sandhi rules in Zhenjiang dialect make no reference to their domain structure. However, the phonological domain structure of quick-tempo tone sandhi diagnoses the mapping from CP to the prosodic constituent ι, and the variabilities in it diagnoses ι restructuring in violation of CP-ι correspondence.

Due to the individualized control of breath, length and other factors, the application of tone sandhi in Zhenjiang dialect on the sentential level in quick tempo is so flexible that it is frequent that a CP maps into n-ary ιs in violation of CP-ι correspondence which is manifested through the variabilities of sandhi readings. The restructuring of ι in Zhenjiang dialect is not random, but sensitive to the integrity of the syntactic constituent, for the right boundary of a restructured ι always aligns with the right boundary of an XP.

As a typical North Wu dialect, Shaoxing dialect also has two layers of tone sandhi rules. T. S. I in Shaoxing dialect takes prosodic constituent ω as its working domain. The prosodic structure well-formedness constraints, BINMIN and BINMAX impose strict requirements on the size of the phonological domain of T. S. I, which conversely attests to the match / mismatch between the syntactic word X and the prosodic word ω. As metrical feet compose ωs, a right-prominent metrical stress pattern is inherited in a ω and then regulates the sandhi patterns of T. S. I in the sense that in Shaoxing dialect the metrically right-prominent stress pattern is realized through the choice of tone on stressed syllables. Not only is T. S. I the phonetic realization of right-prominence on the ω level, but also T. S. II is the phonetic realization of metrical stress on the sentential level.

T. S. II in Shaoxing dialect applying in succession to T. S. I is in essence, the ω-juncture rule, which inevitably applies between ωs irrespective of whether a ω corresponds to an entire syntactic terminal element X, or a part of a syntactic terminal element X. As morphosyntactically complicated as the contexts of application of T. S. II are, the CP is the largest syntactic constituent in which T. S. II can be observed. Following the Match Theory, if a syntactic constituent CP matches with a prosodic constituent ι, then T. S. II is a ω-juncture phonological phenomenon which has its domain of application defined through ι.

The process of T. S. II is actually a balance between phonetics, metrical stress, prosodic structure well-formedness constraints and phrasal prominence. Metrical stress patterns are still visible by the time T. S. II applies, as it is ω-juncture rule in essence. A right-prominent metrical stress pattern requires that a ω ends with a falling tone (hl) or a level tone (h) which are more prominent. But it is very difficult to have the most unmarked falling tone (hl) realized in continuous speech. Level tones are consequently chosen by the final syllables of non-periphery ωs, with falling tones only being possible on sentence final position. With the right prominent metrical stress pattern being observed, the Non-Head Stress Rule reshapes pitch registers of certain ωs regarding what syntactic constituents (i. e. phrase head or non-head) they map from. Both syllables of a di-syllabic ω mapped from the phrase head surfacing with level tones is the compromise between metrical prominence and phrasal prominence. Last but not least, under the pressure of BINMIN, mono-syllabic morphosyntactic constituents incorporate into adjacent ωs to gain legitimate prosodic status.

Wenzhou dialect, a representative dialect of the South Wu family, contains several sets of rules of tone sandhis, whose domains of application are also morphosyntactically-grounded prosodic constituents, i. e. ω and ι, typologically the same as the case of Shaoxing dialect.

For the ω-span tone sandhi in Wenzhou dialect, like what we have seen in

Shaoxing dialect, prosodic structure well-formedness constraints BINMIN and BINMAX assert that an unmarked tone sandhi domain has lower and upper limits on its syllable count. BINMIN and BINMAX are dominant in Wenzhou dialect, hence X-ω correspondence is not always guaranteed. Also the same as with T. S. II in Shaoxing dialect, the domain of application of the other set of tone sandhi in Wenzhou dialect turns out to be a prosodic constituent ι, for it can be witnessed from phrases to clauses, and clause is the largest constituent it applies to.

Simpler than the case in Shaoxing dialect, restriction from metrical stress on tone sandhi in Wenzhou dialect is not obvious. But more complicated than that in Shaoxing dialect, Non-Head Stress Rule is inadequate to explain the ι-level sandhi patterns in Wenzhou dialect. Fundamentally, the Non-Head Stress Rule is also well observed in ι-span tone sandhi in Wenzhou dialect, which also resorts to tonal changes to realize phrasal level stress patterns. In Wenzhou dialect, in the case of ι-span tone sandhi, the low tone (L) is chosen for an accentually demoted syllable. The Non-Head Stress Rule is sensitive to the distinction between head and non-head regarding their abilities to carry phrasal level stress, but in Wenzhou dialect, adjuncts are distinct from arguments on stressability as well. In consequence, the Stressability Hierarchy: adjunct > argument > head, is promoted.

ι-restructuring is witnessed in Wenzhou dialect as well. In contrast to Zhenjiang dialect, the construction of an ι in Wenzhou dialect is sensitive to the prosodic grouping of functional categories. Functional categories (mono-syllabic ones, to be specific) are prosodically so weak that they are not qualified to participate in ω-span tone sandhi, but only cliticize to their lexical hosts and surface with neutral tones. An immediate result of cliticization of functional categories is the recursion in ω. Cliticization of functional categories is not random: ι boundaries tolerate both encliticization and procliticization; but inside an ι, while encliticization is still permissible, procliticiztion is not accepted. This conditioned cliticization then may lead violation to syntactic-prosodic constituency correspondence in the sense that the clitics and their lexical host may not belong to the same syntactic constituent.

In the prosodic hierarchy, the Strict Layer Hypothesis expresses the idea that all the φs included in a clause join to form an n-ary branching ι which defines the prosodic domain of a clause(Nespor & Vogel 2007). But the tone sandhis in Shaoxing dialect and Wenzhou dialect have significantly demonstrate that the Strict Layer Hypothesis is violable: All the ωs included in a clause skipping the level φ, join to form an n-ary branching ι. This does not essentially mean that there is no level φ in these two dialects, but just that the phonology of tone sandhis does not predict the existence of level φ.

Chapter 6

Typology

6.1 Summary

In this book, I have sought answers to the construction of phonological domain structure of tone sandhi in some Chinese dialects, namely Tianjin dialect, Shaoxing dialect, Yuncheng dialect, Xiamen dialect (Zhangzhou dialect and Chenghai dialect), Zhenjiang dialect and Wenzhou dialect. Sandhi patterns, outputs of the application of tone sandhi rules, together with supplementary phonetic clues and perceptual denotation, diagnose the span and the structure of each independent tone sandhi domain. The tone sandhi domains in these eight dialects cannot be directly predicted from morpho-syntactic structure, but are defined through prosodic constituents ω, φ and ι, grounded in the Match theory. Basically, the prosodic domain structures of tone sandhis in these dialects are derived from syntax-prosody constituency correspondence (S-P correspondence), but language-particular prosodic structure well-formedness constraints, syntactic properties and tone sandhi rules may interact with S-P correspondence.

In Chapter 3, I discussed tone sandhis operating on the ω level. In the first place, observing the Match theory, the working domain of tone sandhi in

Tianjin dialect, Shaoxing dialect (T. S. I to be specific) and Yuncheng dialect corresponds to a ω. Secondly, due to prosodic structure well-formedness constraints, the phonological domain structure of the application of tone sandhi in all these three dialects uniformly exhibits divergences from the syntactic word / X in terms of the size of ω. Thirdly, language-specifically, ω in Tianjin dialect ranges from dis-yllabic to tri-syllabic, in Yuncheng dialect it ranges from di-syllabic to quarto-syllabic, and in Shaoxing dialect (T. S. I) it ranges from dis-yllabic to penta-syllabic. A typology of the ω-defined tone sandhi domains then arises:

Table 6.1 Typology of size of ω

Dialect	(...)ω					
	(σ)ω	(σσ)ω	(σσσ)ω	(σσσσ)ω	(σσσσσ)ω	(σσσσσσ)ω
Shanghai Dialect (T. S. I)	√	√	√	√	√	?
Tianjin Dialect		√	√			
Yuncheng Dialect		√	√	√		
Shaoxing Dialect (T. S. I)		√	√	√	√	?
Wenzhou Dialect (T. S. I)		√	√	√	√	√

In Chapter 3 I have demonstrated that mono-syllabic ωs are highly marked. However, they do exist. It is repeatedly reported in Xu, Tang & Qian (1981), Selkirk & Shen (1990), Qian (1992), Zhu (2006) and others that, in Shanghai dialect, there are mono-syllabic ωs which constitute domains of tone sandhis on their own. Also according to Xu, Tang & Qian (1981) and Zhu (2006), in Shanghai dialect, a ω can extend as long as five syllables.

Wenzhou dialect, also a dialect of the Wu family, resembling Shaoxing dialect and Shanghai dialect, also has a large inventory of ω. Hexa-syllabic ωs are reported in Wenzhou dialect even though examples are rather rare and restricted to the translation of foreign names. Variations in the size of domain of tone sandhi in these dialects reveal that on the ω-level, syntactic constituent and prosodic constituent correspondence may be undermined by prosodic structure markedness constraints. Equally importantly, I will also propose that the variations in the size of the domain of tone sandhis are due to the variations in markedness reduction in terms of the size of ω, which I will elaborate in the form of constraint ranking in Section 6.2.

Besides the restrictions from prosodic structure markedness constraints and S-P / P-S correspondence constraints, tone sandhi rules on their own may express requirements on their domain structure. In Yuncheng dialect, I have demonstrated that tone sandhi rules are sensitive to the rightmost di-syllabic immediate morphosyntactic constituent within a ω and this may produce an apparently strange phenomenon that tone sandhi does not always start to work from the very right edge of a ω. Hence, the tone sandhi in Yuncheng dialect typically exemplifies that the construction of the domain of application of phonological rules may not entirely depend on the interaction between prosodic structure markedness constraints and syntactic-prosodic constituency correspondence constraints (in the most common case); phonological rules would also address properties of their domain structure.

In Chapter 4 I have examined the tone sandhi in the South Min family, taking Xiamen dialect as the representative dialect. Despite the differences in phonetic realizations of tones, the processing of tone sandhi and the construction of the domain of tone sandhi are rather consistent among dialects of the South Min family, at least we can witness the uniformity in Xiamen dialect, Zhangzhou dialect and Chenghai dialect. In Xiamen dialect, the right edge of a domain of tone sandhi always aligns with the right edge of an XP (X = lexical category), whereas it is unpredictable whether the left edge of a domain of tone sandhi aligns with the left edge of an XP headed by lexical elements or by a functional elements. Hence, by the end of Chapter 4 we arrive at a temporary conclusion that tone sandhi domains in Xiamen dialect are expressed through prosodic constituent φ. But the corresponding relationship between XP and φ is severely undermined because it is only for sure that φ always aligns with XP on the right edge, contrastively the left edge of φ may align with the left edge of either a lexical-element-headed phrase or a functional-element-headed phrase, which stretches beyond the explanation of the Match theory. The Match Theory holds that the corresponding relationship exists between the lexical-element-headed phrases and the prosodic constituents, with functional elements and their maximal projections excluded, which is stated as Lexical Category Condition (LCC). A more generalized mechanism is required to count this systematic phonological phenomenon in the South Min family. I will propose an "extended" version of correspondence constraint MATCH-XP-φ in Section 6.3 to formulate the phonological domain structure of tone sandhi in Xiamen dialect.

Chapter 5 is about ι-domain tone sandhi. In this chapter I have examined three dialects, two of which belong to the Wu family, i.e. Shaoxing dialect (T.S.I) and Wenzhou dialect. The other one is Zhenjiang dialect, a Mandarin-based dialect, nevertheless greatly influenced by the Wu family.

The Wu family differs from other dialectal groups in the sense that Wu dialects typically possess two separate layers of tone sandhi rules which apply in succession, e.g. Shaoxing dialect and Wenzhou dialect. As T.S.I in both Shaoxing dialect and Wenzhou dialect takes ω as its working domain, the T.S. II domain in both dialects are defined through ι. Shaoxing dialect and Wenzhou dialect share another remarkable characteristic that T.S.II tends to flatten the pitch contour of the entire string except for the "nucleus syllable(s)". Despite the general tendency of flattening, these two dialects differ in that the flattened pitch contour in Shaoxing dialect is endowed with register feature H, while that in Wenzhou dialect is endowed with register feature L.

Based on empirical evidence, I have argued that T.S.II in Shaoxing dialect is in essence the phonetic realization of metrical stress and phrasal prominence on the sentence level. A right-prominent metrical stress pattern presses the final syllables of non-periphery ωs to surface with level tone h, while sentence final syllables surface with either falling tone hl or level tone h. With the right prominent metrical stress pattern being observed, the Non-Head Stress Rule reshapes pitch registers of certain ωs regarding what syntactic constituents (i. e. phrase head or non-head) they map from. Metrical prominence and phrasal prominence will reach a compromise on the sentence level which is realized and recognized as T. S. II.

T. S. II in Shaoxing dialect chooses high level tone h to fill in the metrical stress position, contrastively, low tone L is chosen for an accentually demoted syllables in Wenzhou dialect. Specifically, in Wenzhou dialect, adjuncts, arguments and phrasal heads differ in their abilities to carry phrasal stress, which can be formally expressed as the Stressability Hierarchy: adjunct > argument > head. So in a sentence, only the most stressable constituents can keep the sandhi form gained from T. S. I, but all other constituents will be demoted to low level tone L. To this extent, T. S. II in Wenzhou dialect, typologically similar to T. S. II in Shaoxing dialect, is the realization of phrasal prominence.

Tonal contour fallening is also witnessed in quick-tempo Zhenjiang dialect. Within an ι, only the right-most two syllables undergo tone sandhi rules regularly, but all the syllables to the left of the penultimate will surface with the middle level tone M. It is still unclear what triggers the neutralization in quick-tempo Zhenjiang dialect. I would temporarily attribute this to the principle of *end-weight*[①] which is a syntactic concept.

Table 6.2 T. S. II in Shaoxing dialect, Wenzhou dialect and quick-tempo T. S. in Zhenjiang dialect

		Shaoxing Dialect	Wenzhou Dialect	Zhenjiang Dialect
Triggers	Metrical Stress	√		
	Phrasal Stress	√	√	√
Phonetic Diagnosis	Sandhi Patterns	Stressed σs: promotion to h	Unstressable σs: demotion to L	Pre-penultimate σs: demotion to M

In Chapter 5 I have also discussed the restructuring of prosodic constituents in ι. Due to individualized control of breath, length and other factors, the

---

① In syntax, the principle of end weight means that the long elements, e. g. NP, are put at the end of the sentence, and keep the subject as short as possible.

application of tone sandhi in (quick tempoed) Zhenjiang dialect and Wenzhou dialect on the sentential level is so flexible that it is frequently the case that a CP maps into n-ary ιs in violation of CP-ι correspondence. (See Table 6.3)

Restructuring of ι in Zhenjiang dialect is not random but sensitive to the integrity of syntactic constituency, for the right boundary of a restructured ι always aligns with the right boundary of an XP.

In Wenzhou dialect, mono-syllabic functional elements are prosodically too weak to participate in ω-span tone sandhi, but only cliticize to their lexical hosts in the form of neutral tones. Though the cliticization of functional elements takes place on the ω level, ι asserts restriction on the direction of cliticization. Especially inside an ι, procliticization is not accepted. Situations like this may lead to violation of the S-P correspondence constraint MATCH-X-ω in the sense that the clitics and their lexical host may not belong to the same syntactic constituent.

Table 6.3 Restriction to S-P correspondence from the tone sandhi rules

Zhenjiang Dialect	
Trigger	The control of breath in fast speech is individualized.
Formalization	XP)ι >> MATCH-CP-ι
Example	[[wo [tɕiŋ-ka [tsɔ-saŋ]] [[tsɔ -ji] [pa [tʰa] [sɛ̃n [kʰuɛ[tɕʰ ĩ]]]]])ι)ι)ι)ι I today morning already BA him three CL money I have already given him three dollars this morning.
Wenzhou Dialect	
Trigger	Procliticization on the ω-level is not accepted ι-internally.
Formalization	*((X)ω(c X)ω)ι >> MATCH-X-ω
Example	[soŋ [beŋ [bøy-dʒ-tɕəu] [ha [boŋ-jau] ((L-L)ω(L-HM-MH)ω H)ω(L-L)ω)ι give CL wine to friend give (my) friend a bottle of wine

(continued)

	Xiamen Dialect
Trigger	The head that an adjunct adjoins to is phonetically covert.
Formalization	COVERT-HEAD >> MATCH-XP-φ
Example	[[Ting sio-tsia]$_{NP}$# [**kai-tsai**]$_{AdvP}$# [tse [tsit pan ki]$_{NP}$#]$_{VP}$]$_{TP}$ ( )$_{φ}$ ( )$_{φ}$ (( )$_{φ}$)$_{φ}$ Ting Miss fortunately take this CL flight Fortunately, Miss Ting took this flight.
	Yuncheng Dialect
Trigger	T. S. rule is sensitive to the rightmost di-syllabic IC within a ω.
Formalization	BINARITY, INTERGRITY OF IMMEDIATE CONSTITUENT
Example	[duan [[xii-lian] shui]$_{NP}$]$_{VP}$ # T. S. # ( )$_{ω}$ carry wash face water carry wash water

Restructuring of prosodic constituents is also witnessed on the φ level. In Xiamen dialect I have proved that an adjunct may initiate a domain of application of tone sandhi if and only if the head it adjoins to has no overt phonetic value. Losing the media that relates the adjunct to the subordinate phrase, the adjunct phrase drifts apart from the tone sandhi process initiated by an XP to its right, and initiates another tone sandhi domain on its own. (See Table 6.3)

Restructuring of the prosodic constituents is frequent but not random. In essence, tone sandhi rules state language-particular requirements on ι restructuring. An extreme example is Yuncheng dialect. In Yuncheng dialect, apparently the domain of tone sandhi may not coincide with either a Prosodic Word or a syntactic word, because tone sandhi can only be activated by the right-most di-syllabic immediate constituent within a ω. Phenomena listed in Table 6.3 suggest that the control over the construction of tone sandhi domain from tone sandhi rules can be witnessed in every level of the prosodic domain of tone sandhi.

In the following two sections, I will elaborate on the interaction between syntactic-prosodic constituency correspondence and prosodic structure well-formedness constraints, and the influence on syntactic-prosodic constituency correspondence from properties of syntactic structure in the form of constraint ranking.

6.2 Prosodic Properties and S-P/P-S Correspondence

6.2.1 Size of ω Markedness Hierarchy

Hayes (1995) reasons that in the Prosodic Hierarchy, the pure rhythmic unit, namely the foot, is universally minimally bi-moraic or bi-syllabic, as a consequence, a ω, consisting of minimally one Ft, must itself be minimally bi-syllabic. Selkirk (2011:468) developed and formalized Hayes's idea into two sets of prosodic markedness constraints: BINMIN (ω, Ft) and BINMAX (ω, Ft). BINMIN (ω, Ft) sets the lower limit to the size of a ω which requires that a ω minimally consists of a bi-syllabic Ft, BINMAX (φ, ω) on the other hand sets the upper limits to the size of a ω which requires that a φ maximally consists of two Fts. Hence, size effects on ω are transmitted from a lower level of the prosodic constituent that immediately composes it, namely the Ft.

Lü's (1963), Feng's (1996) and Wang's (2000) successive studies on rhythmic grouping in Chinese predict that, theoretically, a legitimate ω could be minimally di-syllabic and maximally hexa-syllabic (as shown in Figure 6.1).

BINMIN bans mono-syllabic Ft, so a mono-syllabic ω is not permitted as a consequence. If a mono-syllabic constituent does have to stand on its own (e.g. focalized, topicalized), phonetic compensations (e.g. rhyme lengthening, insertion of an empty beat, etc.) are compulsory. It is obvious that these phonetic resolutions are ad hoc, but incorporation into di-syllabic Ft in juxtaposition thus producing tri-syllabic Ft (Figure 6.1 b) is the most unmarked phonological option. (Feng, 1996) Hence, legitimately, in Chinese a Ft could be di-syllabic and tri-syllabic, while a tri-syllabic Ft is more marked than a di-syllabic one as long as the former comes into existence relying on the latter.

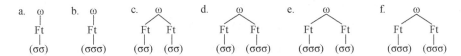

Figure 6.1   Typology of the size effects of ω

Observing BINMAX (ω, Ft), theoretically, in Chinese, a ω could be maximally hexa-syllabic in the sense that being composed of two tri-syllabic Fts (as shown in Figure 6.1 f). Hexa-syllabicness is obviously the most marked status of a ω since it is composed of two marked Fts which in turn expresses the upper limit of ω. Then from di-syllabicity to penta-syllabicity, the markedness of ω increases one by one, which is empirically testified to in Chinese dialects. In Chapter 3 I have proved that the phonological domains of tone sandhi in Tianjin dialect, Yuncheng dialect and T.S.I in Shaoxing dialect are defined through ω. Sandhi patterns in these dialects reveal that: in Tianjin dialect, ω ranges from di-syllabic to tri-syllabic; in Yuncheng dialect, ω ranges from di-syllabic to quarto-syllabic; in Shaoxing dialect, ω ranges from di-syllabic to penta-syllabic (a penta-syllabic ω is the longest ω witnessed in our investigation). Both theoretical and empirical evidence enables me to postulate a ω markedness hierarchy in terms of its size:

(6.1) Size of ω Markedness Hierarchy

$$|(\sigma)_\omega > (\sigma\sigma\sigma\sigma\sigma\sigma)_\omega > (\sigma\sigma\sigma\sigma\sigma)_\omega > (\sigma\sigma\sigma\sigma)_\omega > (\sigma\sigma\sigma)_\omega > (\sigma\sigma)_\omega|$$

The size of ω markedness hierarchy in (6.1) tells that on the one hand, the mono-syllabic ω is the most undesired ω; on the other hand, markedness increase is in proportion to ω length. In Chapter 2 I have introduced that the place of articulation markedness hierarchy is related to a set of output constraints (see 2.6 for reference), analogously, the size of ω markedness hierarchy is also related to a set of output constraints:

(6.2) Output Constraints for Size of ω

a) $*\{(\sigma)_\omega\}$: Assign a violation for each $(\sigma)_\omega$.

b) $*\{(\sigma)_\omega, (\sigma\sigma\sigma\sigma\sigma\sigma)_\omega\}$: Assign a violation for each $(\sigma)_\omega$ and each $(\sigma\sigma\sigma\sigma\sigma\sigma)_\omega$.

c) $*\{(\sigma)_\omega, (\sigma\sigma\sigma\sigma\sigma\sigma)_\omega, (\sigma\sigma\sigma\sigma\sigma)_\omega\}$: Assign a violation for each $(\sigma)_\omega$, each $(\sigma\sigma\sigma\sigma\sigma\sigma)_\omega$ and each $(\sigma\sigma\sigma\sigma\sigma)_\omega$.

d) $*\{(\sigma)_\omega, (\sigma\sigma\sigma\sigma\sigma\sigma)_\omega, (\sigma\sigma\sigma\sigma\sigma)_\omega, (\sigma\sigma\sigma\sigma)_\omega\}$: Assign a violation for each $(\sigma)_\omega$, each $(\sigma\sigma\sigma\sigma\sigma\sigma)_\omega$, each $(\sigma\sigma\sigma\sigma\sigma)_\omega$ and each $(\sigma\sigma\sigma\sigma)_\omega$.

e) $*\{(\sigma)_\omega, (\sigma\sigma\sigma\sigma\sigma\sigma)_\omega, (\sigma\sigma\sigma\sigma\sigma)_\omega, (\sigma\sigma\sigma\sigma)_\omega, (\sigma\sigma\sigma)_\omega\}$: Assign a violation for each $(\sigma)_\omega$, each $(\sigma\sigma\sigma\sigma\sigma\sigma)_\omega$, each $(\sigma\sigma\sigma\sigma\sigma)_\omega$, each $(\sigma\sigma\sigma\sigma)_\omega$ and each $(\sigma\sigma\sigma)_\omega$.

f) $*\{(\sigma)_\omega, (\sigma\sigma\sigma\sigma\sigma\sigma)_\omega, (\sigma\sigma\sigma\sigma\sigma)_\omega, (\sigma\sigma\sigma\sigma)_\omega, (\sigma\sigma\sigma)_\omega, (\sigma\sigma)_\omega\}$: Assign a violation for each $(\sigma)_\omega$, each $(\sigma\sigma\sigma\sigma\sigma\sigma)_\omega$, each $(\sigma\sigma\sigma\sigma\sigma)_\omega$, each $(\sigma\sigma\sigma\sigma)_\omega$, each $(\sigma\sigma\sigma)_\omega$ and each $(\sigma\sigma)_\omega$.

Together, the output constraints in (6.2) express the size of ω markedness hierarchy. For example, $(\sigma)_\omega$ is more marked than other ωs, and $*\{(\sigma)_\omega\}$ is violated by $(\sigma)_\omega$ but not by other ωs like $(\sigma\sigma\sigma\sigma\sigma\sigma)_\omega$, $(\sigma\sigma\sigma\sigma\sigma)_\omega$, $(\sigma\sigma\sigma\sigma)_\omega$, $(\sigma\sigma\sigma)_\omega$ or $(\sigma\sigma)_\omega$. $(\sigma\sigma\sigma\sigma\sigma)_\omega$ is never less marked than $(\sigma\sigma\sigma\sigma)_\omega$, so every constraint that $(\sigma\sigma\sigma\sigma)_\omega$ violates is also violated by $(\sigma\sigma\sigma\sigma\sigma)_\omega$ (i.e. $*\{(\sigma)_\omega, (\sigma\sigma\sigma\sigma\sigma\sigma)_\omega, (\sigma\sigma\sigma\sigma\sigma)_\omega\}$, $*\{(\sigma)_\omega, (\sigma\sigma\sigma\sigma\sigma\sigma)_\omega, (\sigma\sigma\sigma\sigma\sigma)_\omega, (\sigma\sigma\sigma\sigma)_\omega\}$). In this way relative markedness relations are translated into violations of the size of ω output constraints.

6.2.2 Markedness Reduction and Preservation

It is widely accepted in the phonological literature that there are markedness hierarchies. For example, there are obstruent voicing markedness hierarchy, place of articulation markedness hierarchy, manner of articulation markedness hierarchy, segmental sonority hierarchy and so on. It is also held that hierarchical markedness relations are invariant across languages, but individual languages and even individual processes can collapse markedness distinctions. (de Lacy 2006) It is indeed the case that tolerance to marked targets varies from language to language as we have seen that Tianjin dialect, Yuncheng dialect and Shaoxing dialect vary in their permission for the maximal size of ω.

De Lacy's (2006) Markedness Theory primarily addresses three phonological phenomena: markedness reduction, preservation, and conflation. Marked elements can be singled out for preservation, thus obscuring the effects of markedness reduction. Consequently, markedness effects are only clearly visible when preservation is irrelevant. Formally, the interaction between faithfulness constraints and output constraints determines to what extent the marked elements can be preserved. Before we dig into markedness reduction and preservation in terms of the size of ω in Tianjin dialect, Yuncheng dialect and Shaoxing dialect, let us first figure out the mechanism of markedness reduction taking "default" consonant epenthesis in Mabalay Atayal, which is thoroughly and subtly elaborated upon de Lacy (2006), for illustration.

It is reported that in Mabalay Atayal, when a word is underlyingly vowel-final, like in many languages, [ʔ] is inserted in word-final position:

(6.3) Mabalay Atayal Final [ʔ] Epenthesis (de Lacy 2006: 83)
    (a) /an-βakħa/→[βa. nak. 'hɐʔ]   cf. [βak. hɐ-. 'un], *[βak. hɐ. 'ʔun]
        break + {perfective}   break + {trans. loc.}
    (b) /am-satu/→[sa. ma. 'tuʔ]   cf. [sa. tu-. 'an]
        send + {intrans.}   send + {trans. loc.}
    (c) /sinħi/→[sin. 'ħəʔ]   cf. [sin. ħə-. 'un]
        believe + {intrans.}   believe + {trans. pat.}
    (d) /m-paŋa/→[ma. pa. 'ŋaʔ]   cf. [pa. ŋa-. 'an]
        carry on back + {intrans.}   carry on back + {trans. loc.}
    (e) /am-sβu/→[sa. ma. 'βuʔ]   cf. [βu-. 'an]
        shoot + {intrans.}   shoot + {trans. loc.}

It is observed that the final syllable of a word is always stressed, and so proposes that [ʔ] epenthesis is motivated by the need for a stressed syllable to be heavy. Epenthesis in Mabalay Atayal is therefore motivated by a prosodic requirement which is formalized into constraints "ALIGN-'σ-R and STRESS-TO-WEIGHT". Mabalay Atayal allows many consonants in coda position [p t k ʔ s x h m n ŋ h j w], but only [ʔ] is epenthesized. According to the place of articulation markedness hierarchy / PoA "|dorsal > labial > coronal > glottal |" (which has actually been introduced in Chapter 2, see (2.5) for reference), [ʔ] and [h] are therefore the least marked of all consonants. The choice of [ʔ] can be formalized through the ranking of the output-oriented constraints: *{dors} >> *{dors,lab} >> *{dors,lab,cor} >> *{dors,lab,cor,gl} (also see (2.6) for reference):

Tableau 6.1 Mabalay Atayal final [ʔ] epenthesis

/sinhi/	*{dors}	*{dors,lab}	*{dors,lab,cor}	*{dors,lab,cor,gl}
sin.'hik	*!	*	***	****
sin.'hip		*!	***	****
sin.'hit			***!	****
☞sin.'hiʔ			**	****

Being the least-marked segment in terms of PoA, [ʔ] is chosen as the epenthetic segment, because there is no PoA constraint which favors [k], [p], or [t] over [ʔ]. If [ʔ] is illegal, then there is no other segment qualified for epenthesis. Hence, PoA output constraint *{dors,lab,cor} must outrank all other output-oriented constraints that contradict it. Meanwhile, prosodic constraints "ALIGN-'σ-R and STRESS-TO-WEIGHT" must outrank *{dors,lab,cor,gl}, otherwise epenthesis would be blocked; the faithfulness constraint MAX-IO must outrank all the PoA constraints in order to prevent the deletion of [t], [p], and [k].

To summarize, default consonant epenthesis in Mabalay Atayal presents a situation in which the effects of markedness reduction are clearly visible. In Mabalay Atayal, segmental markedness in terms of PoA is reduced to the lowest level, for the high-ranking of *{dors, lab, cor} prevents all segments except for [ʔ] from being epenthesized in word-final position. But it is not always the case that only the least marked element surfaces, marked elements can be singled out for preservation, thus obscuring the effects of markedness reduction. Variation in the size of ω witnessed in Chinese dialects typically exemplifies markedness preservation.

6.2.3 Markedness Preservation and X-ω / ω-X Correspondence

In this subsection, I will deliver a typological account of the size effects of ω in the form of constraint-ranking as far as Tianjin dialect, Shaoxing dialect and Yuncheng dialect are concerned. In Chapter 3 I have demonstrated that T.S.I in Shaoxing dialect typically takes ω as its phonological domain of application. The Match Theory predicts that ω is mapped from the syntactic word X (X = N, A, V). The corresponding relationship between X and ω can be formalized into the correspondence constraints (also see 2.3 for reference):

(6.4) i. MATCH-X-ω: An X must corresponds to a ω on both edges.

ii. MATCH-ω-X: a ω must corresponds to an X on both edges.

iii. DEP-X-ω: Correspondent X and ω have identical syllable numbers.

In Shaoxing dialect, the phonological domain of T.S.I proves that a legitimate ω in Shaoxing dialect is di-, tri-, quarto- and penta-syllabic, which in consequence, witnesses both matching and mismatching between an X and a ω on the dimension of constituent's size: A ω could be as long as, shorter than or longer than an X. With reference to the size of ω markedness hierarchy: | (σ)$_\omega$ > (σσσσσσ)$_\omega$ > (σσσσσ)$_\omega$ > (σσσσ)$_\omega$ > (σσσ)$_\omega$ > (σσ)$_\omega$ |, the two most marked ωs, i.e. (σ)$_\omega$ and (σσσσσσ)$_\omega$ are not favored in Shaoxing dialect[①], while (σσσσσ)$_\omega$, (σσσσ)$_\omega$, (σσσ)$_\omega$ are all preserved in Shaoxing dialect in parallel position with the most unmarked (σσ)$_\omega$. This significantly implies that output constraints *{(σ)$_\omega$} and *{(σ)$_\omega$, (σσσσσσ)$_\omega$} outrank *{(σ)$_\omega$, (σσσσσσ)$_\omega$, (σσσσσ)$_\omega$}, *{(σ)$_\omega$, (σσσσσσ)$_\omega$, (σσσσσ)$_\omega$,

---

① There are no cases of hexa-syllabic ω found in our investigation.

(σσσσ)_ω}, *{(σ)_ω, (σσσσσσ)_ω, (σσσσσ)_ω, (σσσσ)_ω, (σσσ)_ω} and *{(σ)_ω, (σσσσσσ)_ω, (σσσσσ)_ω, (σσσσ)_ω, (σσσ)_ω, (σσ)_ω}, so as to have (σ)_ω and (σσσσσσ)_ω eliminated but have (σσσσσ)_ω, (σσσσ)_ω, (σσσ)_ω and (σσ)_ω preserved:

Tableau 6.2 Markedness reduction and preservation in the size of ω in Shaoxing dialect

	*{(σ)_ω}	*{(σ)_ω, (σσσσσσ)_ω}	*{(σ)_ω, (σσσσσσ)_ω, (σσσσσ)_ω}	*{(σ)_ω, (σσσσσσ)_ω, (σσσσσ)_ω, (σσσσ)_ω}	*{(σ)_ω, (σσσσσσ)_ω, (σσσσσ)_ω, (σσσσ)_ω, (σσσ)_ω}	*{(σ)_ω, (σσσσσσ)_ω, (σσσσσ)_ω, (σσσσ)_ω, (σσσ)_ω, (σσ)_ω}
(σ)_ω	*!	*	*	*	*	*
(σσσσσσ)_ω		*!	*	*	*	*
☞((σσσσσ)_ω			*	*	*	*
☞((σσσσ)_ω				*	*	*
☞((σσσ)_ω					*	*
☞((σσ)_ω						*

Hence, the relative ranking in (6.5) between the output constraints guarantees that di-, tri-, quarto- and penta-syllabic ω are preserved in Shaoxing dialect:

(6.5) Markedness Reduction and Preservation in the Size of ω in Shaoxing Dialect:

*{(σ)_ω}, *{(σ)_ω, (σσσσσσ)_ω} >> *{(σ)_ω, (σσσσσσ)_ω, (σσσσσ)_ω},
*{(σ)_ω, (σσσσσσ)_ω, (σσσσσ)_ω, (σσσσ)_ω}, *{(σ)_ω, (σσσσσσ)_ω, (σσσσσ)_ω, (σσσσ)_ω, (σσσ)_ω}, *{(σ)_ω, (σσσσσσ)_ω, (σσσσσ)_ω, (σσσσ)_ω, (σσσ)_ω, (σσ)_ω}

Observing the high-ranking of *{(σ)_ω, (σσσσσσ)_ω}, a compound longer than penta-syllabic will be split into two or more ωs leading to violation of correspondence constraint MATCH-ω-X, i.e. (6.4) ii which bans the insertion of more ωs:

Tableau 6.3 [tsʰẽ tɕie? liẽ huø̃ vẽ̆ kuE] Spring Festival Gala Evening

[tsʰẽ tɕie? [liẽ huø̃ [vẽ̆ kuE]]]	*{(σ)ω}	*{(σ)ω,(σσσσσσ)ω}	MATCH-ω-X
a. (tsʰẽ tɕie? liẽ huø̃ vẽ̆ kuE)ω		*!	
☞b. (tsʰẽ tɕie?)ω (liẽ huø̃ vẽ̆ kuE)ω			*

The complex compound [tsʰẽ tɕie? liẽ huø̃ vẽ̆ kuE] maps into two ωs thus super long ω (candidate a in Tableau 6.3) are eliminated at the expense of violating MATCH-ω-X.

In Shaoxing dialect, correspondence constraints MATCH-ω-X and MATCH-X-ω intend to guarantee isomorphism between X and ω to the greatest extent while observing the premise that the parsing of ω is legitimate:

Tableau 6.4 [tɕia-lɒ-sɿ bæ̃-li ɦiaŋ-lɒ pɒ-ɕiẽ] Teacher Jia applies for endowment insurance.

[tɕia-lɒ-sɿ bæ̃-li ɦiaŋ-lɒ pɒ-ɕiẽ]]]	*{(σ)ω}	*{(σ)ω,(σσσσσσ)ω}	MATCH-ω-X	MATCH-X-ω
a. (tɕia-lɒ-sɿ bæ̃-li)ω (ɦiaŋ-lɒ pɒ-ɕiẽ)ω				*!
b. (tɕia-lɒ-sɿ)ω (bæ̃-li ɦiaŋ-lɒ pɒ-ɕiẽ)ω		*!		*
c. (tɕia-lɒ-sɿ)ω bæ̃-li)ω (ɦiaŋ-lɒ)ω (pɒ-ɕiẽ)ω			*!	
d. (tɕia-lɒ-sɿ bæ̃-li)ω (ɦiaŋ-lɒ)ω (pɒ-ɕiẽ)ω			*!	*!
☞e. (tɕia-lɒ-sɿ)ω (bæ̃-li)ω (ɦiaŋ-lɒ pɒ-ɕiẽ)ω				

Both candidates a and b in Tableau 6.4 violate MATCH-X-ω for, instead of mapping into an independent ω on its own, the verb [bæ̃-li] is parsed with either [tɕia-lɒ-sɿ] or [ɦiaŋ-lɒ pɒ-ɕiẽ]; on the contrary, Candidate c is ruled out because compound [ɦiaŋ-lɒ pɒ-ɕiẽ] is split into two separate ωs in violation of MATCH-ω-X. Candidate d is eliminated in violation of both MATCH-X-ω and MATCH-ω-X. Candidate e wins without violating any constraints. The example in Tableau 6.3 demonstrates that if there is no need for an X breaking up into more ωs, then MATCH-X-ω must be well observed. So it deserves clarification that MATCH-X-ω entails that the integrity of X is supposed to be maintained to the greatest extent, under that *{(σ)ω} and *{(σ)ω,(σσσσσσ)ω} are not violated. Whereas, if *{(σ)ω} and *{(σ)ω,(σσσσσσ)ω} cannot be guaranteed, MATCH-ω-X and MATCH-X-ω will be sacrificed:

Tableau 6.5 [tɕia-lɒ-sɿ [ma [tɕiŋ-tɕi seʔ-ɦioŋ-vɒŋ]] Teacher Jia bought affordable housing.

[tɕia-lɒ-sɿ [ma [tɕiŋ-tɕi seʔ-ɦioŋ-vɒŋ]]]	*{(σ)ω}	*{(σ)ω, (σσσσσσ)ω}	MATCH-ω-X	MATCH-X-ω
☞a. (tɕia-lɒ-sɿ ma)ω(tɕiŋ-tɕi seʔ-ɦioŋ-vɒŋ)ω				*!
b. (tɕia-lɒ-sɿ ma)ω(tɕiŋ-tɕi)ω(seʔ-ɦioŋ-vɒŋ)ω			*!	*!
c. (tɕia-lɒ-sɿ)ω(ma tɕiŋ-tɕi seʔ-ɦioŋ-vɒŋ)ω		*!		*
d. (tɕia-lɒ-sɿ)ω(ma)ω(tɕiŋ-tɕi)ω(seʔ-ɦioŋ-vɒŋ)ω	*!		*	
e. (tɕia-lɒ-sɿ)ω(ma)ω(tɕiŋ-tɕi seʔ-ɦioŋ-vɒŋ)ω	*!			

Candidates c and d are eliminated because they both contain ωs with undesirable size; Candidate a defeats b since b violates both MATCH-ω-X (i. e. [tɕiŋ-tɕi seʔ-ɦioŋ-vɒŋ] split into two ωs) and MATCH-X-ω (i. e. [tɕia-lɒ-sɿ] and [ma] map into a single ω).

So, in Shaoxing dialect, output constraints *{(σ)ω} and *{(σ)ω, (σσσσσσ)ω} eliminate the two most marked mono- and hexa-syllabic ωs at the expense of S-P / P-S correspondence, while the other four output constraints *{(σ)ω, (σσσσσσ)ω, (σσσσσ)ω}, *{(σ)ω, (σσσσσσ)ω, (σσσσσ)ω, (σσσσ)ω}, *{(σ)ω, (σσσσσσ)ω, (σσσσσ)ω, (σσσσ)ω, (σσσ)ω}, *{(σ)ω, (σσσσσσ)ω, (σσσσσ)ω, (σσσσ)ω, (σσσ)ω, (σσ)ω} are even lower ranked so as to have penta-, quarto-, tri- and di-syllabic ωs preserved. Size effects of ω in Shaoxing dialect can be schematically presented in the form of constraint ranking as shown in (6.6):

(6.6) ω Structure Well-formedness Overrides S-P/P-S Correspondence in Shaoxing Dialect:

*{(σ)ω}, *{(σ)ω, (σσσσσσ)ω} >>

MATCH-X-ω, MATCH-ω-X >>

*{(σ)ω, (σσσσσσ)ω, (σσσσσ)ω}, *{(σ)ω, (σσσσσσ)ω, (σσσσσ)ω, (σσσσ)ω}, *{(σ)ω, (σσσσσσ)ω, (σσσσσ)ω, (σσσσ)ω, (σσσ)ω}, *{(σ)ω, (σσσσσσ)ω, (σσσσσ)ω, (σσσσ)ω, (σσσ)ω, (σσ)ω}

Mono- and hexa-syllabic ωs are not allowed in Shaoxing dialect, while markedness reduction in terms of ω size in Tianjin dialect is much more severe in the sense that the phonological domain of tone sandhi in Tianjin dialect proves that a legitimate ω in Tianjin dialect is restricted to di-syllabic and tri-syllabic in length. This significantly implies that the output constraints *{(σ)_ω}, *{(σ)_ω, (σσσσσσ)_ω}, *{(σ)_ω, (σσσσσσ)_ω, (σσσσ σ)_ω} and *{(σ)_ω, (σσσσσσ)_ω, (σσσσσ)_ω, (σσσσ)_ω} outrank *{(σ)_ω, (σσσσ σ)_ω, (σσσσσ)_ω, (σσσσ)_ω, (σσσ)_ω} and *{(σ)_ω, (σσσσσσ)_ω, (σσσσσ)_ω, (σσσσ)_ω, (σσσ)_ω, (σσ)_ω}, so as to have (σ)_ω, (σσσσσσ)_ω, (σσσσσ)_ω and (σσσσ)_ω eliminated but have (σσσ)_ω and (σσ)_ω preserved:

Tableau 6.6 Markedness reduction and preservation in the size of ω in Tianjin dialect

	*{(σ)_ω}	*{(σ)_ω, (σσσσσσ)_ω}	*{(σ)_ω, (σσσσσσ)_ω, (σσσσσ)_ω}	*{(σ)_ω, (σσσσσσ)_ω, (σσσσσ)_ω, (σσσσ)_ω}	*{(σ)_ω, (σσσσσσ)_ω, (σσσσσ)_ω, (σσσσ)_ω, (σσσ)_ω}	*{(σ)_ω, (σσσσσσ)_ω, (σσσσσ)_ω, (σσσσ)_ω, (σσσ)_ω, (σσ)_ω}
(σ)_ω	*!	*	*	*	*	*
(σσσσσσ)_ω		*!	*	*	*	*
(σσσσσ)_ω			*!	*	*	*
(σσσσ)_ω				*!	*	*
☞((σσσ)_ω)					*	*
☞((σσ)_ω)						*

The relative ranking in (6.7) between the output constraints guarantees that only di- and tri-syllabic ω are preserved in Tianjin dialect:

(6.7) Markedness Reduction and Preservation in the Size of ω in Tianjin Dialect:
*{(σ)_ω}, *{(σ)_ω, (σσσσσσ)_ω}, *{(σ)_ω, (σσσσσσ)_ω, (σσσσσ)_ω},
*{(σ)_ω, (σσσσσσ)_ω, (σσσσσ)_ω, (σσσσ)_ω} >> *{(σ)_ω, (σσσσσσ)_ω, (σσσσσ)_ω, (σσσσ)_ω, (σσσ)_ω}, *{(σ)_ω, (σσσσσσ)_ω, (σσσσσ)_ω, (σσσσ)_ω, (σσσ)_ω, (σσ)_ω}

Observing the high-ranking of $*\{(\sigma)_\omega\}$, the mono-syllabic syntactic constituent will incorporate into adjacent prosodic constituents leading to violation of correspondence constraint MATCH-X-ω, i. e. (6.4) i which bans deletion of ωs:

Tableau 6.7 Tianjin dialect: [tʰa ɕiəu ʃəu iən tɕi] He mended (the) radio.

[tʰa [ɕiəu [ʃəu iən tɕi]_{NP}]_{VP}]_{CP}	$*\{(\sigma)_\omega\}$	$*\{(\sigma\sigma\sigma\sigma\sigma\sigma)_\omega\}$	$*\{(\sigma\sigma\sigma\sigma\sigma)_\omega\}$	$*\{(\sigma\sigma\sigma\sigma)_\omega\}$	MATCH-X-ω
a. (tʰa)_ω(ɕiəu)_ω(ʃəu iən tɕi)_ω	*! *	**	**	**	
b. (tʰa ɕiəu ʃəu iən tɕi)_ω			*!	*	**
c. (tʰa)_ω(ɕiəu ʃəu iən tɕi)_ω	*!	*	**	**	*
☞d. (tʰa ɕiəu)_ω(ʃəu iən tɕi)_ω					*

The correspondence constraint MATCH-X-ω which prohibits deletion of ωs is not observed since the highly-ranked output constraint $*\{(\sigma)_\omega\}$ does not tolerate mono-syllabic ωs, so Candidates a and c in Tableau 6.7 are eliminated. Candidates b and c also lose to Candidate d for penta- and quarto-syllabic ωs are not accepted in Tianjin dialect as well.

In order to remedy the defects of mono-syllabic prosodic constituents, epenthesis is also accepted even though it is an ad hoc solution:

Tableau 6.8 Tianjin dialect: [ɕiəu ʃəu iən tɕi] (to) mend (the) radio

[ɕiəu ʃəu iən tɕi]_{NP}]_{VP}	$*\{(\sigma)_\omega\}$	$*\{(\sigma\sigma\sigma\sigma\sigma\sigma)_\omega\}$	$*\{(\sigma\sigma\sigma\sigma\sigma)_\omega\}$	$*\{(\sigma\sigma\sigma\sigma)_\omega\}$	DEP-X-ω
a. (ɕiəu)_ω(ʃəu iən tɕi)_ω	*!	*	*	*	
b. (ɕiəu ʃəu iən tɕi)_ω				*!	
☞c. (ɕiəu Φ)_ω(ʃəu iən tɕi)_ω					*
☞d. (tʰa ɕiəu)_ω(ʃəu iən tɕi)_ω					*

Candidates a and b in Tableau 6.8 are ruled out for containing mono- and quarto-syllabic ωs respectively. In Candidates c and d, an empty beat and a syllable is inserted in respectively in violation of DEP-X-ω; however, both are tolerated since the highly-ranked output constraints $^*\{(\sigma)_\omega\}$, $^*\{(\sigma)_\omega, (\sigma\sigma\sigma\sigma\sigma\sigma)_\omega\}$, $^*\{(\sigma)_\omega, (\sigma\sigma\sigma\sigma\sigma\sigma)_\omega, (\sigma\sigma\sigma\sigma\sigma)_\omega\}$ and $^*\{(\sigma)_\omega, (\sigma\sigma\sigma\sigma\sigma\sigma)_\omega, (\sigma\sigma\sigma\sigma\sigma)_\omega, (\sigma\sigma\sigma\sigma)_\omega\}$ are satisfied.

Resembling Shaoxing dialect, interaction between output constraints and correspondence constraints will parse complex compounds or coordinate strings longer than tri-syllabic into more than one ω:

Tableau 6.9 Tianjin dialect: [tʃuən ɕia tɕʰiəu tuəŋ] spring summer autumn winter

[tʃuən ɕia tɕʰiəu tuəŋ]	$^*\{(\sigma)_\omega\}$	$^*\{(\sigma)_\omega, (\sigma\sigma\sigma\sigma\sigma\sigma)_\omega\}$	$^*\{(\sigma)_\omega, (\sigma\sigma\sigma\sigma\sigma\sigma)_\omega, (\sigma\sigma\sigma\sigma\sigma)_\omega\}$	$^*\{(\sigma)_\omega, (\sigma\sigma\sigma\sigma\sigma\sigma)_\omega, (\sigma\sigma\sigma\sigma\sigma)_\omega, (\sigma\sigma\sigma\sigma)_\omega\}$	MATCH-ω-X
a. (tʃuən ɕia tɕʰiəu tuəŋ)_ω				*!	
b. (tʃuən)_ω (ɕia tɕʰiəu tuəŋ)_ω	*!				*
☞ c. (tʃuən ɕia)_ω (tɕʰiəu tuəŋ)_ω					*

Observing the high-ranking of $^*\{(\sigma)_\omega\}$, $^*\{(\sigma)_\omega, (\sigma\sigma\sigma\sigma\sigma\sigma)_\omega\}$, $^*\{(\sigma)_\omega, (\sigma\sigma\sigma\sigma\sigma\sigma)_\omega, (\sigma\sigma\sigma\sigma\sigma)_\omega\}$ and $^*\{(\sigma)_\omega, (\sigma\sigma\sigma\sigma\sigma\sigma)_\omega, (\sigma\sigma\sigma\sigma\sigma)_\omega, (\sigma\sigma\sigma\sigma)_\omega\}$, the coordinate string [tʃuən ɕia tɕʰiəu tuəŋ] in Tableau 6.9 is split into two o ωs (i.e. Candidate c) leading to the violation of correspondence constraint MATCH-ω-X, i.e. (6.4) ii, which bans the insertion of more ωs.

So, in Tianjin dialect, output constraints $^*\{(\sigma)_\omega\}$, $^*\{(\sigma)_\omega, (\sigma\sigma\sigma\sigma\sigma\sigma)_\omega\}$, $^*\{(\sigma)_\omega, (\sigma\sigma\sigma\sigma\sigma\sigma)_\omega, (\sigma\sigma\sigma\sigma\sigma)_\omega\}$ and $^*\{(\sigma)_\omega, (\sigma\sigma\sigma\sigma\sigma\sigma)_\omega, (\sigma\sigma\sigma\sigma\sigma)_\omega, (\sigma\sigma\sigma\sigma)_\omega\}$ prohibit mono-, hexa-, penta- and quarto-syllabic ωs at the expense of S-P / P-S correspondence, while the other two output constraints $^*\{(\sigma)_\omega, (\sigma\sigma\sigma\sigma\sigma\sigma)_\omega, (\sigma\sigma\sigma\sigma\sigma)_\omega, (\sigma\sigma\sigma\sigma)_\omega, (\sigma\sigma\sigma)_\omega\}$, $^*\{(\sigma)_\omega, (\sigma\sigma\sigma\sigma\sigma\sigma)_\omega, (\sigma\sigma\sigma\sigma\sigma)_\omega, (\sigma\sigma\sigma\sigma)_\omega, (\sigma\sigma\sigma)_\omega, (\sigma\sigma)_\omega\}$ are even lower ranked so as to have tri-syllabic and di-syllabic ωs preserved. The size effects of ω in Tianjin dialect can be schematically presented in the form of constraint ranking as shown in (6.8):

(6.8) ω Structure Well-formedness Overrides S-P/P-S Correspondence in Tianjin Dialect:

*{(σ)_ω}, *{(σ)_ω, (σσσσσσ)_ω}, *{(σ)_ω, (σσσσσσ)_ω, (σσσσσ)_ω}, *{(σ)_ω, (σσσσσσ)_ω, (σσσσσ)_ω, (σσσσ)_ω} >>

MATCH-X-ω, MATCH-ω-X, DEP- X-ω >>

*{(σ)_ω, (σσσσσσ)_ω, (σσσσσ)_ω, (σσσσ)_ω, (σσσ)_ω}, *{(σ)_ω, (σσσσσσ)_ω, (σσσσσ)_ω, (σσσσ)_ω, (σσσ)_ω, (σσ)_ω}

Reduction in markedness in terms of the size of ω in Yuncheng dialect seems to be "sandwiched" between Shaoxing dialect and Tianjin dialect, for the upper limit of syllable count of ω in Yuncheng dialect is four: the tone sandhi domain in Yuncheng dialect is defined through ω which does not exceed four syllables in length. Analogously, size effects of ω in Yuncheng dialect can be formalized into a constraint schema as shown in (6.9):

(6.9) ω Structure Well-formedness Overrides S-P/P-S Correspondence in Yuncheng Dialect:

*{(σ)_ω}, *{(σ)_ω, (σσσσσσ)_ω}, *{(σ)_ω, (σσσσσσ)_ω, (σσσσσ)_ω} >>

MATCH-X-ω, MATCH-ω-X >>

*{(σ)_ω, (σσσσσσ)_ω, (σσσσσ)_ω, (σσσσ)_ω}, *{(σ)_ω, (σσσσσσ)_ω, (σσσσσ)_ω, (σσσσ)_ω, (σσσ)_ω}, *{(σ)_ω, (σσσσσσ)_ω, (σσσσσ)_ω, (σσσσ)_ω, (σσσ)_ω, (σσ)_ω}

The last problem that needs clarification is the restriction on the arbitrary parsing of ω. Shaoxing dialect and Tianjin dialect exemplify two extremes. In Shaoxing dialect, a justifiable ω not only satisfies the output constraints asserting requirements on its size but also has a feasible semantic interpretation, which I attribute to the fact that Shaoxing dialect has a relatively large inventory of ω in terms of the size of ω. Hence, the integrity of immediate constituency[①] (which

---

① Analogously, this concept is stated as "Sense Unit Condition" in Selkirk (1984: 291).

I express with constraint "IIC") is able to be observed alongside the parsing of ω. See Tableau 6.10 for illustration:

Tableau 6.10 [tsʰẽ tɕie? liẽ huø̃ væ̃-kuE] Spring Festival Gala Evening

[tsʰẽ tɕie? [liẽ huø̃ [væ̃-kuE]]]	IIC	*{(σ)ω}	*{(σσσσσσ)ω}	Match-ω-X
a. (tsʰẽ tɕie? liẽ huø̃ væ̃-kuE)ω			*!	
b. (tsʰẽ tɕie? liẽ)ω (huø̃ væ̃-kuE)ω	*!			
☞c. (tsʰẽ tɕie?)ω (liẽ huø̃ væ̃-kuE)ω				*

Candidates b and c in Tableau 6.13 both have legitimate ω parsing in terms of size, while Candidate b is still ruled out because it fails in observing IIC. ①

Contrary to Shaoxing dialect, the integrity of immediate constituents in Tianjin dialect is significantly sacrificed during the process of ω parsing because severe reduction of markedness in terms of ω size forcibly cuts strings into successive di- and tri- syllabic prosodic fragments. So in sharp contrast to Shaoxing dialect, constraint IIC in Tianjin dialect ranks below the output constraints *{(σ)ω} and *{(σ)ω, (σσσσσσ)ω}, *{(σ)ω, (σσσσσσ)ω, (σσσσσ)ω} and *{(σ)ω, (σσσσσσ)ω, (σσσσσ)ω, (σσσσ)ω}. See Tableau 6.11 for illustration:

Tableau 6.11 Tianjin dialect: [ku uən-xua tɕiɛ] old culture street

[[ku [uən-xua]] tɕiɛ]]	*{(σ)ω}	*{(σσσσσσ)ω}	*{(σσσσσ)ω}	*{(σσσσ)ω}	*{(σσσ)ω}	IIC	Match-ω-X
a. (ku uən-xua tɕiɛ)ω			*!				
b. (ku)ω (uən-xua tɕiɛ)ω	*!	*	*	*			*
c. (ku uən-xua)ω (tɕiɛ)ω	*!	*	*	*			*
☞d. (ku uən)ω (xua tɕiɛ)ω						*	*

---

① There is no more independent evidence motivating the ranking between IIC and the output constraints *{(σ)ω} and *{(σ)ω, (σσσσσσ)ω}. So temporarily, it is irrelevant whether IIC ranks above or parallels with *{(σ)ω} and *{(σ)ω, (σσσσσσ)ω}.

Candidate d in Tableau 6.11 contrasts with Candidates a and c in violating constraint IIC in the sense that the immediate constituent [uən xua] is split into two separate ωs in Candidate d; whereas, Candidates a, b and c are still eliminated for containing ωs with illegitimate size. ①

6.3 Syntactic Properties and Construction of pph

In Chapter 4 I have delivered a detailed analysis of sentence level tone sandhi in the South Min family, exemplified by Xiamen dialect, Zhangzhou dialect and Chenghai dialect, whose domains of application are defined through PPh / φ. In Xiamen dialect, the left edge of a domain of tone sandhi always aligns with a XP (X = lexical category); meanwhile, conditioned by the direction of syntactic branchness, a domain of tone sandhi extends leftward until if meets another XP (X = lexical category). However, the conclusion we arrived at in Chapter 4 only draws part of the entire picture.

First, S-P / P-S constituency correspondence constraints assume that syntactic constituents correspond to prosodic constituents on both edges. Tone sandhi in Xiamen dialect diagnoses the alignment between XP and φ on their right boundaries. So what is the situation on the left boundaries?

Second, theoretically, it has not been made clear why functional words can participate in the processing of tone sandhi since LCC (see 2.1 for reference) states explicitly that prosodic computations are restricted to lexical syntactic elements and their projections, at least on the level of ω and φ.

Third, if words belonging to functional categories are allowed to participate in prosodic parsing, then: 1) what is the mechanism of promoting them to prosodic computation? 2) moreover, what is their prosodic status? 3) do they map into prosodic constituents as the lexical ones do, or cliticize to prosodic

---

① There is no more independent evidence motivating the ranking between IIC and correspondence constraint MATCH-ω-X. So temporarily, it is irrelevant whether IIC ranks above or parallels with MATCH-ω-X.

constituents initiated by the lexical ones?

Fundamentally, S-P / P-S constituency correspondence constraints identify the construction of φs mapped from XP (X = lexical category). The merging of recursion in φ due to the undominance of MATCH-XP-φ explains why Xiamen dialect as a right-branching language is characterized by ALIGNMENT-XP-R-φ-R. So, in Section 6.3.1 I will demonstrate how MATCH-XP-φ regulates the mapping from XP to φ in Xiamen dialect, and figure out the limitation of MATCH-XP-φ in the sense that it fails in computing the prosodic parsing of phrases headed by functional words.

Empirically-based study drives Werle (2009: 259) to develop a very important proposal that (at least in Bosnian Serbian and Croatia / BSC) "... φs correspond not to maximal projections of lexical heads, but to their extended projections". Namely, in BSC, it is not the XP (X = lexical category) itself but extended projection of X^0 (e.g. [Prep [XP]]$_{PrepP}$) that maps into a φ. Werle's (2009) generalization about φ formation is of great theoretical importance in that functional word headed phrases are endowed with legitimate prosodic status as independent φs. Inspired by Werle's (2009) deduction, I propose a generalized XP-φ correspondence constraint to account for the prosodic parsing of functional headed phrases in Xiamen dialect which will be examined in detail in Section 6.3.2.

6.3.1 XP-φ Correspondence

In Chapter 4 we have seen that the right edge of a tone sandhi domain in Xiamen dialect always aligns with the right edge of a lexical headed phrase. Following the Match Theory, S-P constituency correspondence constraint MATCH-XP-φ (also see 2.3 for reference) predicts that a syntactic XP (X = lexical category) corresponds to a prosodic constituent φ. In consequence, this correspondence constraint will convert syntactic representations like (6.10) into recursive φ-domain representations:

(6.10) a. [[Ting sio-tsia]$_{NP}$[t'iaq-k'i [p'ue-k'aq]$_{NP}$]$_{VP}$]$_{TP}$
Ting Miss　　tear up　envelope
Miss Ting tore up the envelope.
a'. (Ting sio-tsia)$_\varphi$(t'iaq-k'i (p'ue-k'aq)$_\varphi$)$_\varphi$
b. [[Ting sio-tsia]$_{NP}$[k'ua([tsit-pai]$_{PreP}$[dian-yã]$_{NP}$]$_{VP}$]$_{TP}$
Ting Miss　　　　watch　one time　　　movie
watch the movie once
b'. (Ting sio-tsia)$_\varphi$(k'ua(tsit-pai (dian-yã)$_\varphi$)$_\varphi$

(6.10) a' to b' demonstrate that tone sandhi in Xiamen dialect takes each φ as its working domain: Every right boundary of a φ activates the processing of tone sandhi which marches leftward without recognizing the left boundaries of the φs and is only to be blocked in the face of another right boundary of φ, then this φ activates another tone sandhi process. Recursion in φ does not influence the processing of tone sandhi which is only sensitive to the right edge of φ; meanwhile, this recursively-built φ corresponds to syntactic structure to the greatest extent, even though the prosodic structure well-formedness constraint NONRECURSIVITY (NRC) is violated:

Tableau 6.12　Xiamen dialect: [[**Ting sio-tsia**]$_{NP}$[**t'iaq-k'i** [**p'ue-k'aq**]$_{NP}$]$_{VP}$]$_{TP}$
Miss Ting tore up the envelope.

[[Ting sio-tsia][t'iaq-k'i [p'ue-k'aq]]]	PARSE-σ	MATCH-XP-φ	NRC
☞a. (Ting sio-tsia)$_\varphi$(t'iaq-k'i (p'ue-k'aq)$_\varphi$)$_\varphi$			*
b. (Ting sio-tsia)$_\varphi$ t'iaq-k'i (p'ue-k'aq)$_\varphi$	*!*		
c. (Ting sio-tsia)$_\varphi$(t'iaq-k'i)$_\varphi$(p'ue-k'aq)$_\varphi$		*!	

Candidate c in Tableau 6.12 is eliminated because the phrase head [t'iaq-k'i]$_V$ is parsed into a φ which will wrongly predict that [t'iaq-k'i]$_V$ initiates an independent tone sandhi domain. Candidate b does not violate MATCH-XP-φ, but it is still ruled out as it has two syllables left prosodically unparsed in the violation of PARSE-σ (Kager 2000: 153) which obligatorily requires every syllable to participate in prosodic grouping. Candidate a is the optimal choice, for it satisfies both highly ranked constraints PARSE-σ and MATCH-XP-φ, even though its recursion is in violation of NRC.

MATCH-XP-φ states the correspondent relationship between lexical word headed phrases and the prosodic constituent φ, and the prosodic parsing of all the examples demonstrated above is not interfered with those functional words.

(6.11) a.　[[lao tsin-a-po]$_{NP}$#[**m**[xiong-sin]$_{VP\#}$]$_{NegP}$]$_{TP}$.　　*Syntactic structure*
　　　a'.　(　　　　　)$_φ$　?　(　　　　)$_φ$　　　　　　　*Prosodic parsing*
　　　　　Old lady　　　　　not　believe
　　　　　The old lady doesn't believe.
　　　b.　[[ying-ko]$_{NP}$#[**e**[kong-we]$_{VP}$#]$_{ModP}$]$_{TP}$　　　*Syntactic structure*
　　　b'.　(　　　　)$_φ$　?　(　　　　)$_φ$　　　　　　　　*Prosodic parsing*
　　　　　parrot　　　can　　talk
　　　　　Parrots can talk.

Functional words negator [m] and modal verb [e] in (6.11) a and b both participate in tone sandhi in the same way as those lexical constituents do. Nonetheless, S-P correspondence constraints, especially MATCH-XP-φ do not assert how these functional ingredients are parsed prosodically (6.11) a' to b'. This theoretical "vacuum" is also witnessed in other phonological processes cross-linguistically, for instance, φ-level accent transfer in Bosnian Serbian and Croatia (BSC).

6.3.2 Defining MATCH-XP-φ

6.3.2.1 Extended Projection and Parsing of φ in BSC

Werle (2009) reported in BSC, in negator-verb and preposition-noun sequences, accents consistently transfer to negators and prepositions from their VP or NP complements. Data in (6.12) exemplify accent transfer from nouns to prepositions in Piva-Drobnjak, a BSC dialect. In (6.12), prepositions get falling accent (a), rising accent (b) or no accent (c):

(6.12) N-to-P Accent Transfer in Piva-Drobnjak BSC (Werle 2009: 189)

a.	pò polju	on field	òd kastīga	from shame
	ù nogu	on leg	dò koljēnā	to knees
	ù planinu	to mountain	ìz grmena	from bush
	ù srijedu	on Wednesday	kòd kotāra	in district
	zà dūg	for debt	mèđu ljūdi	among people
	sà srećōm	with luck	nìza strānu	along side
b.	ù kući	in house	òd više	from above
	pò kući	through house	dò sad	until now
	ù grabāljā	onto rake	sà sūncem	with sun
	ù žitu	in grain	bèz prešè	without hurry
	ù Bosnu	to Bosnia	ispòd grla	under throat
	nà jug	to south	nizà žito	along grain
c.	u sèlu	in village	u svijètu	in world
	u planìni	on mountain	do pónōća	until midnight
	u srijèdi	in middle	iza zúbā	behind teeth

These three patterns of accent transfer reflect the underlying tone of the noun. Underlyingly, if a noun is toneless, it will surface with initial falling tone, and this falling tone will transfer to the preposition to the left of this noun as shown by the cases in (6.12) a; if a noun carries initial tone underlyingly, then the preposition to the left of this noun receives rising tone through spreading as shown by the cases in (6.12) b; if a noun carries noninitial tone underlyingly, then the preposition to the left of the noun remains toneless as shown by the cases in (6.12) c.

Accent transfer indicates that there is no φ boundary between a preposition and its NP complement, rather this preposition phrase shares a φ with its NP complement. The same phonological phenomena take place between negators, complementizers, conjunctions and their lexical phrase complements in BSC. Situations here conflict with the correspondence constraint MATCH-XP-φ which restricts the correspondent relationship between a φ and the maximal projection of a lexical head, i. e. XP (X = lexical category) with phrases headed by functional words excluded.

Based on Grimshow's (1991, 2000, 2005) theory of extended projection, Werle (2009: 259) solves this problem by proposing that φs correspond not to maximal projections of lexical heads but to their extended projections in the sense that a lexical head endows its extended projection with lexicalness. An extended projection is composed of a lexical head and its maximal projection (e. g. N, NP: [[polju]$_N$]$_{NP}$(field)) and one or more superordinate functional projections (e. g. PrepP: [pò[NP]]$_{PrepP}$ (on ...)) which share "nominal" features with its lexical complement (i. e. NP). So, in a preposition-noun sequence, PrepP as an extended projection of N corresponds to an independent φ, e. g. (pò polju)$_φ$ (on field).

Werle's (2009) computation of the construction of φ in BSC underlines Selkirk's (2011: 448 – 449) assumption that, besides prosodic structure markedness constraints, and language-particular phonological properties, language-particular properties in syntactic structure influence the construction of prosodic constituent domain of sentence level phonological phenomena. The tone sandhi in Xiamen dialect is also such a typical case, in that the construction of its prosodic constituent domain requires further specifications of syntactic properties as long as the standard version of the interface constraint MATCH-XP-φ is insufficient in counting the prosodic status of functional headed phrases (as what we have already seen in Section 6.3.1).

6.3.2.2 MATCH-XP-φ in Xiamen Dialect

In Piva-Drobnjak BSC, the correspondence constraint MATCH-XP-φ (X = lexical category) is refined into MATCH-XP-φ (XP = extended projection of lexical head X) to have functional-word-headed phrases accommodated into regular prosodic parsing procedures. Xiamen dialect faces the same problem with Piva-Drobnjak BSC: The phonological domain structure of tone sandhi in Xiamen dialect reveals that functionally-headed phrases participate in the parsing of φ in the same way as those lexical-headed phrases do:

(6.13) Parsing of φ in Xiamen Dialect

a. [[Ting sio-tsia]$_{NP}$ # [m [t'ang [tsiaq [hit [liap [[ts'i-sik]$_{AP}$ [p'iang-ko]$_N$]$_{NP}$]$_{ClP}$]$_{NumP}$]$_{DP}$]$_{VP}$]$_{NegP}$]$_{TP}$ #

Ting Miss   don't eat   that one CL   green   apple

Miss Ting doesn't eat that green apple.

*b. (Ting sio-tsia)$_φ$ m t'ang tsiaq hit liap (ts'i-sik p'iang-ko)$_φ$

*c. (Ting sio-tsia)$_φ$ (m t'ang tsiaq hit liap ts'i-sik p'iang-ko)$_φ$

?d. (Ting sio-tsia)$_φ$ (m (t'ang (tsiaq (hit (liap (ts'i-sik p'iang-ko)$_φ$)$_φ$)$_φ$)$_φ$)$_φ$)$_φ$

The sentence in (6.13) essentially maps into two separate domains of tone sandhi, as shown in (6.13) a: #Ting sio-tsia# and #m t^{h}ang tsiaq hit liap ts'i-sik p'iang-ko#. According to the standard correspondence constraint MATCH-XP-φ, only the two NPs [Ting sio-tsia] and [ts'i-sik p'iang-ko] map into φs, as shown in (6.13) b, because functional words and their projections are not targeted by S-P interface constraints due to LCC (see 2.1 for reference). It is obvious that such a manner of prosodic parsing, even though it perfectly obeys MATCH-XP-φ, would disastrously have left those functional constituents prosodically unparsed, thus depriving them of the right to participate in the processing of tone sandhi.

Prosodic parsing in (6.13) c is also problematic, for MATCH-XP-φ is severely violated in the sense that NP [ts'i-sik p'iang-ko] and those functional constituents altogether map into a single φ. The right edge of this awkward φ aligns with the right edge of NP, while its left edge aligns with the left boundary of NegP. Hence this grouping is not a parsing of φ at all, but simply a description of tone sandhi domains directly in terms of syntactic structures.

The Match Theory predicts a very important generalization about the nature of prosodic structure, namely prosodic constituents may present systematic recursivity and level-skipping for they are constructed corresponding to syntactic constituency. Prosodic parsing in (6.13) d produces a nested φ: NP [ts'i-sik p'iang-ko] maps into the most embedded φ; superordinate functional phrases above this NP map into φ layer by layer from bottom up; this nested mapping process will not stop until another maximal projection of lexical word, i. e. XP (X = lexical category) turns up. As long as tone sandhi in Xiamen dialect is sensitive to the right boundary of φ, then all the right boundaries of these nested φs serve as initiators of tone sandhi. On the other hand, the processing of tone sandhi in Xiamen dialect refers no information from the left boundary of φ, thus the left boundaries do not constitute any obstacles as tone sandhi matches leftward, which will naturally come to an end as soon as another right boundary of φ emerges, for this φ will initiate another domain of application of tone sandhi.

The parsing of the domain of tone sandhi in (6.13) d significantly indicates that the construction of φ in Xiamen dialect resembles that in BSC in that extended projections of lexical heads correspond to φs because a lexical head endows its extended projection with lexicalness. The construction of φ in Xiamen dialect nevertheless differs from that in BSC in that maximal projections of lexical heads themselves correspond to φs as well. This single but nontrivial difference between Xiamen dialect and BSC leads to a typology of prosodic structure: φ in Xiamen dialect is recursive, like the parsing in (6.13) d, while φ in BSC is flat, like the parsing in (6.13) c.

Both empirical and theoretical evidence enable me to propose that in Xiamen dialect correspondence between syntactic phrase and phonological phrase observes constraint MATCH-$\mathscr{X}$P-φ:

(6.14) MATCH-$\mathscr{X}$P-φ: Match XP and its extend projection with a φ separately.

X = lexical categories

The high-ranking of MATCH-$\mathscr{X}$P-φ in Xiamen dialect indicates that the prosodic structure markedness constraint NRC (see 1.7 d for reference) is violated.

(6.15) Ting sio-tsia]$_{NP}$# t'iao-kang]$_{AdvP}$ tsiong p'ue-k'aq]$_{NP}$# t'iaq-k'i]$_{VP}$#

| | Ting | Miss | purposefully | cause | envelope | tear |

Miss Ting purposefully tore up the envelope.

The sentence in (6.15) maps into three independent domains of tone sandhi. Tableau 6.13 shows the optimal prosodic parsing of this sentence evidenced by the sandhi patterns:

Tableau 6.13 Xiamen dialect: [thiao-kang tsiong p'ue-k'aq t'iaq-k'i] **purposefully tore up the envelope**

[[t^hiao-kang]$_{AdvP}$ tsiong [p'ue-k'aq]$_{NP}$ [t'iaq-k'i]$_{VP}$]$_{vP}$	PARSE-σ	MATCH-$\mathscr{X}$P-φ	NRC
☞a. (t^hiao-kangtsiong (p'ue-k'aq)$_\varphi$ (t'iaq-k'i)$_\varphi$)$_\varphi$			**
b. (t^hiao-kangtsiong)$_\varphi$ (p'ue-k'aq)$_\varphi$ (t'iaq-k'i)$_\varphi$		*!	
c. (t^hiao-kangtsiong p'ue-k'aqt'iaq-k'i)$_\varphi$		*!*	
d. (t^hiao-kang)$_\varphi$ (tsiongp'ue-k'aq)$_\varphi$ (t'iaq-k'i)$_\varphi$		*!	
e. (t^hiao-kang)$_\varphi$ (tsiong (p'ue-k'aq)$_\varphi$ (t'iaq-k'i)$_\varphi$)$_\varphi$		*!	*
f. (t^hiao-kang)$_\varphi$ tsiong (p'ue-k'aq)$_\varphi$ (t'iaq-k'i)$_\varphi$	*!		

First of all, Candidate f is eliminated by PARSE-σ for there is one syllable left unparsed prosodically. Candidate b is ruled out because the extended projection headed by [tsiong] does not correspond to a φ. Candidates c and d are eliminated due to the same reason: Either NP [p'ue-k'aq] or VP [t'iaq-k'i] or both have no independent φ correspondent. Candidate e is illegitimate as adjunct [t^hiao-kang] is not included in the φ initiated by the extended projection headed by [tsiong]. Candidate a wins in the end, for both maximal projections of lexical heads [p'ue-k'aq] and [t'iaq-k'i], and extended projection of lexical head [t^hiao-kang tsiong ...] map into independent φs respectively even though NRC is violated.

✻ 6.4 Conclusion

In this book I have examined the relation between syntactic constituency and the prosodic constituent domains of phonological rules exemplified by tone sandhis in Chinese dialects. Substantial sandhi data reveals that the phonological domains of tone sandhis in Tianjin dialect, Shaoxing dialect, Yuncheng dialect, Xiamen dialect (Zhangzhou dialect and Chenghai dialect), Zhenjiang dialect and Wenzhou dialect have to be analyzed through prosodic constituents whose construction are basically grounded in morphosyntactic structure.

The domain structure of tone sandhi proves the existence of the three distinct prosodic levels, namely, PWd, PPh and IP predicted by the Match Theory. On the one hand, language-particular prosodic structure markedness constraints may interact with S-P / P-S correspondence constraints resulting in mismatch between syntactic structure and prosodic structure. On the other hand, syntactic properties may be inherited by prosodic constituents due to the undominance of S-P correspondence resulting in the violation of universal prosodic structure well-formedness constraints. Besides language-particular prosodic and syntactic properties, phonological rules themselves may also express requirements on the construction of their working domain. I will conclude this book with a schema of constraint-ranking:

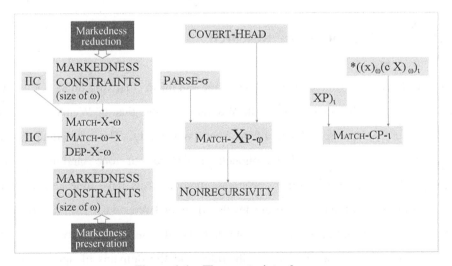

Figure 6.1 The constraint schema

As the Match Theory predicts, the domain of application of tone sandhi in these dialects are defined through prosodic constituents which are mapped from syntactic constituents.

Markedness of the size of ω may be reduced or preserved. At the same time, the integrity of immediate constituent may be as important as, or less important than the size constraints of ω.

Tone sandhi in the South Min family tells us that the maximal projections of functional words also map into φs. With all the syllables parsed prosodically, the domain structure of tone sandhi incurs severe violation of prosodic structure well-formedness constraint NONRECURSITY.

Various factors, like rate of speech, style, constituent length, etc. may result in prosodic constituent restructuring which nevertheless is not randomn at all. Tone sandhi rules assert requirements on the construction of their domains of application. In Xiamen dialect, an adjunct may map into a pph if the head it adjoins to has no overt phonetic value; in Zhenjiang dialect, the ι restructuring takes place on the condition that the right edge of a ι always aligns with the right edge of a XP; in Wenzhou dialect ι restructuring does not allow encliticization. ①

6.5 Areas for Future Research

In this book, I have examined the tone sandhi in Shaoxing dialect which is a representative dialect of the North Wu family, and that in Wenzhou dialect which is a representative dialect of the South Wu family. These two dialects are mutually unintelligible, and the phonetic realization of tone sandhis in both dialects differs from each other; whereas, both dialects have tone sandhis that operate on two distinctive prosodic levels, namely PWd and IP. With regard to the simmilarities and differences in both dialects, it deserves a typological survey of the connection between tone sandhi rules and the domains of application of

---

① It is held in this book that prosodic constituent restructuring by no means indicates the uncertainty of the prosodic status of phonological rules (tone sandhi domain to be specific) which is also explicitly asserted in Nespor & Vogel (2007).

tone sandhi rules in the North Wu family and the South Wu family.

I have already demonstrated that Xiamen dialect, Zhangzhou dialect and Chenghai dialect, which are all the South Min dialects, take PPh as the domain of application of tone sandhi rules. It will be of typological significance of examining the phonological domain structure of tone sandhi in the North Min family.

Bibliography

Abney, Steven. *The English Noun Phrase in Its Sentential Aspect* [D]. Cambridge, Mass.: MIT, 1987.

Anderson, Stephen. *Aspects of the Theory of Clitics* [M]. Oxford: Oxford University Press, 2005.

Aoun, Josph and Li, Y.-H. Audrey. *Essays on the Representational and Derivational Nature of Grammar: The Diversity of Wh-constructions* [M]. Cambridge, Mass.: MIT Press, 2003.

Bao, Zhiming. Chinese tone sandhi [A]. In V. M. Oostendorp, C. Ewen, E. Hume and Kerean Rice (eds.), *The Blackwell Companion to Phonology* [C]. Oxford: Wiley-Blackwell, 2011: 2561-2583.

Bao, Zhiming. *The Structure of Tone* [M]. Oxford: Oxford University Press, 1999.

Booij, Geert. Cliticization as prosodic integration: The case of Dutch [J]. *The Linguistic Review*, 1996, 13: 219-242.

Booij, Geert. Principles and parameters in prosodic phonology [J]. *Linguistics*, 1983, 21: 249-280.

Chao, Yuenren. *A Grammar of Spoken Chinese* [M]. Berkeley: University of California Press, 1968.

Chao, Yuenren. *Studies in the Modern Wu Dialects* [M]. Peiping: Hsinghuacollege Press, 1928.

Chen, Baoxian. Tone sandhi pattern of Xinan dialect in Zhangping County, Fujian Province [J]. *Essays on Linguistics*, 2008, 37: 87-104.

Chen, Mattew Y. A symposium on Tianjin tone sandhi: Introductory remarks [J]. *Journal of Chinese Linguistics*, 1987, 15: 203 – 227.

Chen, Mattew Y. The syntax of Xiamen tone sandhi [J]. *Phonology*, 1987, 4: 109 – 150.

Chen, Mattew Y. *Tone Sandhi: Patterns across Chinese Dialects* [M]. Cambridge: Cambridge University Press, 2000.

Chen, Matthew Y. The paradox of Tianjin tone sandhi [J]. *Chicago Linguistics Society*, 1986, 22: 98 – 154.

Chinese Academy of Social Sciences and Australian Academy of the Humanities. *Chinese language Altas* [M]. Hongkong: Longman Group (Far East) Ltd.,1987.

Chomsky, Noam. Remarks on nominalization [A]. In Roderrick Jacobs and Peter S. Rosenbaum Waltham (eds.), *Readings in English Transformational Grammar* [C]. New York: Ginn & Company, 1970: 184 – 221.

Chomsky, Noam. *Lectures on Government and Binding* [M]. Dordrecht: Foris, 1981.

Cinque, Guglielmo. A null theory of phrase and compound stress [J]. *Linguistic Inquiry*, 1993, 2: 239 – 297.

De Lacy, Paul. The interaction of tone and stress in Optimality Theory [J]. *Phonology*, 2002, 19: 1 – 32.

De Lacy, Paul. *Markedness: Reduction and Preservation in Phonology* [M]. Cambridge: Cambridge University Press, 2006.

Duanmu, San. *The Phonology of Standard Chinese* [M]. Oxford: Oxford University Press, 2007.

Fan, Jiyan. The grammatical function of "de" in adjective-noun construction [J]. *Studies of the Chinese Language*, 1958, 5: 213 – 217.

Feng, Shengli. On the prosodic word in Chinese [J]. *Social Sciences in China*,1996, 1: 161 – 176.

Ghini, Mirco. Φ-formation in Italian: A new proposal [J]. *Toronto Working Papers in Linguistics*, 1993, 2: 41 – 78.

Goldsmith, John. Tone, accent and getting them together [J]. *Berkeley Linguistics Society*, 1987, 13: 88 – 104.

Grimshaw, Jane. Locality and extended projection [A]. In Coopmans Peter, Martin Everaert and Jane Grimshaw (eds.), *Lexical Specification and Insertion* [C]. Amsterdam: John Benjamins Publishing Company, 2000: 115 – 133.

Grimshaw, Jane. *Extended Projection* [D]. MS: Brandeis University, 1991.

Grimshaw, Jane. *Words and Structure* [M]. Stanford: CSLI, 2005.

Gussenhoven, Carlos. Sentential prominence in English [A]. In M. Van Oostendorp, C. Ewen, E. Hume and K. Rice (eds.), *The Blackwell Companion to Phonology* [C]. London: Wiley-Blackwell, 2011:2778 – 2806.

Gussenhoven, Carlos. *The Phonology of Tone and Intonation* [M]. Cambridge: Cambridge University Press, 2004.

Hale, Kenneth and Selkirk, Elisabeth. Government and tonal phrasing in Papago [J]. *Phonological Yearbook*, 1987, 4: 151 – 183.

Hall, Tracy A. The phonological word: A review [A]. In Tracy A. Hall and Ursula Kleinhenz (eds.), *Rhythm and Meter* [C]. Orlando, Florida: Academic Press, 1999: 201 – 260.

Haspelmath, Martin and Sims, Andrea D. *Understanding Morphology* [M]. London: Hodder Education, 2010.

Hayes, Bruce. The prosodic hierarchy in meter [A]. In P. Kiparsky and G. Youmans (eds.), *Rhythm and Meter* [C]. Orlando: Academic Press, 1989: 201 – 260.

Hayes, Bruce. *Metrical Stress Theory: Principles and Case Studies* [M]. Chicago: Chicago University Press, 1995.

Hsu, H. C. Revisiting tone and prominence in Chinese [J]. *Language and Linguistics*, 2006, 7: 109 – 137.

Huang, C.-T. James, Li, Y.-H. Audrey and Li, Yafei. *The Syntax of Chinese* [M]. Cambridge: Cambridge University Press, 2009.

Huang, C.-T. James. Phrase structure, lexical integrity, and Chinese compounds [J]. *Journal of Chinese Language Teachers Association*, 1984, 19: 53 –78.

Hyman, Larry M. The representation of multiple tone heights [A]. In Koen Bogers, Harry van de Hulst and Marten Mous (eds.), *The Phonological Representation of Supersegmentals: Studies on African Languages*[C]. Berlin: Mouton de Gruyter, 1986:109 – 152.

Inkelas, Sharon & Zec, Draga. The phonology-syntax interface [A]. In John A. Goldsmith (ed.), *Handbook of Phonological Theory*[M]. Oxford: Blackwell Publishing, 1995: 535 –549.

Inkelas, Sharon. *Prosodic Constituency in the Lexicon* [M]. New York: Garland Press, 1990.

Ito, J. and Mester, A. Prosodic adjunction in Japanese compounds [A]. In Y. Miyamoto and M. Ochi (eds.), *Formal Approaches to Japanese Linguistics: Proceedings of FAJL* [C]. Cambridge, MA: MIT working papers in Lingua, 2007, 4: 97 – 111.

Ito, J. and Mester, A. Prosodic subcategories in Japanese [J]. *Lingua*, 2013, 124: 20 –40.

Ito, J. and Mester, A. Weak layering and word binarity [A]. In Takeru Honma, Toshiyuki Tabata and Shin-ichi Tanaka (eds.), *A New Century of Phonoloy and Phonological Theory* [C]. Tokyo: Kaitakusha, 2003: 26 –65.

Jun, Sun-Ah. Prosodic typology [A]. In Jun Sun-Ah (ed.), *Prosodic Typology: The Phonology of Intonation and Phrasing* [C]. Oxford, New York: Oxford University Press, 2005: 430 –458.

Kabak, Baris. and Revithiadou, Anthi. An interface approach to prosodic word recursion [A]. In Jenet Grizenhout and Baris Kabak (eds.), *Phonological Domains-Universals and Derivations* [C]. Berlin: Mouton de Gruyter, 2009:105 – 134.

Kager, Rene. *Optimality Theory* [M]. Cambridge: Cambridge University Press, 1999.

Kaisse, Ellen. *Connected Speech: The Interaction of Syntax and Phonology*

[M]. New York: Academic Press, 1985.

Kassimjee, Farida and Kisseberth, Charles. Optimal domains theory and Bantu tonology: A case study from Isixhosa and Shingasidja [A]. In Larry Hayman and Charles Kisseberth (eds.), *Theoretical Aspects of Bantu Tone* [C]. Stanford, California: CSLI, 1998: 33 – 132.

Kisseberth, Charles. On domains [A]. In Jennifer Cole and Charles Kisseberth (eds.), *Perspectives in Phonology* [C]. Stanford, CA: CSLI Publications, 1994: 133 – 166.

Ladd, D. R. Intonationalphrasing: The case of recursive prosodic structure [J]. *Phonology Yearbook*, 1986, 3: 311 – 340.

Li, Rulong. Tone sandhis and neutral tones in Xiamen dialect [J]. *Journal of Xiamen University (Arts & Social Sciences)*, 1962, 3: 78 – 114.

Li, Shiyu. How do the native speakers of Tianjin dialect learn Mandarin? [J]. *Studies of the Chinese Language*, 1956, 4: 24 – 27.

Li, Xiaofan. Levels and classes of tone sandhi in Chinese dialects [J]. *Dialect*, 2004, 1: 16 – 33.

Li, Xingjian and Liu, Sixun. Tone sandhis in Tianjin dialect [J]. *Studies of the Chinese Language*, 1985, 1: 76 – 81.

Liberman, M. and Pierrehumbert, Janet. Intonational invariance under changes in pitch range and length [A]. In M. Aronoff and R. Oehrle (eds.), *Languages Sound Structure* [C]. Cambridge, MA: MIT Press, 1984.

Lin, Jowang. Lexical government and tone group formation in Xiamen Chinese [J]. *Phonology*, 1994, 2: 237 – 275.

Lin, Lunlun. Studies on tones in Chaoshan Cantonese [J]. *Linguistic Research*, 1995, 1: 52 – 59.

Lin, Lunlun. The homophony syllabary of Chenghai, Guangdong Province [J]. *Dialect*, 1994, 2: 128 – 142.

Lin, Lunlun. *Studies on Chenghai Dialect* [M]. Shantou: Shantou University Press, 1996.

Lin, Maocan and Yan, Jingzhu. On the nature of neutral tones in Beijing dialect[J]. *Studies of the Chinese Language*, 1980, 3: 166 –178.

Lombardi, Linda. Coronal epenthesis and unmarkedness [J]. *University of Maryland Working Papers in Linguistics*, 1998, 5: 156 –75.

Lombardi, Linda. Why place and voice are different: constraint-specific alternations and Optimality Theory [J]. *Rutgers Optimality Archive*, 1995: 105.

Lu, Bingfu. The basic function and derived function of "de" as are viewed from its distribution [J]. *Chinese Teaching in the World*, 2003, 1: 14 –29.

Lu, Jilun. A new tone sandhi pattern in Tianjin dialect [J]. *Journal of Tianjin Normal University (Social Sciences)*, 1997, 4: 67 –72.

Lu, Zhiwei. *The Chinese Morphology* [M]. Beijing: Science Press, 1964.

Lü, Shuxiang. A preliminary study of the problem of mono-and di-syllabic expressions in modern Chinese [J]. *Studies of the Chinese Language*, 1963, 1: 11 –23.

Lü, Shuxiang. *Problems in the Analysis of Chinese Grammar* [M]. Beijing: The Commercial Press, 1979.

Lü, Zhenjia. The regularities of tone sandhis in Yuncheng dialect [J]. *Journal of Shanxi Normal University (Social Sciences)*, 1989, 3: 111 –120.

Ma, Qiuwu. More on the paradox of Tianjin tone sandhi [J]. *Contemporary Linguistics*, 2005b, 2: 97 –106.

Ma, Qiuwu. An OT solution to the paradox of Tianjin tone sandhi [J]. *Studies of the Chinese Language*, 2005a, 6: 561 –576.

McCarthy, John and Prince, Alan. Faithfulness and reduplicative identity [A]. In Jill Beckman, Laura Walsh Dickey and Suzanne Urbanczyk (eds.), *Papers in Optimality Theory: University of Massachusetts Working Papers in Linguistics* [C]. Amherst, MA: GLSA, 1995: 249 –384.

McCarthy, John J. and Prince, Alan. *Prosodic Morphology* [M]. MS: University of Massachusetts, Amherst, 1993.

Mei, Zulin. Tones and tone sandhi in the 16th century Mandarin [J]. *Journal of Chinese Liguistics*, 1977, 5: 237 –260.

Milliken, S., et al. Resolving the paradox of Tianjin tone sandhi [A]. In Jialing Wang and Norval Smith (eds.), *Studies in Chinese Phonology* [C]. Berlin: Mouton de Gruyter, 1997: 53 – 80.

Nespor, Marina and Vogel, Irene. *Prosodic Phonology* [M]. Berlin: Mouton de Gruyter, 2007.

Nespor, Marina and Vogel, Irene. *Prosodic Phonology* [M]. Dordrecht: Foris Publications, 1986.

Odden, D. Syntax, lexical rules and postlexical rules in Kimatuumbi [A]. In S. Inkelas and D. Zec (eds.), *The Phonology-Syntax Connection* [C]. Chicego: University of Chicago Press, 1990: 259 – 277.

Payne, David L. *The Phonology and Morphology of AxinincaCampa* [M]. Dallas, TX: SIL, 1981.

Peperkamp, Sharon. *Prosodic Words* [M]. Amsterdam: Holand Academic Graphics, 1997.

Pierrehumbert, Janet and Beckman, Mary. *Japanese Tone Structure* [M]. Cambridge, MA: The MIT Press, 1988.

Prince, Alan and Smolensky, Paul. *Optimality Theory: Constraint Interaction in Generative Grammar* [M]. Oxford: Blackwell, 2004.

Qian, Nairong. *Contemporary Studies on Wu Dialects* [M]. Shanghai: Shanghai Education Publishing House, 1992.

Radford, Andrew. *English Syntax: An Introduction* [M]. Cambridge: Cambridge University Press, 2004.

Seidl, Amanda. *Minimal Indirect Reference: A Theory of the Syntax-Phonology Interface* [M]. London, New York: Routledge, 2002.

Selkirk, E. and Shen, Tong. Prosodic domains in Shanghai Chinese [A]. In Sharon Inkelas and Draga Zec (eds.), *The Phonology-Syntax Connection* [C]. Chicago: University of Chicago Press, 1990: 313 – 337.

Selkirk, E. On the nature of phonological representation [A]. In J. Anderson, J. Laver and T. Meyers (eds.), *The Cognitive Representation of Speech* [C]. Amsterdam: North Holland, 1981: 379 – 388.

Selkirk, E. Sentence prosody: Intonation, stress and phrasing [A]. In John A. Goldsmith (ed.), *The Handbook of Phonolgical Theory* [C]. Oxford: Blackwell, 1995: 550 – 569.

Selkirk, E. The interaction of constraints on prosodic phrasing [A]. In Merle Horne (ed.), *Prosody: Theory and Experiments* [C]. Dordrecht: Kluwer, 2000: 231 – 262.

Selkirk, E. The prosodic structure of function words [A]. In J. L. Morgan and K. Demuth (eds.), *Signal to Syntax* [C]. Mahwah, NJ: Lawrence Erlbaum, 1996: 187 – 213.

Selkirk, E. The syntax-phonology interface. In John Goldsmith, Jason Riggle and Alan C. L. Yu (eds.), *The Handbook of Phonological Theory* (2nd edition) [M]. Oxford: Blackwell, 2011: 435 – 484.

Selkirk, E. *Phonology and Syntax: The Relation Between Sound and Structure* [M]. Cambridge, MA: MIT Press, 1984.

Selkirk, Elisabeth. The role of prosodic categories in English word stress [J]. *Linguistic Inquiry*, 1980, 11: 563 – 605.

Shi, Feng and Wang, Ping. The new changes in Tianjin dialect [J]. In Feng Shi and Zhongwei Shen (eds.) *A Festschrift in Honor of Professor William S-Y. Wang on his 70th Birthday* [C]. Tianjin: Nankai University Press, 2004: 176 – 191.

Shi, Feng. On the tones in Tianjin dialect and the changes [J]. *Studies of the Chinese Language*, 1988, 5: 15 – 24.

Shi, Feng. Tone sandhis in Tianjin dialect [A]. In Feng Shi (ed.), *Studies in Tones and Stops* [C]. Beijing: Peking University Press, 1990:84 – 100.

Shi, Qisheng. The dynamic operation of tone sandhi in Shantou dialect [J]. *Studies of the Chinese Language*, 2011, 4: 334 – 345.

Si, Fuzhen. Head theory and DeP in Chinese [J]. *Contemporary Linguistics*, 2004, 1: 26 – 34.

Snider, K. Tonal upstep in Krachi: Evidence of a register tier [J]. *Language*, 1990,66:453 – 474.

Tang, Sze-Wing. *Formal Chinese Syntax* [M]. Shanghai: Shanghai Educational Publishing House, 2010.

Ting, Pang-hsin. Some aspects of tonal development in Chinese dialects, Bulletin of the Institute of History and Philology [J]. *Academia Sinica*, 1982, 4: 629-644.

Trask, R. L. *A Dictionary of Phonetics and Phonology* [M]. London / New York: Routledge, 1996.

Trubetzkoy, Nikolai S. *Grundzüge der Phonologie* [M]. Göttingen: Vandenhoeck and Ruprecht, 1939.

Truckenbrodt, Hubert. On the relation between syntactic phrases and phonological phrases [J]. *Linguistic Inquiry*, 1999, 30: 219-255.

Truckenbrodt, Hubert. *Phonological Phrases: Their Relation to Syntax, Focus and Prominence* [D]. Oxford: MIT, 1995.

Vogel, Irene. The status of the Clitic Group [A]. In J. Grijzenhout and B. Kabak (eds.), *Phonological Domains: Universals and Deviations* [C]. Berlin / New York: De Gruyter, 2009: 15-46.

Vogel, Irene. The status of the clitic group. In Jenet Grizenhout and Baris Kabak (eds.), *Phonological Domains, Universals and Derivations* [C]. Berlin: Mouton de Gruyter, 2009.

Wang, Futang. *A Study of Shaoxing Dialect* [M]. Bejing: Language and Culture Press, 2015.

Wang, Jialing. On tone sandhi and neutral tone in the Tianjin dialect within the framework of Optimality Theory [J]. *Studies of the Chinese Language*, 2002, 4: 363-383.

Wang, Jialing. The typology of the pitch of the neutral tone in Chinese dialect [J]. *Nankai Linguistics*, 2006, 1: 1-10.

Wang, Xiaomei. Tone sandhi rules in tri-syllabic sequences in Tianjin dialect [J]. *Studies of the Chinese Language*, 2003, 2: 165-192.

Wang, Hongjun. Phonological word and phonological phrase in Chinese [J]. *Studies of the Chinese Language*, 2000, 6: 525-575.

Wang, Hongjun. *Chinese Nonlinear Phonology* [M]. Beijing: Peking University Press, 2008.

Werle, Adam. *Word, Phrase and Clitic Prosody in Bosnian, Serbian and Croatian* [D]. Amherst: University of Massachusetts Amherst, 2009.

Wu, Zihui. *A Study of Shaoxing Dialect from the Perspective of Wuyue Culture* [M]. Hangzhou: Zhejiang University Press, 2007.

Wu, Zongji. The intonational changes on sentential level in Mandarin [J]. *Studies of the Chinese Language*, 1982, 6: 419 –450.

Xiong, Zhongru. A DP structure headed by De [J]. *Contemporary Linguistics*, 2005, 2: 148 –165.

Xu, Baohua, Tang, Zhenzhu and Qian, Nairong. Tone sandhi in the Shanghai dialect (a new variety) [J]. *Dialect*, 1981, 2: 145 – 155; 1982, 2: 115 – 128; 1983, 3: 197 –201.

Xu, Liejiong and Langendoen, Terence. Topic structures in Chinese [J]. *Language*, 1985, 61: 1 –27.

Yang, Xiuming. *A Study of Tones and Regional Cultures of Zhangzhou* [M]. Beijing: China Social Sciences Publishing House, 2010.

Yang, Wei and Yang, Naijun. *Shaoxing Dialect* [M]. Beijing: International Cultural Publishing Company, 2000.

Yip, Moria. Contour tones [J]. *Phonology Yearbook*, 1989, 6: 149 – 174.

Yip, Moria. *Tone* [M]. Cambridge: Cambridge University Press, 2002.

Yuan, Jiahua. *Outline of Chinese Dialects*, 2nd edition [M]. Beijing: Language and Cultural Press, 2001.

Yue-Hashimoto, Anne Oi-kan. Tonal flip-flop in Chinese dialects [J]. *Journal of Chinese Linguistics*, 1986, 14: 161 – 182.

Zhang, Jie. Tones, tonal phonology, and tone sandhi [A]. In C.-T. James Huang, Y.-H. Audrey Li & Andrew Simpson (eds.), *The Handbook of Chinese Linguistics* (First Edition) [C]. Chichester, West Sussex, UK: John Wiley & Sons, Inc, 2014: 443 – 463.

Zhang, Jisheng. *The Phonology of Shaoxing Chinese* [D]. Amsterdam: LOT,

2006.

Zhang, Zhenxing. Tone sandhis in Yongfu, Zhangping dialect [J]. *Dialect*. 1983, 3:175 – 196.

Zhang, Zhenxing. Subgrouping of Min dialect [J]. *Dialect*, 1985, 3: 171 – 180.

Zhang, Hongnian. Tone sandhis of Zhenjiang dialect [J]. *Dialect*, 1985, 3: 191 – 204.

Zhang, Jisheng. A study of correlation between linguistic distance and mutual intelligibility among Wu dialects in light of feature specification [J]. *Studies of the Chinese Language*, 2015, 6: 498 – 508.

Zhang, Jisheng. Representation of the right-prominent metrical structure of Shaoxing dialect [J]. *Linguistic Sciences*, 2013, 3: 269 – 276.

Zheng-zhang, Shangfang. Tone sandhis in Wenzhou dialect [J]. *Studies of the Chinese Language*, 1964, 21: 106 – 152.

Zheng-zhang, Shangfang. The phonetics of retroflex suffixation in Wenzhou dialect I [J]. *Dialect*, 1980, 4: 245 – 262.

Zheng-zhang, Shangfang. Variations of neutral tones in Wenzhou dialect, Zhejiang Province [J]. *Dialect*, 2007, 1: 1 – 3 – 115.

Zheng-zhang, Shangfang. *Dialect Chorography of Wenzhou* [M]. Beijing: Zhonghua Book Company, 2008.

Zhu, Xiaonong. *A Grammar of Shanghai Wu* [M]. Unterschleim/Munich: Lincom Europa, 2006.